COMBAT TALONS IN VIETNAM

Number 154
Williams-Ford Texas A&M University
Military History Series

MC-130E #64–0547, call sign "Romeo Charlie" on one of its last landings. (Photo courtesy of Ron Rowe)

COMBAT TALONS IN VIETNAM

Recovering a Covert Special Ops Crew

JOHN GARGUS

Texas A&M University Press
College Station, Texas

First edition

This paper meets the requirements of ANSI/NISO Z39.48–1992 (Permanence of Paper).
Binding materials have been chosen for durability.
Manufactured in the United States of America

Library of Congress Cataloging-in-Publication Data

Names: Gargus, John, author.
Title: Combat Talons in Vietnam : recovering a covert special ops crew / John Gargus.
Other titles: Williams-Ford Texas A&M University military history series ; no. 154.
Description: First edition. | College Station, Texas : Texas A&M University Press, [2017] | Series: Williams-Ford Texas A&M University military history series ; number 154 | Includes bibliographical references and index.
Identifiers: LCCN 2016046716| ISBN 9781623495121 (cloth : alk. paper) | ISBN 9781623495138 (ebook)
Subjects: LCSH: Gargus, John. | Vietnam War, 1961-1975—Aerial operations, American. | Special operations (Military science)—Vietnam. | United States. Air Force—History—Vietnam War, 1961-1975. | Vietnam War, 1961-1975—Missing in action—United States. | Vietnam War, 1961-1975—Casualties—United States. | Hercules (Turboprop transports)—History—20th century. | Airmen—United States—Biography.
Classification: LCC DS558.8 .G37 2017 | DDC 959.704/348—dc23 LC record available at https://lccn.loc.gov/2016046716

This book is dedicated to the memory of the S-01 crew members.

GEAN P. CLAPPER
CHARLES P. CLAXTON
EDWARD J. DARCY
WAYNE A. ECKLEY
DONALD E. FISHER
JACK MCCRARY
EDWIN N. OSBORNE JR.
FRANK C. PARKER III
GERALD G. VAN BUREN
GORDON J. WENAAS
JAMES R. WILLIAMS

Men go to war assuring themselves and their families that they will return home safely and that everything will be all right. They know very well that there are inevitable casualties, but they reassure themselves that these realities of war will befall someone else. They suppress the fears of coming back home in a casket or a rubber body bag. Those who have any misgivings about their possible fate visualize themselves as coming home with proper military honors and being buried among their family ancestors.

Not many men concern themselves with the possibility of getting captured by the enemy. All branches of service conduct escape and evasion and survival as prisoner of war training to prepare those whose wartime assignments could cause them to be captured by the enemy. Once again, getting captured and enduring everything that one experienced during days of training was something that would happen to someone else.

No one plans to become a missing in action person for years and years even though appropriate legal and personal counseling to prepare soldiers for such unforeseen separation is available. A soldier's family should be prepared to cope with the many difficult legal, financial, and insurance problems that accompany a loved one's missing in action (MIA) status. A soldier's dependents should also be aware of the efforts our country makes to maintain that status until they can be declared killed in action (KIA) and eventually brought home for an appropriate funeral.

Not one of the eleven men to whom I dedicate this book anticipated what happened to them. They led reasonably comfortable lives in the war zone where they performed interesting but highly classified and challenging missions. They planned to come home to continue their flying careers in other assignments. But on one night they failed to return from a clandestine flight over North Vietnam and we heard nothing about them for twenty-five years. They were declared as missing in action for the first ten years before their status was changed to killed in action. Then, after fifteen more years, their crashed aircraft was located. Finally, it took eight more years to excavate their remains, positively identify some of them, and return all recovered human parts for a burial in one common casket with full military honors at Arlington National Cemetery.

Contents

Illustrations

COMBAT TALONS IN VIETNAM

Introduction

This book tells the story of the first Combat Talon C-130 aircraft and the airmen who flew them in Vietnam. Their hazardous missions flown over North Vietnam were so highly classified that only the highest echelons of service commands knew of their existence. Airmen who flew them and their supporting ground crews were sworn to secrecy. They could not talk about their work with other soldiers and could not keep their families informed about their flights. Consequently, their contributions to the war did not become known until many years later when their accomplishments were officially declassified.

This book began as a story I wrote in 1998 for the families of eleven Combat Talon crew members lost on a clandestine mission over North Vietnam. It had happened thirty-one years before in 1967, but because of the secrecy of the operations, the families were told only that their loved ones failed to return from a nighttime mission. Over the years practically all secret operations of the Vietnam War became declassified, and the story of the eleven men and their fate could finally be told. Because I participated in the planning for the mission of this lost aircraft, the Air Commando Association community of Fort Walton Beach, Florida, asked me to write a story that could be presented to the families at the dedication of a memorial pedestal for the fallen crew at the Hurlburt Field's Memorial Air Park. Two years later, the remains of the crew were interred in a common grave at Arlington National Cemetery.

At the funeral, many of my attending colleagues, who knew that I had pursued the trail of the lost crew by visiting the Central Identification Laboratory in Hawaii and the Air Force Mortuary Services in San Antonio, Texas, asked me to write a follow-up story about how the aircraft crash site was located and how the crew's remains were identified and processed for interment. First, I consulted with the families about doing it. Most of them were grateful for what they had learned from my story and were also satisfied with the crash site discovery information they received through the official casualty notification channels. Nevertheless, my friends urged me to continue the story for those veterans who either knew or had served with the eleven lost friends. My presentations on their fate at periodic reunions were not enough. However, at those gatherings I learned a lot about our lives in Vietnam from those who preceded my one-year assignment there as well as from those who followed me. Consequently, I gathered enough stories to incorporate the lost crew account into a book about the men who served during the first operational employment of Combat Talons in Vietnam.

I began to write relying on my own background and experiences in special operations. Then I supplemented stories of my urging friends with solicited accounts of those whom I had never met but whom I was able to reach by e-mail or telephone. The result is this book's account from the perspective of many who served in the early Combat Talons. It is not a Combat Talon history in Vietnam. That history was expertly written by Col. Jerry Thigpen in his *The Praetorian STARShip*. This book will only complement his history with accounts of airmen who lived it.

We have learned a lot about the Vietnam War since the time of the stories of this book. Operations then were so secret that individual crews did not know what kind of missions other crews were flying. We were committed to secrecy and warned not to share information about our flights with others. However, after several different missions, each crew learned a great deal about what kind of special operations we were conducting over North Vietnam. All that time, the loyal ground maintenance crews remained uninformed. They could form their own conclusions by observing what was happening around the Talons they serviced, but they did not have a need to know what the missions were. Only the commanders and mission planners knew the upper echelon bosses at the Studies and Observations Group (SOG). Once at that level of information, they had no need to know what kind of special operations other branches of SOG were conducting. All they needed to know was that they were the SOG's airlift support arm. Such secrecy ensured that if one of the crews was shot down, the survivors would not be able to divulge much about the mission and command structure of the organization.

Today, we can learn about the SOG and its secret operations from many declassified sources. Each reader needs to keep in mind that I am placing the events of this book within the time span in which they were occurring and avoiding the benefits of the hindsight that we now possess. Because I also had an assignment as a mission planner, I was exposed to more information than what was sharable with crew members. In spite of that, I was also kept in the dark about things I did not need to know.

To place our existence in Vietnam in its proper context, I also need to address the growing pains the special operations units experienced when the war began and how the military commands responded to the urgent operational needs of their days. The mere existence of these units presented problems for the higher echelons of their respective commands and services. They were like specially cut pieces of a picture puzzle that did not fit anywhere. Their shapes required adjustments to the sides of their intended surrounding pieces. Military doctrines took a long time to incorporate them into their folds. Combat Talons survived this process because of their special operations value. They evolved into the most reliable and up-to-date aircraft platforms in the Air Force inventory.

The conclusion of this story comes almost five decades after the tragic aircraft loss, with the dedication of the Combat Talon Memorial at Hurlburt Field in Florida. There, etched in stone, this monument records the names of crew members and tail numbers of all Combat Talon aircraft losses to the present day.

1

Attraction to Special Operations

Unconventional Warfare

Unconventional warfare has been with us ever since men began fighting with sticks and stones. They always tried ingenious ways to outwit each other, often resorting to stealth and deception. Then, when men learned how to fly airplanes, the art of war entered into a dimension that existed only in the dreams of those who had wished they could fly. Today we have not yet explored everything we can do with the improving airborne capabilities and the rapidly expanding technological discoveries that allow us to fly remotely from anywhere and to everywhere in the world.

Frontal assault territorial wars may become the traditional conflicts of the past that we will see reenacted only in the movies. We are now experiencing subtler insurgencies for subverting and crippling governments of nations. Advances in aircraft and engine designs have opened up opportunities for future unprecedented special operations.

Aviation was still in its infancy during World War I when aircraft were short-ranged and too small to operate far behind the fixed front lines. This changed during World War II when more advanced aircraft made it possible to spread hostilities far behind the still-fixed territorial front lines and deliver disastrous firepower to the enemy's war-making industrial capacity at home. Imaginative clandestine long-range incursions into the enemy's air space expanded the horizons of special operations. Hostile guerilla forces could be inserted into vital strategic locations inside the territories controlled by the enemy.

Special Operations in World War II

I witnessed the emerging airborne special operations as a ten-year-old boy in 1944. We lived in central Slovakia, which rebelled against the Germans in what became known as the Slovak National Uprising. My father was a first lieutenant in the Slovak Army Reserve. He became the deputy commander of his unit; it was headquartered in the county seat only about 12 miles from our home village. Complementing his reserve army soldiers were local and Russian partisan units. Local partisans were recruited from nearby villages, and the Russians, who were well trained for operations behind enemy lines, were either air landed at the only local air base or were parachuted in. My godfather headed one of the locally recruited guerrilla bands, or as we called them, partisan bands.

On good weather nights there was much overhead air traffic. Russian transport aircraft, Li-2s (copies of US C-47s), brought in either resupplies or new troops. Because of the distance from the airdrome, we were in the area that received reinforcements and war supplies via parachutes. Late one October evening we heard an aircraft that flew lower than the others, and it seemed like it flew right up our street. I remember that my mother and I both sat up startled in our beds, disturbed by the unusually loud noise. My mother recalled that the sound of this aircraft stopped suddenly. When we awoke the next day, one partisan on horseback announced to all in our village that a Russian aircraft had crashed into the hill above our village. That was the low-flying aircraft we had heard the night before.

Out of the twenty-one men aboard, who expected to land at the airdrome farther to the west, only three survived. The rest were brought to the village fire station where women with local midwife/nursing skills cleaned their bodies. They washed the blood out of their hair and faces so that my father and godfather could photograph them for some future use. Some of the village men brought their shaving blades and gave the dead faces their final shaves. When my father noticed me among the curious boys who were hanging around, he told me to go home. That was a stern order I could not refuse. However, once I knew that he had gone back to his Astra headquarters, I returned to peek through the window of the fire station. I should have not done that. To my dying days I will remember the rows of neatly laid out bodies of young Slovak and Russian men who had lost their lives for a cause they believed in. I did not know then that my fate would one day present me with an opportunity to serve as an American airman flying resupplies for guerillas in some faraway country in Southeast Asia.

I returned to my native village in Czechoslovakia in 1990 after the collapse of the Communist regime. Then, as an air force veteran, I returned to the 1944 aircraft crash site to pay respect to the eighteen men who died there. My home villagers built a small memorial at the spot, and I saw ample evidence that the site has been having frequent visitors. I am including a photograph of me examining a small piece of aircraft wreckage that still covered the site. I want the reader to note the difference between this forty-six-year-old piece of wreckage and the lack of similar pieces of Combat Talon at the crash site in North Vietnam. When I, as a boy, took a small piece of aluminum tubing as a souvenir from the crash site, I hid it from my mother because I knew that I had done something wrong. As the photograph shows, that site remains a well-respected place to this day.

Author is examining one of the pieces of a Russian Douglas 17 that are still available at the World War II crash site. (Photo by John Gargus)

That was in Europe on the eastern, Russian, front. The US Office of Strategic Services (OSS) conducted similar operations in support of partisans in Yugoslavia. On the western front the OSS carried out successful special operations with allied Jedburgh teams that supported the French resistance forces. And in the Far East, the Air Commandos waged a successful campaign in the China-Burma-India theater. There they infiltrated and air-supplied thousands of fighters against the Japanese in areas that were not accessible by any other means but air. However, in spite of all those successes, once the war ended, the victorious special operations units were disbanded, and the imaginative men who developed as-needed tactics were dispersed throughout the military or returned back to civilian life. Their special operations talents were no longer needed.

Korea and the Cold War

Just a few years later the United States was involved in another multinational conflict—in Korea. Once again, men with prior experience and novices alike responded to carry out makeshift, as-needed, special air operations with readily available conventional aircraft. They proved their value to the whole war effort, but as soon as that armistice was reached, their vital services were no longer needed.

After Korea the focus shifted to nuclear confrontation with the Soviet Union. Emphasis was on strategic bombing and missile delivery of atomic weapons. If there was a future war, it would be one of massive retaliation and mutual annihilation. Neither side would dare to start one. This produced a frightening stalemate.

Even though a full-scale nuclear war seemed like a suicidal option, the geopolitical struggle for people's minds continued. The Iron Curtain divided Europe into western North Atlantic Treaty Organization (NATO) countries and communist Warsaw Pact countries. The rest of the world, notably former colonial but now newly independent countries in Asia and Africa, was up for grabs. The communists were determined to subvert governments of economically stressed nations or to intervene wherever domestic unrest surfaced. President Kennedy's response to this development was to provide counterinsurgency assistance to friendly nations. This created an immediate need for foreign-language-speaking qualified personnel who could interface with native populations and provide them with necessary training in weapons and tactics. The US Army Green Berets, who were already involved in assisting countries in Latin America, had a head start in this area. The US

Air Force, which was still in its infancy, was focused on its massive retaliation clout with strategic bombers and intercontinental ballistic missiles. It was slower to respond to the newly emerging counterinsurgency needs. All types of vintage aircraft, especially helicopters, were needed to connect with pockets of populations in remote areas.

Early in 1961 the air force established a Combat Crew Training Squadron (CCTS) nicknamed Jungle Jim at Eglin Air Force Base. The squadron's specific mission was to train friendly forces in aircraft they would acquire from the US surplus inventory. The squadron's Detachment 2, which was nicknamed Farm Gate, deployed to Bien Hoa, Republic of Vietnam, in November 1961 to train the Vietnamese Air Force in counterinsurgency tactics.[1] Farm Gate's airmen wore distinctive Australian-style air commando jungle hats.

In 1962 the air force continued to expand its counterinsurgency role by establishing the Special Air Warfare Center (SAWC) at Eglin Air Force Base. It absorbed the assets of the CCTS that were already committed in Vietnam and created Mobile Training Teams (MTTs) that spread throughout Latin America where the Green Berets had already established their foothold.[2]

It wasn't just the absence of dedicated aircraft for special operations; the Department of Defense (DOD) neglected to plan ahead and establish a permanent joint service organization to orchestrate effective special operations support for the conventional military forces. Consequently, once the United States became involved in Vietnam, the government came to another starting point for creating an organization that would do the job.

Vietnam

It became obvious that limited, insurgency-type wars needed dedicated aircraft to conduct special operations in support of other branches of service. The aircraft had to be capable of flying cargo and personnel at low altitudes deep into the enemy-controlled air space. They had to avoid detection by the enemy's radar, whose improving electronic technology would threaten their survivability. Also, their successful employment needed to be orchestrated into the overall war strategy of other conventional forces.

In 1963 the DOD got down to serious business and developed a concept under OPLAN 34A that addressed special operations requirements in intelligence collection, psychological operations, political pressure, resistance operations, and physical destruction. President Lyndon B. Johnson approved it. However, there were some political problems with its implementation. The plan was aimed at expanding the unconventional war into North Vietnam, with the hope that once we posed a serious threat to the North Vietnamese economic and political infrastructure at home, they would cease their infiltration activities into the south. The US military assistance to the Republic of Vietnam through the Military Assistance Command, Vietnam (MACV) was limited to counterinsurgency operations in the south. To implement the plan's clandestine operations against North Vietnam, the DOD had to create a special group directly under the Special Assistant for Counterinsurgency and Special Activities (SACSA) to conduct four types of operations: maritime, psychological warfare, airborne, and normal air.[3]

The original name of this Special Operations Group (SOG) was soon changed to the Studies and Observations Group, which retained its SOG acronym. It was located in Saigon where the DOD retained operational control of it, ensuring that its clandestine activities were consistent with the politics and war strategies of Washington. The MACV was kept out of the chain of command, and the SOG's leadership was vested in an army colonel. Operations conducted by SOG were so highly classified that very few officials even at the highest level of command in Vietnam were aware of their existence.

SOG's operations required long-range transport aircraft that could carry out clandestine insurgency and psychological operations into North Vietnam. Available and suitable aircraft had to be modified to assume this new role. The Fairchild C-123 transport was chosen for this role under a program called Big Safari. This little-known program was created to bypass the normal time-consuming procurement bidding and contract awarding process in order to expedite urgent modifications of limited numbers of aircraft for specific purposes. Modification of six C-123s under a project named Duck Hook and later renamed Heavy Hook is a good example of Big Safari's many special aircraft modifications. Modification of six airframes with enhanced low level compatible navigation equipment and electronic countermeasures (ECM) to detect enemy radar was performed at Lockheed Air Service in Ontario, California. None of the installed systems were designed specifically for the Heavy Hook C-123. They were off-the-shelf items already employed in other aircraft. Four of these modified C-123s became operational at Nha Trang in 1964.[4]

From its inception SOG wanted a newer and heavier aircraft, such as the C-130. Consequently, the air force directed in 1965 that fourteen of its new production line C-130s should be modified through Big Safari also at Lockheed Air Service in Ontario, California, for employment in special operations under the project name Stray Goose. This program incorporated experiences of prior conflicts that employed C-47s, B-17s, B-24s, B-29s, and many others and came out with the first airframe specifically dedicated to special operations missions.[5] This was definitely a great leap forward. Later, the modified aircraft became known as Combat Talons. Their periodic follow-on modifications kept up with the emerging technology and unconventional warfare needs and provided the Air Force Special Operations Forces (AFSOF) with many years of service, to the present day.

Lure of Special Operations

I followed the evolution of special operations while I served as assistant professor of aerospace studies in the Air Force Reserve Officer Training Corps (AFROTC) detachment at Texas A&M University during 1964–67. At that time the school was an all-male university whose special feature was the requirement for all able-bodied first- and second-year students to be enrolled in either the Army or Air Force ROTC. Almost three thousand young men participated in this program. Students in the third and fourth year had military contracts and received commissions as second lieutenants upon completion of their individual baccalaureate programs. Texas A&M was proud of being the second-largest producer of career officers, after the US Military Academy at West Point. Besides teaching courses in aerospace studies, I was an advisor to about 140 young men in two Air Force Cadet squadrons.

I often wondered how I could fit special operations into my air force career. My undergraduate studies focused on international relations, specifically on the struggle between the USA and USSR. Then I began my postgraduate studies at Texas A&M, learning Spanish and focusing on the Unites States' relationship with Latin America. Surely, I could be useful in some future unconventional role assignment.

One of the school's instructional features was the showing of a monthly documentary film on what was new in the air force. My growing interest in special operations received a substantial boost in 1966 when I saw a film segment on the Fulton Recovery System, a new project experimenting with a specially configured C-130 aircraft that could pick up people from the ground. It was something I wanted to become involved in. One of my colleagues was equally interested in this because before coming to Texas A&M, he had served in Hawaii where he flew in special C-130s that snatched secret surveillance satellites in midair after they reentered into the earth's atmosphere over the Pacific Ocean. The war in Vietnam was escalating, and there was no doubt in our minds that this system was used to rescue soldiers from behind enemy lines. We also knew that at the end of our tour of duty at Texas A&M we would be sent to fly in Vietnam in who knows what type of aircraft. By volunteering for this program, we could be assured that our one-year tour there would be in the aircraft of our choice. My friend, Lt. Col. Tom Hines, had a good friend in the nearby Air Force Military Personnel Office at Randolph Air Force Base who was responsible for Vietnam assignments. We decided to pay him a visit.

Before driving to San Antonio, we coordinated with our wives. By volunteering for this newly established program, we could end up with a shortened tour at Texas A&M, but we would gain by going to Vietnam in an aircraft of our choice. Since we were guaranteed a follow-on one-year tour in Vietnam anyway, this seemed to be a pretty good plan. Our wives agreed. Tom's friend, who had also served at Texas A&M before our time, was not as enthusiastic about our desire to jump into this new program. He asked us to rethink our plans. The program called for pilots and navigators with many hours of flying experience. To be an aircraft commander, one needed at least three thousand hours in a C-130. Navigators also needed that much time, but their flying time could be in many other aircraft. Tom had so much C-130 time that he, as a lieutenant colonel, could qualify for an operations officer of the unit. That was exactly what he wanted. There was also another catch. He told us that the new unit could expect a loss of one-third of its crew and that the survivors would most likely end up in the special operations loop for as many as eight years by filling follow-on special operations assignments in Europe, Stateside, and then back in the Pacific.

We did not change our minds, and Tom promised that he would get in touch with a number of his pilot and navigator buddies and have them volunteer for this program.

Combat Talons in Vietnam and Beyond

The rest of the story in this book is told from my personal perspective enhanced by numerous accounts of my colleagues who assisted me with their documented inputs. We served together in the lowest echelon of our commands where we, as worker bees, executed every task and mission as best as we could, believing that we were contributing significantly to the anticipated victory in Vietnam. We knew that there were some command problems due to our highly classified top secret posture and that this affected our blending into the overall wartime effort. But that odd feature of our existence did not concern us at that time. After all, we were obligated to contribute only one year of our careers to this war and then expected to return to hopefully normal peacetime assignment. Now, decades after that war, we have good historical hindsight, and because this story concludes in 2015, I need to dwell on what was happening all around us during that war and how the Combat Talons survived the spurting evolution of the air force's special operations.

The Combat Talon story cannot be told without including details of the impact Gen. William W. "Spike" Momyer had on the unconventional warfare in Vietnam. He is well known today for being an authority on air force doctrine and tactical air power, as well as for his personal dislike of special operations and their effective employment of obsolescent aircraft. He did not like the popular image the air commandos assumed after their reestablishment in 1961. Shortly after he became the commander of the Seventh Air Force in Vietnam in 1966, he banned the Australian-style bush hats along with distinctive baseball caps and insignias of past units that the commandos wore. Momyer claimed that special uniforms should not have been authorized. The first commander of the 14th Air Commando Wing, Col. Gordon Bradburn, recalled that Momyer commented to him that he was going to "educate you guys back into the Air Force."[6]

Colonel Bradburn's 14th ACW at Nha Trang and Col. Harry C. "Heinie" Aderholt's 56th ACW at Nakhon Phanom, Thailand, were not the favorite wings of Momyer's Seventh Air Force. Colonel Aderholt's biography, *Air Commando One*, which is lauded by the retired air commando community, addresses the conflicts between him and Momyer.[7] These wing-level adversities did not affect the SOG mission of the Stray Goose detachment at Nha Trang. There was a problem between the Seventh Air Force and the SOG because that command level was kept out of the loop, which did not sit well with Momyer. This was partially rectified by a memorandum of understanding on 26 October 1967 that established the office of Deputy Commander for Special Operations (DCSO) under the commander of the 14th ACW. Under it, the operational control of the Stray Goose detachment and the Heavy Hook First Flight flowed from SOG through the DCSO. The DCSO became responsible for administration and supervision of assigned personnel, flying safety, adherence to air force regulations, and for performance of other air force normal service functions.[8] Was that part of "educating you guys back into the Air Force?"

Initially, the Stray Goose Detachment 1 belonged to the 314th Troop Carrier Wing based at Ching Chuan Kang Air Base in Taiwan, and the 14th ACW at Nha Trang was obligated to provide it with base facilities. Obviously, more command adjustments were necessary. This was corrected on 15 March 1968 when Detachment 1 of the 314th TCW was renamed as the 15th Air Commando Squadron (ACS) and transferred to the Nha Trang based 14th ACW commanded by Col. John M. Patton. This did not change the new squadron's mission. The squadron remained under the DCSO, Col. David Collins. However, that was not all. There was another name change on 1 August 1968. At that time both the squadron and the wing lost their "commando" designation. The squadron became the 15th Special Operations Squadron, and the wing became the 14th Special Operations Wing. Lieutenant General Momyer approved this name change. He was promoted to a full general and took over the Tactical Air Command later in 1968. He retired in 1973 and spent five years writing the authoritative book on doctrine, strategy, and tactics, *Air Power in Three Wars*.[9] He lived to see the transfer of the special operations air forces from the Tactical Air Command to the Military Airlift Command in 1983 and the establishment of the Air Force Special Operation Command (AFSOC) as an independent air force major command in 1990. The Combat Talons survived all these evolutionary changes to the special operations. Vietnam's Combat Talon unit, nicknamed Combat Spear, remained within the Pacific Command (PACOM). The training unit in the States, nicknamed Combat Arrow, ended up in the AFSOC, and a new Combat Knife was introduced into the European Command (EUCOM). (General William W. "Spike" Momyer passed away at the age of ninety-five in 2012.)

2

Stray Goose Training

Pope Air Force Base, North Carolina

Tom Hines and I were somewhat surprised when our tour of duty at Texas A&M was curtailed before the end of the academic year. Our reassignment orders were not very clear. The eventual unit of assignment was Detachment 1 of the 314th Troop Carrier Wing, PACAF at APO San Francisco. (APO San Francisco, 96205, was the US Post Office address for Nha Trang Air Base in the Republic of Vietnam.) With my orders, I would start transitional training into C-130s at Pope Air Force Base (AFB) in North Carolina after the Easter holidays. This would be done in a Rotational Training Unit (RTU) that took in all rated specialties from pilots to loadmasters and introduced them to their new aircraft—a transport C-130. Then I was to remain at Pope Air Force Base and begin follow on Project Stray Goose training, starting in June.

I did not waste any time after arriving at Pope AFB. Right after signing in at the RTU, I went to the squadron that had four special C-130s on the far end of the ramp watched over by armed guards. They had to be the Stray Goose aircraft. I identified myself as a future student and wanted to speak to some of the instructors. I learned much later that the officer who told me to cool my heels and wait for my time to come was not even in the program. When he told me: "Major, you don't yet have the need to know anything about the Stray Goose," he was correct. I had to wait until the day my Stray Goose training program started.

In the meantime, I continued with my introductory C-130 training. Knowing that I would be in North Carolina for at least four months, I rented a home and brought in my whole family—wife Anita and children Dolores, John, Julie, and Alice—from Bryan, Texas. The oldest, first grader Dolores, experienced her first of many school transplantations. As I flew, I observed minimal activity along the closely guarded Stray Goose aircraft. The talk was that they flew at night. After a while the word spread that I was one of those who would stay at Pope AFB and fly in one of those aircraft. Then my classmates began to ask me questions about what I knew about that mysterious program. I know what some of them must have thought of me. "This guy volunteered for a program he knew nothing about!" That part was right. But there was nothing wrong with my motivation.

Stray Goose

Once I reported for the Stray Goose training I reconnected with Lt. Col. Tom Hines, who did his C-130 refresher training at Stewart Air Force Base in Tennessee. He was good to his word. He recruited some of his prior crew members for the program. Two of them would be on my Vietnam-bound crew. Maj. Bob Rosser, a highly experienced C-130 pilot, became my aircraft commander, and Capt. Hugh McCormick, from his assignment as a satellite cone snatcher in Hawaii, became my companion navigator. Stray Goose C-130s required eleven crewmembers: three pilots, two navigators, one navigator/electronic warfare officer (EWO), two flight engineers (FEs), two loadmasters (LMs), and one radio operator (RO). We would train together as a crew because this special operations aircraft required exceptional crew coordination. We were the eleventh crew trained by the 779th Troop Carrier Squadron's Stray Goose instructors. The first six were numbered Stray Goose 1 through 6 (SG-1 through SG-6). After that the numbering restarted with S-01. My crew number became S-05.

"Stray Goose" was the name assigned to the air force's 1965 project to modify fourteen new production C-130E models for employment in future special operations. The first four aircraft went to the 779th Troop Carrier Squadron at Pope Air Force Base where they were used to train crews for their operational employment in the Vietnam War. Instructors for these aircraft were trained in the Lockheed Air Service facility in Ontario, California. That is where the special navigational and electronic countermeasures systems were installed and flight tested. Their training was an integral part of the Stray Goose project. C-130s modified under the Big Safari program were named Combat Talons, however, the Stray

Goose name persisted among the newly trained crews that were going to fly them in Vietnam. My 1967 assignment orders for a one-year tour in Vietnam directed me to start with a "Project Stray Goose" training at Pope Air Force Base.

The first six Vietnam-bound crews deployed with their four new aircraft to the 314th Troop Carrier Wing (TCW) at Ching Chuan Kang (CCK) Air Base in Taiwan. There they became members of this wing's Detachment 1. They arrived with a mascot that was not a goose but a duck named Maynard. Two crew members raised it from an "egg size" baby to a short-lived adult alcoholic bird. Perhaps this duck inspired the no-longer-remembered designers of their new unit's logo, which was a comic book caricature of an angry goose with a spear in its beak.

Why the spear? These, eventually fourteen new MC-130E (I)s were dispersed to three global locations. Pope Air Force Base's training unit was named Combat Knife. The just-deployed four aircraft unit to CCK became Combat Spear, and the yet to be formed future unit in Germany was going to become Combat Arrow. These unit names, Knife, Spear, and Arrow, would remain their permanent Combat Talon names even though their air force unit designated names and numbers would change as they all moved from one location to another with corresponding reassignments to new parent wings.

Old timers have fond memories of Maynard. Stories about him are told at reunions, and they become embellished with imaginary feats. However, his short biography that follows is all true. Lt. David Mattingly got a baby duckling as an Easter present from his girlfriend and named him Maynard. He was a cute little fellow who never realized that he was a duck because

Duck Maynard has no resemblance to the stray goose on the original depiction of the first Combat Talon mascot logo. (Composite by John Gargus, photo of Maynard by David Mattingly)

he spent all his time in the company of Mattingly and his roommate Lt. Bill Guenon. They had to coax him into a pool of water and urge him to swim. As a land-based baby growing up very fast in the bachelor officers' quarters (BOQ) he exhibited fear of water. But with some coaxing, he got accustomed to being in the water and to the lifestyle of his two human roommates. They took him everywhere they went, attracting much attention in the bars and restaurants they frequented. That is where he acquired a taste for rum and coke and medium rare steaks. He was pretty well grown up and white feathered when it came time for the first contingent of Stray Goose crews to depart for Vietnam. By that time, even though he was not a goose, all regarded him as a Stray Goose mascot and deployed with him to CCK in Taiwan.

Maynard attracted the attention of a reporter when Mattingly and Guenon took him for a waddling walk in Honolulu, their first overnight stop on the way to Taiwan. He was photographed, and the interview the reporter had with his human companions appeared in the *Honolulu Star Bulletin*. It would have been just a cute duck story about soldiers taking a duck to their wartime assignment if the story had not identified them as members of a Stray Goose project. That was the first time this classified project name appeared in newsprint. Even though this incident did not lower the boom on the security leakers, we heard plenty about it during our training at Pope AFB. We were cautioned not to attract any attention to ourselves and to our project.

Maynard's antics caused his owners many interesting problems with military authorities. Embellished barroom stories about him abound to this day. But, as expected, Maynard became an alcoholic. Friendly doctors who examined him diagnosed him with sclerosis of the liver. He died of it before reaching his first full year. The crew encased him in an aluminum pan and dropped him into the Gulf of Tonkin during a leaflet drop from 18,000 feet.

The "Stray Goose" name began to fade during the Vietnam War. US troops who served in Vietnam resorted to calling Combat Talon aircraft "Blackbirds" because of their dark jungle canopy color. Only those crews assigned to Combat Spear units persisted in using the name Stray Goose. Tactical manuals that were eventually published for the MC-130E (I) fleet by the Tactical Air Command referred to them only as Combat Talons. However, the Stray Goose name and the original logo are still alive today and will survive in the annals of aviation history thanks to the Stray Goose

Composite photo shows two Combat Talons on a low-level flight. Note the successful camouflage. The shadow of the bottom aircraft is more visible than its fuselage. (USAF photo)

International organization established in 1993 by six early commanders of the Combat Spear unit in the Pacific.

"Blackbirds" was the name given to our Stray Goose aircraft by the Special Forces we supported. Later, "Blackbirds" became the popular name for the spy SR-71 supersonic aircraft that provided our forces with high altitude photography. However, at the time of this story the SR-71s were still highly classified. The dark jungle canopy paint scheme that made the Stray Goose aircraft look black from a distance went out of style after Vietnam when other operational camouflage colors became necessary. Today, only the old timers who flew them refer to them as Blackbirds.

Our training was unlike anything I experienced before. Because of the TOP SECRET classification of almost everything inside of the aircraft, we did not have any books or flight manuals to study. While parked on the ramp, the aircraft were secured by an armed guard who allowed only those individuals to enter the clearly marked restricted area who had specifically authorized access to them. Classroom note taking was discouraged. All learning was by listening, observing, and doing.

Our instructors were excellent. They understood the capabilities of the aircraft, but none of them had seen any service in Vietnam. They would not say anything about the missions we would fly once we arrived there, even though our training gave us plenty of clues about what we would end up doing. As far as they were concerned, everything about our future missions was classified and they would not talk about it. They would not even tell us where we would be based. We learned from other Pope C-130 crew members who went to Southeast Asia on temporary duty (TDY) assignments that our parent 314th Troop Carrier Wing was based at Ching Chuan Kang (CCK) Air Base in Taiwan. Pope TDY crews were assigned there while they flew throughout Southeast Asia. Perhaps we would be based in Taiwan.

We began our Stray Goose training with a fascinating demonstration flight in which the instructors showed what the aircraft could do at low levels. We also observed ground to air extraction by the Fulton Recovery System both from inside of the aircraft and then from the ground up.

My most impressive experience was the realization about what the terrain following radar (TFR) could do. Our instructors flew the aircraft into a straight but very narrow valley that could almost be described as a gorge. TFR was set to fly at 500 feet above the ground. They put the flight controls on autopilot and let us observe the downhill ride. The valley floor below was uneven, which caused the radar to fly us somewhat higher, but we were told that the nearest obstacle below would not have us closer to it than the preselected altitude of 500 feet. I was standing behind the copilot's seat with my eyes fixed at the terrain off our right wing. At 230 knots of ground speed (GS) the hillside on our right whizzed by rapidly and the distance of our right wing tip from the tree-lined hillside was stretching and narrowing as we sped forward. One instructor pointed out to me that I was standing about 66 feet from the tip of the right wing and that TFR gave us about 100 feet of minimum clearance to the closest lateral obstacle, measured from the center of the aircraft. That would be just 35 feet of wingtip clearance. Terrain following at such close distances is not meant to be done on autopilot. Our flight was just a demonstration ride to show us what kind of clearances we could expect from the TFR.

I compared the wingtip clearance we experienced to an everyday occurrence on interstate highways. Imagine doing 60 to 65 miles per hour in the fast left-hand lane. You are likely to be about 35 feet away from the trees that line the highway. If you look to your left, the trees whiz by your

A view of the flyby terrain and trees that seem to pass so close to the wing tips. (USAF photo, composite by John Gargus)

car rapidly, almost in a blur. Now, if you could quadruple your speed to 265 mph, you would see the trees or terrain go by as fast as they go by the wingtip of an aircraft that moves four times as fast at its normal terrain following speed.

APQ-115 Terrain Following Radar (TFR)

Terrain following flight is a simple concept that became a reality once the military developed radar and computer technology to the point where they could be combined into an operational system. Blind people learn to use sticks to assist them in walking on uneven and obstacle-filled terrain. They use their walking canes to touch the ground along their intended path, feeling for obstacles as well as dips and rises in the terrain. They adjust their pace and steps accordingly. The aircraft we were training to use is much like a blind person; the only difference is that it is airborne and must maintain forward flying speed without touching the ground. It must fly over the terrain ahead at desired altitudes. The aircraft's probing cane is a narrow pencil radar beam that scans the intended flight path over the ground. Return signals from this radar beam provide accurate distances to the obstacles ahead and their elevations relative to the aircraft's in-flight altitude. What is needed is a timely command to the pilot to tell him when he should begin to climb, descend, or resume level flight in order to negotiate the terrain ahead at a desired aboveground clearance. A computer can accomplish this if it is given two more pieces of critical information. The first is the ground speed of the aircraft, which is required to calculate the needed start climb and dive commands. The second is the wind drift. The center of the narrow radar beam's scan must not be straight ahead of the aircraft along its longitudinal axis. It has to center on the projected track of the aircraft over the ground. The effect of the wind drift has to be offset to the left or right of the nose of the aircraft. Both of these vital inputs are available from the Doppler radar. They are fed into the integrated terrain following computer that calculates the timing of needed up and down commands to correspond to the terrain ahead. The drift information is needed for slaving the middle of the radar beam sweep on the centerline of the projected aircraft's path over the ground. That was the terrain following technology of the Stray Goose and the follow-on Combat Talons.

Now declassified and well known as Combat Talons, these first-generation aircraft were truly special pieces of equipment. In a typical special operations manner, they were equipped with systems that were already available for other experimental or developing projects and that were put together to perform a mission that had not existed before. Terrain following radar was a new type of computerized radar developed for the newest fighter aircraft. It was designed to permit the aircraft to penetrate into hostile territory at low altitudes where they could avoid detection by enemy's early warning radar. The technology was quite primitive by today's standards. Because it was designed for small jet aircraft with operational air speed twice that of a C-130, the radar operated in the low spectrum of its optimum range. We could not use it for terrain following at air speeds below 160 knots because below that slow speed the computer would go into memory operation and give the radar a FAIL indication. It worked well at a C-130 normal operational ground speed of 230 knots.

Each Stray Goose crew had three pilots, two navigators, two flight engineers, two loadmasters, and one each electronic warfare officer (EWO) and radio operator. Three pilots were necessary because of the strain on the two pilots in the seats who had to monitor the console and manipulate the throttles. To avoid fatigue, pilots in the left seats had to switch at periodic intervals. The aircraft commander would occupy the right-hand, normally the copilot, seat. The third pilot, who alternated with the pilot in the left seat, was used as a map reader standing behind the left-hand seat.

For all practical purposes, terrain following flying was like flying a sustained instrument landing system (ILS). Pilots had to fly by the attitude direction indicator's (ADI's) pitch bar that received commands based on radar terrain returns and the horizontal situation bar that received inputs from the Doppler cross track. Pilots in the left seat had to monitor the radar scope for visual terrain signals and manipulate engine throttles to maintain the desired ground speed. During daytime, well-placed cockpit windows allowed them to verify approaching terrain, but on a dark night, this was impossible. They could not fix their eyes to the outside through the ever-present glare of the cockpit's amber lights and not risk losing focus on the instruments by which they had to fly. For that reason, it became the standard practice to have the first pilot fly in the left seat and have the aircraft commander sit on the right. This was the only way he could command his eleven-member crew. Flying in the left-hand seat he could not take time away from the instruments to focus on even a routine in-flight problem. He did not have a radar scope on the panel in front of him when he sat on the right, but he could terrain follow by monitoring his ADI and the Doppler ground speed indicator. He had the complete control of the aircraft whenever the pilots on the left switched with each other.

Flying at desired ground speeds instead of air speeds had certain advantages. Pilots had to monitor their Doppler ground speed indicators and keep one hand on the engine throttles so that they could manipulate them to maintain the desired ground speed during ADI commanded climbs or descents. It helped the navigators to attain greater timing precision. They would simply tell the pilot what ground speed to fly to reach a given turning point with accuracy measured in seconds. For airdrops, the navigators could monitor and control the time-to-go display to arrive within five seconds to a desired drop point. The APQ-115 terrain following radar was poor for mapping, especially at low altitudes where we could fly at preselected terrain following altitudes of 250, 500, and 1,000 feet. It wasn't practical to switch from a terrain following mode to a mapping mode to look for targets when low altitude concealment behind elevated terrain features was desired. For that reason, there were two navigators on board. One would operate the radar and related navigational aids from the navigator's console. The other navigator would map read, standing on the right-hand side behind the aircraft commander.

Terrain following in the Combat Talons required great concentration and crew participation. The navigator seated at the console had to monitor everything on his console and follow the flight progress on his chart. He had a more complete control of the TFR and had to inform the pilots whenever he switched the available radar scope presentations. He monitored the Doppler radar and updated it as necessary. Because the TFR was designed to scan only a limited space ahead of the aircraft, and the flights were always so close to the ground, it was very limited in its mapping capability. For that reason, almost all updates to Doppler radar came from the map-reading navigator or the third pilot. The third pilot stood on the left behind the pilot and the navigator behind the aircraft commander. They would call corrections to the radar navigator, saying such things as: "We are .2 mile to the left," or "I have us .3 of a mile short." Normally, both would agree with the call and the radar navigator would reset the Doppler that would immediately show up on the ADIs if the correction was left or right of track.

Each flight had three identical navigational charts in the cockpit. Each map reader held his in his hand. Each was carefully folded or rolled up to show just the area over which the aircraft flew at that time. The radar navigator had his spread out on his worktable. We used Air Operations Charts of 1 to 250,000 scale and others that were as detailed as 1 to 50,000. Each leg of flight was from 20 to 60 nautical miles in length. The whole route of flight, with many changes of headings, was drawn by a solid line that had a tick mark every mile from the turning point ahead to its start at the preceding one. Some preferred to have a bigger tick mark at each 5-mile interval and still a larger one at 10 miles. This made it easier especially for the map readers who didn't have a tabletop and had to refold their charts periodically as the flight progressed. That way they could quickly glance at the decreasing distance to go counter in the cockpit and compare it to the distance on the map and to the terrain they observed through the windows. One nautical mile, or 1 knot, is equal to 1.1508 statute miles that we use to measure distances on highways. The normal operational speed of 230 knots is equal to 265 miles per hour.

The 230 knot ground speed corresponded nicely to the nautical mile distances ticked on our charts. Each nautical mile corresponded to 1 knot of ground speed. This was convenient and easy to correlate with our charts. At that comfortable C-130 ground speed we flew at almost 4 nautical miles (nm) per minute or 1 nm every fifteen seconds. It made it easier for the navigators to tell the pilots at what ground speed they needed to fly in order to meet the time of arrival at a turning point. As the pilots increased or decreased the requested ground speed, the computer's time-to-go would indicate the precise arrival time and if all else went well, the on the ground checkpoint could normally be reached within five seconds of scheduled time. That was the accuracy we could only dream of before flying by ground speed. That also helped us on airdrops. We could reach our initial point with the same accuracy, but then the aircraft would have to slow down and start flying indicated air speed through the air mass that was also moving with the direction of the wind. That relatively short period of flight caused small adjustments to the timing of a "green light" drop command.

"Short Look"

Part of our day and night terrain following flights included an execution of a simulated psychological leaflet drop. We called this maneuver "short look." We flew it on the longest leg of our flight over the western mountains of North Carolina. It ran from a prominent turning point west of Charlotte and ran north to another point west of Hickory. We had a designated high altitude drop line that ran more than 10 nm and a desired wind vector. Airdrop would occur at a given minimum altitude that could vary from 20 to 30,000 feet depending on the encountered wind velocities. So, if the desired winds were experienced at 22,000 feet, the climb would stop there. If not, it was necessary to go higher.

The maneuver would begin by terminating the TFR flight and accelerating to the maximum air speed possible within the surrounding air mass. The pilots would advance the throttles to full power and the aircraft would begin to shake as it surged to the maximum attainable velocity. Once that point was reached, the pilot would raise the nose of the aircraft and perform a maximum rate of climb to the needed altitude. Once the radar navigator determined that the desired altitude and the wind vector were met, he would call for a level off and preparation for the drop. Once at proper air speed, the ramp would be opened and a simulated leaflet airdrop would begin. Typically, a box of leaflets would be jettisoned about every ten seconds.[1]

At any point during the drop sequence either one of the instructors (pilot or navigator) could call for an emergency abort. This simulated a call that would normally come when over hostile territory from the electronic warfare officer (EWO) who had detected that the aircraft was about to be attacked by anti-aircraft artillery (AAA), or surface to air missiles (SAMs). Response to that call had to be immediate. The drop would be aborted. The pilot would execute a swift defensive maneuver. He would close the ramp, reduce the power to idle, retract the flaps, lower the nose, and bank 60 degrees in any direction. The aircraft would quickly attain speed of over 300 knots, and hopefully, the enemy's radar lock-on would be broken. Return from this rapid fall through the skies to normal terrain following mode was tricky. The navigator had to monitor the rapidly decreasing altitude as well as the terrain below. He would have to call for a timely level off so that the aircraft was at least at a minimum safe altitude from which it could descend farther and resume terrain following flight.

Two significant phenomena occurred during a "short look" that affected the crew and anything in the aircraft that was not securely tied down. First, when the pilot initiated the rapid fall from the drop altitude, everyone experienced brief weightlessness, and if not strapped to a seat, would float up to the ceiling. The same thing happened to everything on the navigator's table. Loose pencils, erasers, books, as well as all loose things, would float up and then fall to the floor when the normal gravity was reestablished. Then, when the navigator called for the level off, the opposite effect manifested. Rapid increase in gravitational forces made everyone extremely heavy, and often those standing up were forced down to the floor on their hands and knees. Severity of that gravitational force depended on how the pilot handled the pull-up and level off.

Once the "short look" was over the navigator was busy checking the accuracy of the flight instruments while the others in the cockpit were picking up lost pencils or whatever flew about during the moment of weightlessness. The TRF always failed during this unusual operation. Its antenna could not handle the stress of the gravitational forces from the dive recovery. Normally, it righted itself and the FAIL warning light went away. A bigger problem was when the compass gyros tumbled. This made the gyro slaved compasses unreliable, and that marred the accuracy of other navigational instruments. Fortunately, this did not happen very often.

The short look maneuver was designed for psyops (psychological operations) leaflet drops in a hostile air space. Dropped leaflets were designed to influence the minds of targeted military and civilian populations with propaganda information that would lead them to doubt their cause and question the motives and capabilities of their leaders.

Fulton Recovery System

Inflight recovery of objects from the ground was not a new idea. Aircraft began to pick up mail packages early in the 1920s. Then during World War II the US Army Air Force showed interest in picking up personnel from behind enemy lines. After that the newly independent US Air Force continued experimenting with the All American Aviation System in C-47s, but it was not until Robert Edison Fulton Jr. developed his Skyhook Surface to Air Recovery System (STARS) that a personnel pickup became an operational option. In 1964 the air force decided to modify some of the new production C-130E models with the Skyhook STARS. Because the early Stray Goose crews got to meet Mr. Fulton during their training at Pope AFB, they preferred to call his invention as the Fulton Recovery System. The Lockheed C-130, model E became the air force's MC-130 E(I), also known as the Stray Goose and Combat Talon aircraft.

Very simply, the Fulton Recovery System was designed to pick up personnel or packages that were moored to a helium-filled balloon by a 500-foot-long lift line. Modified aircraft had to fly under the balloon, snatch the lift line into a locking device in its nose, and then pull the trailing line with suspended cargo into the aircraft with ramp-mounted winches. Normal operation envisioned a precision airdrop of a recovery kit to a person, or persons, on the ground, or a special kit adopted for recovery from the water. The receiving person then had twenty minutes to prepare for a pickup because the aircraft would return precisely twenty minutes later. This would happen if there was no radio communication between the aircraft and the person on the ground. In a permissive environment it would be safe to use radios, and the time of pickup could be adjusted to suit the person on the ground. The recovery kit could also be dropped by any other capable aircraft, even an F-4, or it could be included

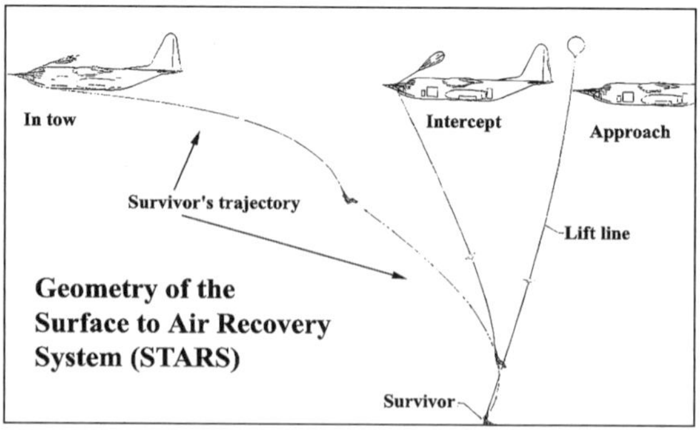

The geometry of the trajectory followed by a person or package picked up by Mr. Fulton's Surface to Air Recovery System. Initial lift-off is in the direction of the aircraft before the intercept. Consequently, the picked-up package can clear a nearby 30-foot tree before it follows the path of the towing aircraft. (Sketch from Robert E. Fulton's "One Man Caravan" with overprint by John Gargus)

in a normal resupply bundle air-dropped to the infiltrated teams. In that case, communication with the aircraft about the pickup time would become necessary.

A Fulton Recovery kit for personnel contained three numbered packages and a pressurized helium container with easy-to-follow instructions that were printed in simple English with comic book quality illustrations. The number one container had either one or two winter-type flight suits with parachute-like harness sewn into the fabric. Users were instructed to put on the suit and connect the harness to a snap on package number three, which contained the lift line. Then they were to tie together lines coming out of packages two and three. After that they were to plug in the hose of the pressurized helium container to the carefully unfolded balloon from package number two and inflate it. With that done, the balloon could be released slowly until it reached the maximum height permitted

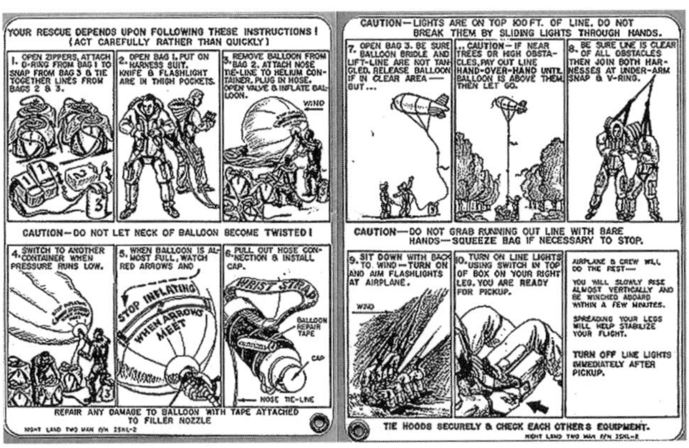

These simple illustrated instructions, laminated in protective plastic, were included in each Fulton Recovery kit. (Photo by John Gargus)

About to be picked up passenger gets ready for his ride. (Scanned photo from a Fulton Recovery System brochure)

by the full length of the 500-foot lift line from package number three. The lift line was specially braided with numerous strong nylon threads, which gave it a desirable capability to stretch and reduce the impact of gravitational forces on the individual. Experienced parachutists, who had been picked up, claimed that the g-forces they experienced were less than those felt in a parachute jump. The final step users had to take was to sit down with their back toward the wind, face the incoming aircraft, and wait for the most memorable pickup and ride.

The most distinguishable feature of a Stray Goose C-130 was the outer rigging of the STARS equipment. All modified aircraft had noticeably different looking noses. Built into the nose section, on the top part of the radome, were retractable yokes and connectors for removable propeller guide cables called fending lines. When installed for a recovery they stretched from the root of the yoke to the outboard end of each wingtip. They were embedded with sharp cutting blades that were spaced at regular intervals. These blades would sever the lift line in case the pilot failed to fly into it within the spread of the extended yokes. This ensured that the missed lift line did not make contact with the aircraft's propellers. Pilots seldom missed. When the yokes were fully extended they formed lobster-like antennas with a 24-foot-wide opening for the lift line to slide into a locking sky anchor in the nose of the aircraft.

Not visible were the easily installable internal components of the Fulton Recovery System that would be positioned on the ramp within the twenty-minute time period between the recovery kit drop and the scheduled pickup. These components included a rack for two hydraulically operated reel-in winches, an A-frame platform for elevating the pickup lift

A close view of a Combat Talon radome with retracted yoke arms. When the yoke is extended, the arms will guide the intercepted balloon tethering lift line into the sky hook locking mechanism. (Photo by John Gargus)

line, ramp air deflectors and guards, lift line retrieval hooks, and various personnel safety tie-down harnesses.

Everyone on the crew got involved in a pickup. First of all, the navigator had to come up with the existing wind direction at 500 feet above the ground and direct the aircraft to the pickup spot. The aircraft would have to slow down and fly into the wind on its pickup approach. One of the navigators would strap himself to the floor with a safety restraining harness and pull in the cockpit cabin's escape hatch. Then everyone in the cockpit would start looking for the moored balloon and the three small red flags that were embedded in the lift line just below it. Nighttime pickup was more challenging. The approach directions would be the same, but everyone would be looking for three bluish strobe lights instead of red flags. Once spotted, everyone wanted assurance from the pilot in the left seat that he had the lift line markers in sight and did not need any more help in getting to it. The pilot on the right took over the control of the throttles and maintained the 135 knot indicated air speed. After that the pickup pilot had both of his

Combat Talon at the moment of lift line intercept. (711th SOS photo)

hands free to aim for the middle marker. He could not be more than 12 feet left or right of the lift line. I never saw one miss.

At the moment of intercept, the balloon would rip open with the sharp jerk on the lift line, and everyone inside could hear a sharp slap as the top portion of the lift line made contact with the roof of the aircraft. It was much louder at night when the fragile glass strobe lights slammed into the aircraft. Then, the navigator, who opened the overhead escape hatch, had to pull the loose end of the lift line inside of the cockpit. Once he had the balloon side of the line inside, he had to remove any remaining strobe light glass and cut off the hardened pig tail that had connected it to the now-deflating and free-floating balloon. At times this proved to be a challenging task. This was when the end of the lift line would be too far to the right side of the escape hatch and the navigator had to stick the upper part of his body out of the aircraft as far as the restraining strap would allow him to go. Then he would have to use the walking-cane-like hook to snatch the loose line and pull it inside of the cockpit. The hook was also tied to the cockpit floor. Such a windy maneuver got rid of one's dandruff better than any brand of shampoo.

At the same time the navigator was taking care of the top of the lift line, two loadmasters, who were also strapped to the ramp with restraints that would prevent them from falling out, were also hanging over the side and fishing for the other end of the line that would float several feet below the aircraft. They used a suspended torpedo-shaped bomb with hooks on each side to engage the trailing line. The fishing hook bomb was connected to the upper winch that was used to reel it inside of the aircraft along with the snatched lift line. Working together, the loadmasters tied down the lift line to a cleat bar on the ramp, and once it was secured in two places, the pilot was instructed to release the sky anchor so that the loadmasters could pull the balloon end of the lift line through it and then along the bottom of the aircraft and onto its opened rear ramp. The end of the lift line was entered through the top pulley of the A frame that was still flat on the floor of the ramp. Once the picked-up load was reeled to the edge of the ramp, the top winch was used to raise the A frame, which elevated the picked-up load in trail load above the edge of the ramp and permitted the rescued person to enter the aircraft in a standing-up position.

Four people worked in the back of the aircraft. The loadmasters worked the end of the ramp and handled the lift line. One of the flight engineers worked as the hydraulic winch operator. (This was the main reason for having two flight engineers on each crew.) The third pilot became the safety observer. He monitored everything that was happening on the ramp. He made sure that the loadmasters were properly secured to the aircraft during the lift line retrieval and that they had the line secured in two places at all times before the final winching-in of the person in tow. Both loadmasters and the flight engineer wore helmets and restricted their communications to well-rehearsed hand signals that were understood by the safety observer. The safety observer stayed out of the way and was on the headset so that he could communicate with the crew giving a play-by-play-type narration of the goings on in the rear of the aircraft. Consequently, coordination by hand signals was very important. The loadmasters needed to have both of their hands free and could not be reaching for and depressing mike buttons to talk.

The electronic warfare officer and the radio operator did not have a direct role during the Fulton Recovery. The STARS was installed for use inside a hostile air space. That is when the EWO had to be on his toes monitoring his console and headset for signs of enemy threats. The radio operator's console was just to the left of the EWO's position. He was needed to be ready for any emergency radio transmission that could come up at any moment. Once in Vietnam, the EWOs would train the radio operators as their competent assistants to monitor various electronic signals that the aircraft's electronic countermeasures (ECM) equipment could detect. Their dual position was located just behind the aircraft's bulkhead, and it was closed off by a heavy duty curtain that protected the TOP SECRET ECM systems from the view of those who had no need to know. We kept the curtain closed even when we did not have any passengers riding with us. It was quieter behind the curtain than anywhere else in the back of the aircraft.

We could not run a full cycle of Fulton Recovery at any of the four Fort Bragg drop zones. Drop times had to be scheduled well ahead and coordinated with many other activities that were always going on there either on the ground or in the air. Coming back twenty minutes later for a pickup would require more time reserved for the drop zone. In addition, moored balloons 500 feet above any drop zone would interfere with other air traffic at other nearby zones. So, we dropped loads that simulated Fulton Recovery kits at Fort Bragg drop zones and did the balloon pickups from a rented small field on a farm south of the drop zones. Ground crews, consisting of loadmasters from other crews, used one large storage shed for the balloons and other needed equipment. A life-size rubberized dummy that could be folded into a seated position served as a pickup passenger. To ensure that we did not destroy a new balloon at every pickup, the ground crews designed an ingenious system for dual tethered balloons. A smaller, about quarter size, balloon was tied to the normal size recovery balloon by an about 200-foot-line and then moored to the ground by a parallel 500-foot line. The top of the lift line was weakened to tear upon impact so that it would break just below the balloon and the intact balloon would rise to the additional 200-foot height allowed by the length of the line that tethered it to the smaller balloon. The ground crew would then pull down both balloons for use at the next pickup. Normally the large balloon had to be deflated so that it would fit back in the storage barn. Escaping helium gas would get inhaled by the handlers who would then talk funny until the helium effect on their vocal cords wore off.

ECM Equipment

Stray Goose electronic countermeasures (ECM) equipment was the most sensitive TOP SECRET equipment installed on the aircraft. That was the reason why the EWO's and radio operator's positions were hidden behind the heavy curtain. EWO's ECM console was not a single system. It had an array of round scopes with numerous control knobs. Each displayed signals from sensors that detected electromagnetic energy striking various aircraft antennas. Consequently, the EWOs could monitor the enemy's ground-based early warning and tracking, as well as anti-aircraft weapon directing radars. Their displays showed the strength and the origins or directions of received energy signals. Because each radar beam had its own peculiar audio signal, they could identify exactly what type of radar was displayed on their scopes and what kind of threat it was posing. All those were passive systems. They also had a system for detecting airborne interceptor radars. Here they could manipulate the received signals and disrupt them. Hopefully they would confuse the attacking pilot's radar depiction of the aircraft he was tracking and assist the Stray Goose to evade the pursuer. EWOs also controlled a chaff dispensing system that, when energized, would create a very large and growing radar return on enemy's radar scopes. In addition to that, they operated state of the art tape recorders for recording and annotating audio signals from detected radars. In this manner, they became collectors of electronic intelligence (ELINT) that could be used for future mission planning and training.

EWOs were navigators with additional training in electronics and in the latest systems designed to detect enemy radar threats. Their training capability at Pope AFB was very limited. They could monitor every type of radar available along the TFR training routes over the Southeast United States but to prepare for Southeast Asia (SEA), they had to resort to listening to classified ELINT recordings received from Vietnam. Thanks to the training requirements of the Georgia National Guard whose F-102 interceptor pilots needed target aircraft to pursue, it was possible to schedule mutual training high level flights. That gave the EWOs opportunities to exercise the counter-interceptor capability of their equipment. Needless to say, they could not practice chaff dispensation in the US air space.

Detachment 1 Commander's Visit

One day, well into our training, we received a surprise visitor. He was Lt. Col. Don Britton, the commander of our future unit. He was interesting to talk with, but he would not tell us anything about our future missions. We did not yet have the need to know. We would learn everything once we arrived in Vietnam. There was always a chance that some of us would not complete our training and end up not going to war. By that time in our training we knew pretty well what we would be doing in Vietnam. Where else but over North Vietnam would we be challenged by Soviet-made radars and anti-aircraft weapons? There were none in the south at that time of the war. There were fighter pilots who faced being captured after ejecting from their crippled aircraft. Surely, we were destined to save some of them with our Fulton Recovery System.

He did tell us that the detachment he commanded started its operation at CCK Air Base in Taiwan, but soon after that they moved to Nha Trang Air Base in Vietnam. All his stories centered on the living facilities at Nha Trang. We learned that the officer crew members lived downtown in a rented hotel where they had their own dining facility and a rooftop bar. The hotel was occupied solely by the detachment's officers, and all members were kept in reasonable isolation from other air force units for security reasons. The enlisted crew members lived in designated facilities on base.

Survival Training

Finally after more than ninety hours of flying, more than thirty hours of which was at night, our Stray Goose training was completed. We now needed to put our family businesses together and proceed to the prisoner of war survival training at Fairchild Air Force Base near Spokane, Washington. After that we would fly from the West Coast to Clark Air Base in the Philippines where we would attend jungle survival training. Then we would fly to Saigon and on to Nha Trang.

The POW survival training took me back to the days of my youth and awakened concerns for my family in communist Czechoslovakia. My parents and younger brother and sister still lived there. How many more bad things could happen to them if I ever became a POW in North Vietnam? Since I was viewed in Czechoslovakia as a traitor for my unauthorized departure, I could be extradited if I was captured alive.

Instructors, who confronted me during the first interrogation that followed a make believe capture after a night escape and evasion exercise, focused on my foreign origin. They either learned about it from my personnel file or detected my foreign accent. I didn't voice anything more than the required name, rank, and service number during the interrogation. That should not have been enough for them to suspect me as one from some Slavic European country. But that is what they focused on. "Where are you from?" and "Where were you born?" Those were the same phrases I kept hearing. At times they were repeated in Russian. One of the interrogators would use Russian on me and also spoke it to his colleague, even though I concluded that the other one did not speak it. He would just nod his head and dadadad, saying "Da" and "Da" in agreement. I did not give any indication that I understood what was being said. Nevertheless, once they gave up trying, the Russian speaking interrogator called me "*tovarishch*" (communist word for comrade-in-arms) and said that they'd see me again.

My escorting guard replaced the hood over my head. The hood was just a sack of thick nylon fibers made for building sandbag barriers to control rising waters during flooding. Poking me in the ribs with what simulated a bayonet, he directed me to another room in the courtyard. Once there, two other guards forced me into a small pie-shaped box that was about 3 feet high and 2 feet wide at the opening. The side walls were about 3 feet long and met forming a sharp wedge. I had no idea what was going on.

Once they managed to have my whole body inside, they shut the guillotine-like drop door behind me. I was down on my knees and sat on my heels. I was bent over and could stretch my arms out to feel around the inside of the box. My shoulders were at an angle because at that point the box was too narrow for me to straighten them out. I took off my hood and tried to make myself as comfortable as I could. It seemed to me that there were many boxes like mine and that they were connected like pieces in a pie pan. I heard some noises, uncomfortable sobs of others who were in the same predicament as I, or the sounds might have been piped in for our torment. Occasionally, the guards would bang on top of the boxes, commanding us to be quiet. I was not making any noises, so the fact that they banged on my box showed me that the moaning sounds had to be piped in. I have no idea how long they kept me in the box. Sometimes I heard someone being forced into a box and sometimes others who were ordered to get out and straighten up.

I was really tired of my uncomfortable folded-up position in the box when the entry door suddenly opened. I eased out of the box and felt pain all over my body. I was prompted to straighten up. I could see my two tormenting guards in the semidarkness of the room. They got upset because I had removed my hood, and one of them had to bend down and get it out of the box. Once rehooded, they led me away and I tried to stretch as many sore muscles as I could before we reached another room where they took off my hood.

"*Ai tovarishch*, are you ready to talk now?" Those were the same two interrogators greeting me. I gave them my name, rank, and service number once more. They bought that, but next they wanted me to pronounce my name in my native tongue. Then they had other questions about my origins, and when they got tired of me the escorting guard put the hood back on my head. The parting words of the interrogators were that they would see me as soon as I got ready to talk. They put me back in the box.

I am sure that this time the box they put me in was somewhat smaller than the first one. I didn't fit in as well. Nevertheless, I managed to wiggle my body in until I attained what became my most comfortable position. I heard the same noises, and because of the repetition, I was sure that they were being played back from a tape. I don't know how long I was in the box this time. I was very sleepy and I was losing sense of the time.

After they took me out of the box, they walked me here and there for a while. That was good because I had more time to exercise my stiffened muscles. When we paused at a door, I was sure that I would be entering a new place. I was wrong. Once the sack was removed from my head, I stood in front of the same two interrogators.

They were more hostile in their approach. "Are you ready to talk to us now?" When he repeated the same in Russian, he no longer used the polite (plural) "you" but a familiar "you" in addressing me. Once again I gave no indication that I detected anything different. To encourage my cooperation they promised that I would be able to eat and get some sleep if I decided to talk. If I didn't, they would see me again. Neither one of them, nor I, was going anywhere. They were at home and I was their rude guest.

Back to the box we went. This time I knew that the box was smaller. I had some difficulty in getting in. They poked me in the buttocks as I was wiggling my body in. Then, before I was all the way in, they pushed the sliding door down. My left foot was in the way and the door hit me on my instep. I felt a sharp pain and let out a scream. I was sure that they broke my foot. Their response was to push my injured foot inside the box. I was in trouble now. My foot was in pain and I couldn't reach it to feel the extent of the injury. The discomfort I felt over my whole body from being in this smaller box soon overcame the pain in my foot. My only hope was that this box confinement would not last very long.

Once this ordeal ended and I was led away, I felt pain with every step. The guards did not notice anything, and when we stopped in front of a door I was ready to talk to the interrogators about my injury. But that did not happen. I was pushed inside a booth, and as they locked the door behind me, they told me that I was not to communicate with anyone and that I could not go to sleep. Once alone, I was able to feel around my booth in complete darkness. It was about twice the size of a telephone booth. There wasn't enough room in it to lie down. I sat down immediately and removed my left boot and sock. I couldn't see anything, but I felt that it was already swollen. It was sore to the touch, but I did not feel any broken bones. I was still feeling my sore foot when the door flew open and the guard shouted at me: "No sleeping," even though he could see that I was examining my foot. He slammed the door and locked it.

I just sat there and as my eyes adjusted to the dark, I noticed that there was some light coming in from around the door that wasn't completely insulated.

I was trying to sleep, but the guard would come by frequently and either bang on my door or sneak up and throw it open. On one such occasion he brought me a bowl of watered-down pea soup and a small piece of bread. The soup portion was about a cup and a half. It tasted good. While I sat there, I discovered another emerging problem. A squatting position in the box caused my hemorrhoids to flare up. Once my mind focused on that situation, I had to stand up to ease the emerging discomfort. I tried to sleep standing up in the corner, with each of my shoulders touching a converging corner wall. That gave my upper body some support and my spread-out legs held me up. I think that I actually got some sleep that way between the frequent times the guard came around to harass me and my neighbors. I kept repeating to myself that this was just training and that we were all supposed to get a taste of how life could be as a POW. It would soon be all over.

Then a guard came in and motioned me to come out. He uttered: "Put on your boots!" when he saw that one of my feet was bare. Surprisingly, I was able to put on the sock and insert my foot inside the boot without much pain. The guard took me back to the interrogation room. The two interrogators I faced this time were different. Sure enough, there must have been a shift change. They had regular working hours, and at that time I no longer had any idea how long I had been there. The first two interrogators were probably back at home sleeping in their beds.

I had a fresh start with these two. They began with the same set of questions. One of them pretended to write down my serial number. He looked at me with interest and asked me to spell my last name. I did that. Then he asked me to repeat my service number. I have no idea what possessed me but I told him "Forty-eight thousand four hundred and ninety-eight A." He almost jumped up from his chair, but the other one was amused. "Are you trying to be funny?"

I had no reply and they did not get anything else out of me. I said nothing about my sore foot. I knew that training would soon be over.

They sent me back to the triangular box. It was a medium-size one. It was definitely larger than the last one I came out of. In spite of the discomfort I think I might have fallen asleep in there because I was startled and did not know where I was when they opened the door and ordered me out. Then I no longer remember whether I went back to the box or the booth after another interrogation session. I know that I faced the same interrogators two more times before the training ordeal came to its end.

When I returned to my room at the bachelor officers' quarters after about sixty hours of sleepless evasion and resistance training I collapsed on my bed and slept for hours. After waking up I took a long shower, during which I examined my foot and my hemorrhoids. The foot appeared okay and seemed to hurt only when I thought about it. I could not say the same about my hemorrhoids. Without any details, they were unbearable. I was glad that our survival training was over. While I shaved in the community bathroom I learned from others that there was a bus that would leave soon for the airport in Spokane. I hurried to pack my belongings and departed. My wife had made plans to meet me in Seattle, where she visited her hometown high school friend. I had met my wife during my navigator training at Harlingen Air Force Base in Texas and got to know her friend very well.

After one night in Seattle we flew to San Francisco. We spent one night in a hotel there and met a navigator friend from Harlingen who was based at Beale Air Force Base. He and his wife showed us some nighttime city sites that included a drive through the hippie Haight-Ashbury district and a theater show featuring female impersonators. Then they took us to their home at Beale where we spent the night. On the next day our friend drove us to Travis Air Force Base for my departure to Clark Air Base and my wife to San Francisco for her return to Texas and our four small children.

Our long flight to the Philippines was the most unpleasant I ever had. After six years of flying in C-118s from McGuire Air Force Base, when I had no problem sleeping in an assigned bunk bed at my scheduled times, I could not sleep sitting up in an airline seat. So once again I went sleepless for a long time and suffered from my worsening hemorrhoid problem. I felt better standing up and walking back and forth in the aisle between the seats.

The jungle survival training started day after our arrival. The first days were in the classroom, and then we went by bus to a new jungle location. One week before there had been a tremendous downpour that caused mudslides in the training camp. Some people were lost in that disaster. So we were led to a pristine jungle area that had not been used before. The day went along fine and we all prepared our hammocks for sleeping at night. Soon it began to rain and we had to stretch our ponchos over the mosquito netting that covered our hammocks. Hungry mosquitos wanted to stay out of the rain as well, so they joined us under our poncho covers. Some found their way through the netting and fed on us during a rainy night. We were on a relatively steep slope and when daylight came we saw several mud balls that had rolled down the slope, picking up decayed jungle floor vegetation. They would roll an inch or two after the rain filled the vacated space behind them as they moved down the hill. Even before we took down our hammocks our instructors informed us that the survival training was canceled. They feared another disastrous mudslide.

Once back in quarters, I showered and discovered with alarm that my hemorrhoids had grown some more. I had to see a doctor about that. But I held off until the morning after our arrival at Nha Trang.

3

Vietnam

Saigon

My arrival in Vietnam was full of surprises. After I claimed my over-stuffed-with-clothing B-4 bag, I followed a line of new arrivals to find out where to go next. My flight to Nha Trang would be on a military aircraft that I needed to pick up about two hours later at Base Operations. So, I wandered around a bit. I soon ended up in what was definitely a Vietnamese section of the airport. I began attracting some attention because I was in civilian clothes among small-statured Vietnamese in uniforms. They all looked very young and everyone seemed to smoke. Soon I came to an open-ended side wing of the building where I saw about thirty Vietcong prisoners squatted down on the floor with armed soldiers guarding them. Their hands were tied behind them. They had very bushy and unkempt hair and many had dirty, angry faces. I saw one that was leaking green goo from his nose. His hands were tied, so he couldn't wipe his face. I got out of there and headed for a place where I found newcomers like me, wearing civvies.

As I walked away, I noticed that there was a bar on the second floor. I went there and found it almost empty. I sat at the bar and asked for the best Vietnamese beer. The bartender provided it with a smile, and as I studied the beer label, he stretched out his hand for payment. I handed him a dollar bill, but he would not take it. He kept saying "Pay MPC. Must pay MPC." I did not understand him, but he soon realized that I was a newcomer who had nothing but US dollars. Finally, he took my dollar bill and instead of giving me coins in change, he handed me three pieces

Five cent Military Payment Certificates (MPCs) New designs with different colors were printed every now and then to reduce the risk of counterfeiting. (Photos by Donald "Dusty" Rhodes; composites by John Gargus)

of multicolored monopoly-game-size money. I examined the blue one that was for 5 cents and had "Military Payment Certificate" printed on it. That was my introduction to the money I'd be using for the next year. The beer I got had two number threes printed on the label. The bartender pointed to the label and repeated several times "Bam y bam, bam y bam." I concluded that this was the brand name. Later I learned that this was Vietnamese for thirty-three.

Finally I headed to Base Operations. It was easy to find because it was the busiest part of the airport. I walked along the ramp, avoiding busy vehicular traffic that consisted of forklifts, all kinds of trucks, and military jeeps. I was greeted at Base Operations by Maj. Karl Wiegand, my crew's 1st pilot, and by Maj. Barney Dowd, S-06 crew's navigator. Three enlisted crew members from Barney's crew were there also waiting for a ride to Nha Trang. Our aircraft arrived shortly. It was a C-123 with the same dark green and black paint scheme as the Combat Talons. As soon as the props stopped rotating, civilians began loading it through the back ramp. I waited for the pilots to come out to the operations building, but I did not see any of them leave the aircraft. Then one American civilian started introducing himself to us saying that they were going to fly us to Nha Trang. He explained that they flew in civilian clothes. That was odd. He was an air force captain accompanied by a Vietnamese who was also wearing casual civilian attire. We were on board the aircraft strapping ourselves in to the cloth bucket seats, when we realized that the whole crew was Asian. The captain we just met was the only American on the crew. Karl Wiegand nudged me and told me that the crew members were Chinese. I shook my head in disbelief, and he said that the captain told him so and that our aircraft commander was also Chinese. With that, I rose from my seat and looked up into the cockpit. He was right. The captain's companion in casual beach clothes we met in Base Operations was sitting in the aircraft commander's seat and the captain was his copilot. So we had a Chinese pilot flying a US aircraft in civilian clothes. What kind of war was this?

Nha Trang

Several of our future companions met us at the aircraft and drove the officers to a downtown hotel in a windowless crew van they called Bread Wagon. Enlisted crew members remained on the base. They had their own Detachment 1 quarters there.

Many officers came out to greet us upon our arrival at the Anh Hoa Hotel. They helped us with our baggage and led us to a large downstairs room in the place they called Hog Heaven. We would stay there that night and move into our assigned rooms the next day. I put my B-4 bag and my navigator's case on one available bed and headed for the dining room for the evening meal that the waiters began serving. The whole officer complement of our crew was already there. We were the last ones to arrive. I ended up sitting at a table with all new faces. Someone ordered a bottle of Lancers wine for our six-man table and we had a fine, plentiful meal. After that everyone went to the rooftop bar for after dinner drinks and more. That evening I consumed more alcohol than I should have. I remember that someone escorted me to Hog Heaven because I would not have found it by myself. I had no trouble finding my bed because my bags were still on top of it. When I stretched out still fully dressed, I resolved that I would not drink that much ever again. I kept that resolution throughout my tour in Vietnam.

Home wing's welcome sign to the Nha Trang Air Base installed after the wing's name change from the Air Commando Wing in August 1968. (Wikipedia photo)

I spent the next day in-processing at personnel, finance, supply, transportation, and finally in the medical dispensary. We had to hand carry all our records, so things moved pretty fast. Most of the time was spent in supply where we were issued the tropical work uniforms we used to fly in. Uniforms had to go to the tailor shop where they sewed on our subdued rank insignia, air force tag, and embroidered our last names above the right breast pockets. Transportation already had my footlocker of clothing and personal items that I had shipped from home before departing for the survival training. Last, I went with my medical records to the hospital where I remained to see a flight surgeon about my troubling hemorrhoid problem.

The doctor who saw me called in others to witness what I had before he informed me that I needed an operation and that if ready I could be air evacuated on that day's flight to the Clark Air Base in the Philippines. I explained to him that this was unacceptable. I was part of an eleven-member crew that trained together and I had to stay with them. We were already scheduled for an in-briefing and an in-country familiarization flight. Fortunately, this flight surgeon knew about our aircraft because he had flown with us on one of the daily shuttles. I questioned him whether my condition warranted being placed on a DNIF (duty not involving flying) status. He said it was his judgment call and that if I were so determined to fly in my condition, he could let it go by. He said that the only thing they could do for my severe hemorrhoid condition was to have me sit in a warm sitz bath twice a day. If that showed no improvement, I would have to go to a hospital for an operation. That settled it. My improvement was slow, but it took well over two months before I was completely back to normal. Very few people knew about this nasty problem until the time of this writing.

Studies and Observations Group (SOG)

We learned a lot during our welcome to Vietnam in-briefing by the staff of our Stray Goose detachment. Conclusions about our intended mission in Vietnam that we formed during our training at Pope Air Force Base were confirmed. We would be infiltrating agents into North Vietnam, resupplying them as needed, and also flying high altitude leaflet drops (short looks). We were curious about the Fulton Recovery missions. They told us that in the previous month of May the SG-2 crew was tasked with a Fulton pickup for a downed crew member. The kit was dropped to him by an F-4 pilot; however, the North Vietnamese recovered the kit and captured the airman before the crew got to the scene. This unusual kit delivery caused our operational headquarters to question future requests for pickups of pilots in North Vietnam. Better accuracy for airdrop of kits was necessary, and the twenty-minute time lapse between the kit drop and scheduled recovery was questioned. Could recoveries be executed in that short time? A loitering C-130 would compromise the pickup site and jeopardize the entire process. Most likely, we could get scheduled only for a pickup of a previously infiltrated team member who needed urgent return back from the enemy territory. By that time in Vietnam, the HH-3 Jolly Green Giant helicopters and A-1E fighter support aircraft had the daytime Search and Rescue (SAR) missions well in hand. Our daytime missions would be shuttling throughout Southeast Asia in support of the Green Berets.

Once I began writing this book, I learned more details about the predicament the unit found itself in during the aborted Fulton Recovery attempt of May 1966. The downed crew member had a leg injury but was otherwise okay. He could communicate using his survival radio. His position was north of Hanoi with the closest enemy air base at Kep. It was too far for the normal SAR by HH-3 Jolly Green Giants and supporting A-1Es from Thailand. It appeared to be a textbook case for a Fulton Recovery rescue. However, a daytime kit drop and recovery with some loiter time in the area looked too suicidal. Nighttime pickup would be safer. An obvious question came up. Could the downed man locate the kit in the dark? There were still other problems with a nighttime pickup. There wasn't a single pilot in the unit who had done it before. Doug Forsythe, unit training officer, his aircraft commander Sam Rose, and the third pilot Dave Mattingly, all from the SG-2 crew, had experimented with nighttime approaches without once engaging the lift line. They were sure that they could pull off a nighttime pickup if another aircraft could airdrop the kit to the downed pilot. Well, it just so happened that Forsythe connected with one F-4 pilot from Da Nang who showed great interest in the Fulton Recovery concept. They discussed the possibility of a kit delivery by an F-4, and he succeeded to get an aircraft for an experimental flight. Mr. Ron Fair, Fulton Recovery Tech Rep, managed to package one kit, padded with plenty of Styrofoam, into a pod that was deliverable without a parachute by an F-4. They flew once and the F-4 hit the spot in the drop zone. The pod did not break up and the kit was functional. All this happened shortly before this emergency arrived. None of it was sanctioned by the commanders of either unit. It was just a try by ingenious special operators who wanted to get things done.

When the actual need for a Fulton Recovery rescue arrived, Sam and his crew believed that they could pull off a nighttime recovery. They stepped up and showed that they had the guts to try it and identified the pilot who could get the kit down to the airman who had been hiding for more than two days. The SOG bought off on this and authorized the rescue. The F-4 pilot got approval from his command and went on to drop the kit at last light so that the downed man could locate it while he still had daylight. The drop was successful, but the North Vietnamese got to him. He had time to warn the rescuers that he was about to be captured.[1]

Our biggest surprise was to learn that we were not the only highly classified special operations flyers in town. The briefing room where we were seated belonged to the First Flight Detachment. Its crews began operations for the Military Assistance Command, Vietnam–Studies and Observations Group (MACV-SOG) in early 1964. They flew the same type of missions in modified C-123s. We both got our operational life from an unconventional warfare plan named OPLAN 34A.

SOG was a super-secret organization based in Saigon. It was always commanded by a US Army colonel. Our SOG commander was Col. Jack Singlaub, who, as a first lieutenant, had distinguished himself as a Jedburgh during World War II in France. As a major during the Korean War, he served as the operations chief for the Joint Advisory Commission, Korea (JACK). The mission of this organization was to collect strategic intelligence and operate an escape and evasion (E&E) network for downed United Nations airmen. This entailed recruitment and insertion of agents far behind enemy lines by airdrops and by boats at sea.[2] What a logical stepping-stone for commanding the SOG in Vietnam one decade later! His Combat Talon claim to fame was that he had himself picked up by the Fulton Recovery System at Camp Long Thanh.

Initially, SOG answered directly to the Joint Chiefs of Staff (JCS) in the Pentagon. More specifically to the Special Assistant for Counterinsurgency and Special Activities (SACSA) who had direct access to the chairman of the JCS.[3] At least, that is the way the command line was envisioned by its creators. Eventually, too many people got involved in the special operations war. They included US ambassadors in Southeast Asia (Vietnam, Laos, and Thailand) and top brass at MACV and the Seventh Air Force.[4]

Unofficial designs for never authorized patches for the Studies and Observations Group and for two of its air assets: the Stray Goose C-130Es and the First Flight's C-123s. (Composite photo by John Gargus)

First Flight

First Flight's facilities were located on a secure north side of the air base that housed the Vietnamese Air Force. Our operations and administration was on the American south side. We did not have TOP SECRET facilities on our side. Since the First Flight's Duck Hook C-123s preceded the Stray Goose MC-130Es by two years, they were well established in their facilities. Because Stray Goose crews began their operations from the faraway CCK Air Base in Taiwan, the First Flight supported them with all classified message transmission they required to fly their missions. That relationship continued once they moved to Nha Trang. We shared their briefing room, which we also used as our mission planning room. They had it swept electronically every now and then by the counterintelligence people from Saigon's SOG to make sure that no one had implanted a listening device. Consequently, we could discuss needed TOP SECRET information about our business. The room had a separate entrance from the courtyard, and we had to go next door to their limited access operations room to get the key whenever we needed the room. A huge TOP SECRET map depicting the Southeast Asia order of battle was mounted on the wall in the operations room. That is where we shared classified communications equipment, notably the teletype that tied us to the SOG. We did not have any of our detachment people working in their building, with the exception of mission planners. Whenever a message came for us and a mission planner was not in their building, they would call our flight operations on the other side of the base and someone would have to come to retrieve it. Those designated pickup messengers were few. Normally our commander or the operations officer would drive a mile across the base to pick up these almost always TOP SECRET messages.

There were two other functions the First Flight performed for us. They would prepare all resupply packages for airdrops, many times with assistance from Saigon-based SOG specialists. The same went for specially built boxes for leaflets and pretuned radios. Pretuned radios were locked on to the station that transmitted news and propaganda from South Vietnamese sources. All our loadmasters had to do was to secure the bundles inside the aircraft. The First Flight personnel also repacked our crew parachutes.

First Flight's C-123s were modified for their unconventional warfare mission by the Big Safari program. The airframes were completely sanitized. This included removing the aircraft numbers and purging all traces of them from official air force records. In addition, all decals and stenciled equipment, as well as part numbers, which could trace them to "made in the USA," were removed.

So much emphasis was placed on the US deniability that the first crews that flew missions into North Vietnam were non-American. They were mostly Chinese from Taiwan who had prior experience in clandestine missions into Red China. Others were Vietnamese. They were brought to Hurlburt Field in the Florida panhandle for training. Chinese/Taiwanese crews were known as "C" crews, Vietnamese were "V" crews, and Americans were "A" crews. Initially, there were only two "A" crews that flew as instructors outside of North Vietnam. In about two years the "V" crews were discontinued and eventually the "A" crews were allowed to fly north. None of the crews wore uniforms. They always wore civilian clothing.[5]

This super-secret handling of the First Flight became a point of many of our discussions. Of course, we couldn't talk about it outside our own circle because at that time this unit and its aircraft did not officially exist. But we would talk among ourselves about carrying out covert operations to the extremes. What other nation had a reason and the means to conduct clandestine operations against the Hanoi regime? How could any intelligent observer in Southeast Asia be fooled into believing that the unmarked C-123s belonged to anyone else but the United States? Just about every military aircraft flying in Vietnam was American made. The aircraft were serviced and fueled by US personnel wherever they landed. Did it make any difference that the air crews flew in civilian clothing? During the day, they flew the same shuttle missions for the same customers as we did in our Combat Talons. Unlike us, they got shot up on some of their missions because they could not fly as low as we did with our terrain following capability, and they could not avoid radar detection as successfully as we could. Nevertheless, they never lost an aircraft while flying over North Vietnam. After one mission they had to make an emergency landing at the

S-05 crew on the beach. *Standing left to right*: Butler, Vallas, McCormick, Rosser, and operations officer Hines. *In the front*: Krueger, Yates, Lewis, Commander Rogers, Ellis, Claxton, and Gargus. Missing is Wiegand. (Photo by Karl Wiegand)

Royal Thai Air Base in Thailand. They were badly shot up with substantial aircraft damage. Several Taiwanese crew members had injuries that needed immediate attention. All we learned about this incident was that it caused a diplomatic problem that was quietly resolved.

First Flight crews lived in a large villa built by what must have been a wealthy Frenchman during the colonial days. It was located on a large plot of tree-covered land across the beachfront road. The view of the building from the well-traveled beach road was obscured by the trees, so the mixed-national occupants in civilian attire enjoyed good privacy. They had their own dining facility and a bar. In that way, their accommodations were comparable to those at our three-story Anh Hoa Hotel.

Day Missions

Our first daytime shuttle flight consisted of routine short distance hops from one base to another. We had an instructor pilot from another crew to guide us along. We started at Tan Son Nhut Air Base in Saigon where we picked up several passengers and cargo that had to be dropped off here and there as we made our way up country to Da Lat, Pleiku, Kontum, Kham Duc, Hue Phu Bai, Da Nang, and then "feet wet" (over water) back to Nha Trang. It seems that each daytime shuttle would involve five or six stops. Normally we had two aircraft flying every day. One would start in Saigon to pick up people who needed to go north, and the other would start north at Khe Sanh or Hue Phu Bai and fly south dropping off people who needed to end up in Saigon. Only those landing locations that were manned by air force personnel had air traffic control facilities. Consequently, outside of Da Nang, Nha Trang, Cam Rahn Bay, and Saigon we were pretty much on our own. Our arrivals at other places were anxiously anticipated events of the day. Pilots would contact someone to verify that the landing field was safe to land on and we went in. There were no "FOLLOW ME" trucks to lead us to a parking spot. Our pilots just taxied in the direction where they saw people or where they had parked during their previous visit. Because there was no ground support at these stops, we would often keep the engines running during loading and off-loading. Many times we would end up landing in isolated places that had Green Beret and Montagnard outposts with narrow dirt strips. We would shut down a couple of engines when on the ground there, but never all four. We didn't want to get stuck in places like that. First Flight C-123s handled most of the air traffic to those jungle outposts. Their wing span was 22 feet shorter than our planes,' and that made a big difference on outposts where the trees appeared to be almost at the edges of dirt runways.

It was unreal to depart from Saigon's Tan Son Nhut Air Base and then less than thirty minutes later land at an isolated Green Beret outpost. We went from what must have been the busiest and most diversified airport in the world to a place where large fixed-wing aircraft seldom went. Observing the air and ground traffic at Tan Son Nhut was mind boggling. Almost every type of aircraft known to the Western world could be seen coming and going. There were helicopters of all kinds, small single-engine aircraft, every type of fighter we had in Vietnam, all types of cargo planes, and a multitude of commercial airliners that were bringing new troops in and taking old troops back to the States. I don't know how the air traffic controllers kept their sanity. They had to direct all types of fixed-wing and rotary aircraft that flew at different air speeds and handle plenty of wartime responses when damaged aircraft requested emergency landings. Ground traffic was also confusing. It was a nose to tail traffic jam on the taxiways with big aircraft dwarfing the small. Other vehicular traffic was also amazing. Motorized vehicles of all types, even motorcycles, ran

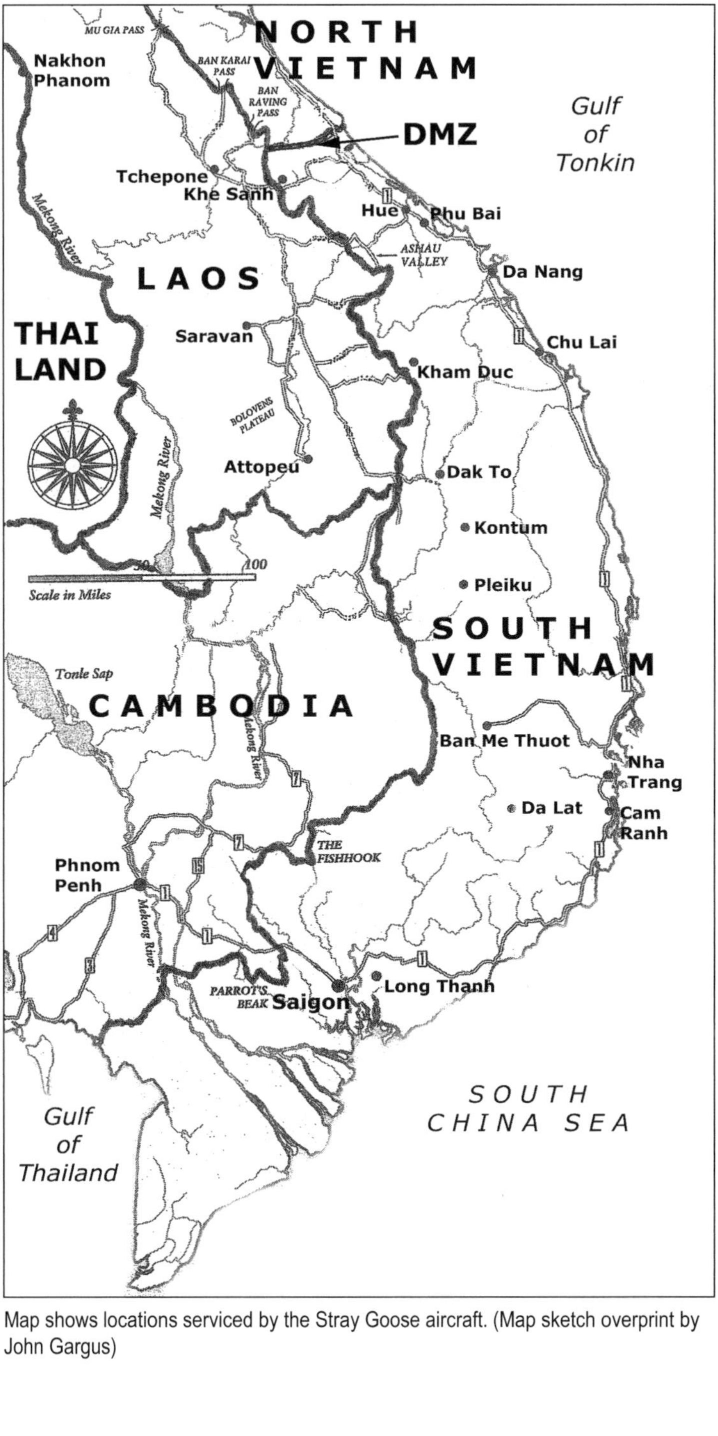

Map shows locations serviced by the Stray Goose aircraft. (Map sketch overprint by John Gargus)

here and there. Cargo that had to be moved somewhere by someone was scattered along the sides of the tarmac waiting for a forklift or a truck. There were also several wrecked aircraft dragged off to the grass on the side of active runways and taxiways so that they would not block the way for moving aircraft and vehicles. It was fascinating to watch everything that went on. However, we were always glad once we lifted off one of the Saigon's runways and headed for one of those unimproved landing strips without the incessant air controller traffic chatter.

We were always welcomed at Green Berets' remote fields. We flew in their mail, and we often had a couple of cases of beer to trade for garden fresh vegetables the natives grew in their area. We bought our cases of San Miguel beer on trips to CCK in Taiwan or at Clark Air Base in the Philippines for little less than $1.50 per case of twenty-four bottles. Our loadmasters kept them on the ramp of the aircraft so they were always cold upon delivery. It was a good trade for two or three crates of vegetables for our kitchens. The best watermelon I ever tasted came from Pleiku. We were disappointed when the only thing they had to trade on that trip were ripe watermelons. Our loadmasters fussed over that, but it was the only time they had to trade cold beer for hot sunbaked watermelons. Our cook Charlie guessed right when he sliced them up. He informed us that they must be from Pleiku where they grew the best ones. His favorite vegetables came from Da Lat.

We often transported live meat on the hoof. I never witnessed us delivering a live buffalo, but hauling pigs and chickens was quite normal. Pigs weighing more than two hundred pounds would be tied up and placed in cocoon-shaped bamboo-woven baskets for easy handling by two men. Sometimes we had three or four of them going to an outpost where they were set free to roam. There were times when the pilots had to remind the people on the ground to clear the runway of a pig or two. Chickens were something else. They had their own native handlers. Four to five chickens were bound together by their feet and carried hanging upside down. The first time I saw something like that was when an overcrowded bus drove past us and I thought that one of the hangers-on was carrying a bouquet of flowers in his free hand. A closer look revealed that he was holding a bundle of colorfully feathered live chickens.

With six crews and four aircraft, we had plenty of idle time on the ground. Almost every week there was one crew out of the country either in Taiwan or in the Philippines. Periodic phase inspections and repairs were performed at CCK in Taiwan, and the crew would stay there for three or four days. Interceptor defense training for electronic warfare officers was flown against the F-102s from Clark Air Base in the Philippines. Even though the whole crew needed to be familiar with interceptor evasive tactics, the focus was on maintaining the proficiency of the EWOs. For economy of this training, a second EWO from another crew would join to make his refresher training trip. Clark Air Base is where we got an ample supply of San Miguel beer for bartering in Vietnam. We acquired much of our "stuff" at CCK Air Base by scrounging from the Morale, Welfare, and Recreation (MWR) people we befriended. That is how we got our replacement ping pong balls and paddles, badminton sets, tennis rackets and balls, pool cues and billiard balls, dart boards, wrestling floor mats, and much weight-lifting equipment. I am sure that we traded some of this overage "stuff" for other things we needed from army and air force neighbors at Nha Trang.

We also made irregular side trips to Thailand's Royal Thai Air Force Bases at Ubon, Korat, Udorn, Takhli, and Nakhon Phanom. SOG scheduled these trips on an as-needed basis and frequently with little advanced notice. Much of the time we were simply providing transportation for people who had business dealings there with Air America and CIA operations in Laos. We never had a trip to Laos, but we transported many Green Berets to Udorn, from where they used other aircraft to fly to their final destinations in Laos. Some of the SOG's infiltration missions originated from Nakhon Phanom. All we knew was that they were of short duration because we would be bringing some of the same teams back to Vietnam on the next day or soon thereafter. The CIA had an isolation facility at Takhli and Air America operated out of Ubon. Air America was an American passenger and cargo airline covertly owned by the US government It operated as a dummy corporation for CIA's operations in Southeast Asia. We shuttled civilians and soldiers between there and Saigon. We had no need to know what they were doing, and none of our passengers ever volunteered any information.

Night Missions

I flew my introductory combat mission with Maj. Walt Pine and his S-03 crew. It was an overwater leaflet drop along the coastline south of Haiphong. It was a pretty routine short-look maneuver well outside of the lethal range of anti-aircraft artillery (AAA) and surface to air missiles (SAMs). The only thing that could reach us would be a MIG-21 interceptor that would have to enter into the Gulf of Tonkin air space, which was dominated by the US Navy from the floating carriers known as "Yankee Station" to the southeast of the leaflet drop.

I remember only two things about that mission. I was looking forward to learning how the radio navigation system Loran-C performed in that area. The coverage looked ideal over the gulf, but it was almost unusable over the North Vietnamese mainland because of the position of transmitters and the geometry of the printed reception lines. Because of the lateness of my addition to the crew, I did not get to participate in the crew's detailed mission planning. I was surprised that Capt. Larry Kelley did not have the mission laid out on a chart that had Loran-C information printed on it. The other thing that surprised me as being strange was the fact that we executed a maximum emergency escape after the drop even though the EWO, Capt. Felix Matusevic, did not issue an emergency warning. I did not expect such an aggressive escape from high altitude and experienced the usual temporary weightlessness. My oxygen mask came off my face as I rose to the ceiling because the flexible goose neck hose from the oxygen regulator was not long enough to reach my face at the cabin ceiling. I managed to land on my feet and allowed myself to kneel down as my body weight multiplied during the recovery. It was a needless in-flight event that put unnecessary stress on the airframe. We could have made a normal rapid descent straight on our drop-heading.

Our crew's first combat mission was very uneventful. We dropped several million leaflets along the Laotian border that were destined to cover the terrain in the vicinity of Thanh Hoa. Then on the night of October 14 our most memorable mission transpired. Our tasking was to drop radios packaged in Styrofoam containers that would float on the water just east of the port of Haiphong. Local fishermen or beachcombers would salvage them and listen to South Vietnamese propaganda broadcasts on a pretuned frequency. As we headed north of Da Nang at 500 feet above the surface of a very calm sea, I unfolded my second chart that had Loran-C lines on it. I was eager to use it on this mission. Because of the calm sea the Doppler radar would not be as accurate as it was over uneven terrain. I was delighted with the Loran-C accuracy and how well it kept us on track.

Then, all of a sudden I heard our pilots exclaim, "What the hell is that?" I glanced at my radar and spotted several ships right on our course. As close as we were to them and their lateral spread left to right, the only

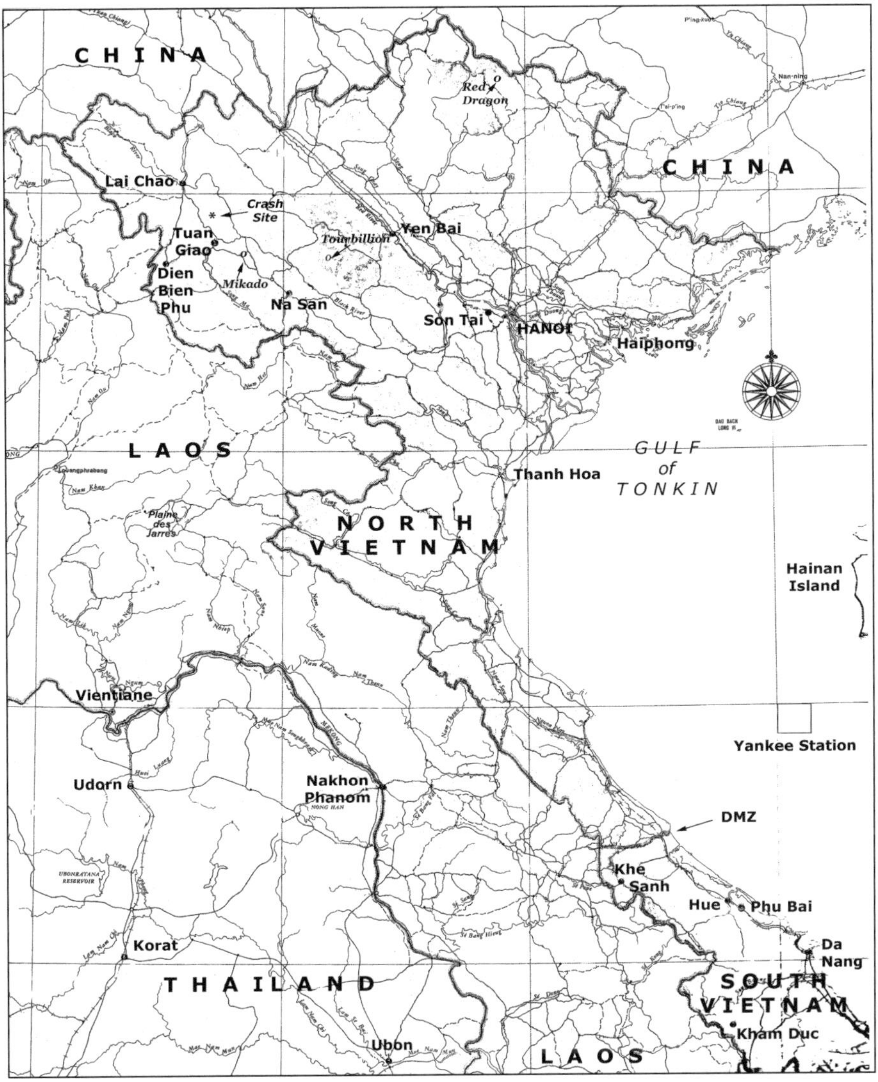

Map shows prominent locations referred to in the text. (Map sketch overprint by John Gargus)

thing the pilots could do was to climb up and fly right over the ships at the Yankee Station. Their cockpit conversation told me that we flew right over one of our carriers. Obviously, the navy had us on their radar and would probably launch an interceptor after us. I was embarrassed by my negligence in not scanning the radar, which was standard for overland flights. I allowed myself to be distracted by the Loran-C. I had a probable Yankee Station position indicated on my other chart. The Yankee Station occupied a 60-square-mile area that would move from one place to another at irregular intervals. We had it plotted just right. We suspected that the navy had not been informed about our operation in their area.

After that unexpected distraction we descended back to 500 feet, and when the time came to turn west toward Haiphong, we went lower to 250 feet. At our initial point, we turned southwest and began to drop the radios. Just as we completed this task, John Lewis, our EWO, issued a warning that he had detected a MIG-21 conical scan radar behind us. He began to work on this return and alerted us for a break to the left upon his command. That came seconds later. The pilots banked sharply to the left and went to full throttles on all four engines. The pursuing interceptor flew past us, and I called for a return to our original southerly escape heading. We also descended to below 100 feet. When John Lewis called that he had the interceptor back on our tail again, our aircraft was already flying past 300 knots and was shaking aggressively. At John's escape command the pilots pulled up the nose of the aircraft and made another steep 60-degree bank turn to the left. Once again the interceptor whizzed by. John related that the interceptor had turned to the right and approached us from the land. He continued to employ the electronic countermeasure systems and dropping chaff prior to each time he told the pilots to break. We anticipated another pass. Lieutenant Colonel Hines, the operations officer, flew with us on this mission in the left pilot's seat. He cautioned about popping up if there was another pass. We had to be much higher than we were at the moment because we needed more altitude to avoid the left wing striking the water during another sharp 60-degree bank turn. John Lewis was not aware of how low we were. He was only listening to the conversations between Hines and me. He was asking the pilots to go even lower, and that is when Hines answered him by saying: "John if I go any lower I will have to start using the windshield wipers."[6] By this time, much of the buffeting we experienced was due to the water effect. We were so low that our airflow was disturbing the water surface in front of the aircraft's nose. The third interceptor pass began a few minutes later. By that time we were all very nervous and hoped to spoil his lock-on again. He shot past us unseen once more and we headed eastward over the gulf. Then there was a long complete silence in the aircraft. Everyone must have been assessing our perilous predicament while expecting John Lewis to come up with another warning. Finally, I broke the silence by asking why we were flying so fast. I had our ground speed at 325 knots and altitude at 50 feet. Tom Hines agreed and asked me for a heading to Da Nang. I gave him a cardinal heading of 180 degrees and quickly obtained our precise position using Loran-C. I had to refine our heading more to the left, and soon after that we were back at 500 feet flying toward Da Nang and then 235 miles farther south to Nha Trang.

The maintenance men who assisted us in parking the aircraft were aghast at the site of it. It was covered with sea salt that altered its dark jungle canopy paint scheme. Stray Goose aircraft were the early users of first-generation "stealth" technology. Besides being painted dark green from the top to camouflage us in flights over the jungle, they were painted sky gray from the bottom to reduce their visibility from the ground up. The paint contained porous sand that absorbed, rather than reflected, radar energy. As large as the C-130 is, the paint reduced its radar signature to that of a much smaller F-4 fighter. The painted skin of the aircraft was rough like a fine sandpaper. That might have reduced speed somewhat because the sandpaper texture increased air friction, but it was worth it. Enemy radar took us for a smaller plane. Lieutenant Colonel Hines ordered our maintenance people to give the aircraft a complete wash down to protect the integrity of the semistealth paint.

John Lewis was in the hot seat during the debriefing. Was he sure it was a MIG-21 and not a navy F-4 from the Yankee Station that challenged us? Both interceptors had very similar conical scan radar that also sounded alike. Even though the navy had a good reason to send someone aloft to see who flew overhead of one of their carriers, John insisted it was not an F-4. It had to be a MIG-21 controlled from the mainland because it came from that direction and returned to overland twice more. John did not have any warning indications from the North Vietnamese radars. All seemed normal and he had not reported any radars tracking on our over-water low level flight. A follow-up with command at SOG headquarters by Maj. Roy Thompson had the navy deny that they pursued anyone. We did not query the North Vietnamese. And of course, if anyone had asked us, we did not fly over the Yankee Station either, and we did not go anywhere near North Vietnam.

My next most memorable and the most difficult mission was a resupply of Team Tourbillon that came one month later. We had to fly over the highest mountains in North Vietnam to get to their drop zone. This drop zone was not on a level terrain. It was on the north facing slope of what was almost a ridgeline that was followed by yet another close ridgeline that rose about 100 feet higher. The drop zone was just at over 3,000 feet in elevation. Our drop flight path to it had to be in a southerly direction coming from the mountains that would have us fly up to almost 10,000 feet. There was no way to get to the drop zone from the opposite direction because the two ridgelines would obstruct the view of the lighted drop zone. Besides that, the aircraft could not accelerate fast enough after the drop to clear the mountains to the north. Consequently, we were confronted with a very unconventional airdrop. It would have to be made either during a descent or from a much higher altitude if we leveled off for the drop at some distance away. We had to figure out the timing of our descent between the mountain peaks so that we could have at least twenty seconds of level flight before the drop. Using US Army topographic charts of 1 to 50,000 scale that showed contour elevations at 20-meter intervals, we plotted our descent on graph paper mile after mile with a 1,000-foot safe clearance above the ground below. This way we came up with altitudes at which we should be at any one mile away from the drop zone. We had to slow down early during our descent to be at a proper drop air speed at least 1 mile out. It looked good on paper. We needed to duplicate it in flight. That required us to be exactly on track because we would be flying between high mountains on the left and right. Our terrain following radar would be disabled because we would fly at below 160 knots, but it would operate in its terrain avoidance mode that would display only those targets that were at, or above, our flight level.

Once we were in the air, all went well. We avoided radar detection and as we reached our highest flight level, just past 10,000 feet, pilots reported scattered cloud formations to the south. That was the direction in which we needed to go. Lieutenant Colonel Hines flew with us again because we were short one pilot. Major Claxton was unable to fly with us that night. Major Rosser, our aircraft commander, was in the right pilot's seat. I was hidden behind a heavy curtain so that my desk lights did not affect the night vision of other cockpit occupants. I could not see the clouds on radar because it scanned only a narrow sector directly ahead of us and we were still heading to the east. Once we turned to the south toward our drop zone the pilots got a better view of what was ahead. The clouds were scattered, and even though some were directly in front of us they did not appear to spill down to the floors of the valleys. Hines wanted assurance that we were exactly on track. We were. So we agreed to abandon terrain following and switched to terrain avoidance. That gave me a 90-degree pie sector scan ahead of the aircraft. At that time there were just a few returns that were ahead of us above flight level. Hines asked how soon we could start descending and slowing down. It was still too soon. Then we entered into a cloud. Pilots could tell that the clouds started at a level not far below us and we were soon out of them. It was then safe for us to start descending. After that, all went well. Pilots kept asking me if we were still on the centerline of our planned flight. I had a good radar presentation on my scope. We were below the high terrain on both left and right. It looked like we had more than 3 miles of clear space dead ahead of us. I asked for a faster descent because my graph paper calculations showed that we were higher than we should have been each mile after descending mile. The radar would not show us anything below, it painted only what was above us to the left and right, and I think that the pilots were hesitant to go down any steeper. Nevertheless, I was 100 percent sure that we were right on track. Targets left and right were at the exact distances I expected them to be. Our other pilot, Major Wiegand, and the map reading navigator, Captain McCormick, were straining their eyes looking ahead for the drop zone signal lights that were supposed to be lined up in the shape of letter L. I do not know who spotted the lights first, but they were visible to all except me. I believe that we stopped descending shortly after the lights were sighted. Pilots leveled the flight and concentrated on attaining proper drop air speed. They saw the lights and made very small adjustments to the flight path to the target. I told McCormick that we were higher than planned. He called the green light that signaled the loadmaster to jettison the four-bundle load. As we expected, all four bundles went long past the ridgeline, landing in the trees on the opposite side of the hill. We should have dropped sooner because we were too high. We learned later from the visiting contact captain from SOG that it took several days for the team to recover what we delivered.

Duty Crew

Our crew could expect to fly at least two daytime shuttles every week. Likewise, every day of the week we had a designated "duty crew" to take care of the hotel. The scheduling officers in the on-base operations office kept careful records of whose turn it was to go on a phase inspection to Taiwan or on a training trip to the Philippines. The same went for the duty crew scheduling. Designated daily crew had to make sure that there was adequate water supply in the rooftop water storage tanks. Now and then it was necessary to truck in a water trailer full of potable water from the base. Normally that task required three people and took more time than anything else that needed to be done. Then there were two operating generators to service. That was done before noon so that switching of power from one to the other did not inconvenience too many people. Diesel fuel and oil levels had to be checked and replenished as needed. Before the newly fired-up generator got connected to the hotel electrical grid, we had to adjust several settings, the most critical of which was the 60-cycle frequency we needed. That frequency kept slipping because of the vibration the generators produced that shook their storage shed. Frequency always slipped downward. It became noticeable when the light bulbs began flickering and one could almost count the cycles per second. That always evoked angry loud cries from several directions: "Duty Crew!" I remember this part of my introduction to duty crew responsibilities. Capt. Gordie Wenaas, navigator from the S-01 crew, was diligent in explaining to us the importance of proper servicing of generators.

The rest of the duty crew responsibility was to service the bar. We had to make sure that there was enough beer and soft drinks in the refrigerators. The ice machine had to be serviced to ensure that we had enough ice for the evening. If we had to make ice at night, we were sure to exceed the electrical capacity of the barroom circuit breaker and lose the lights. The circuit breaker was in a small walk-in space by the door to the bar. It had no lights, so the person who volunteered to restore the lights had to hold a flashlight in his mouth unless he had someone else helping him. To me this was the most dangerous undertaking. We did not have standard US circuit breakers. These were open-faced small plastic boxes with incoming and outgoing wires. The tripping mechanism was a thick-gauge soldering wire that had to be shaped into a letter C and inserted in the place of a similarly shaped wire that had melted or burned through. The repairer had to use a well-insulated screwdriver to pry out the top and bottom end of the burned-through silver wire and replace it with a new one, squeezing it securely into the groove on the back side of the box. Eventually, someone created a tool from a 2 × 4 by rounding off the corners so that a perfect C could be rounded from the soft wire. That someone also cut the wire into just the proper lengths, so that a new C type of fuse could be formed and installed quickly.

Even though we had two barmaids who cleaned the bar, mixed and served drinks, the barroom required major clean up. The barmaids quit working at about 10:00 p.m., but the bar never closed. So we had to prepare everything for the next evening.

Part of the duty crew's responsibility was to make sure that the hired daytime maids performed their jobs well. That was never any problem. They managed to stay busy, and the oldest one was definitely looked up to as their boss. She understood our system and, observing the daily activities at the generators, she knew who was on duty crew that day. So she would come to one of us and identify the problem. It was normally a circuit breaker that burned out while they were ironing. Also it could be a burned-out light bulb in one of the bathrooms or in some common area that needed replacing.

4

Nha Trang Facilities

Reception at Nha Trang Air Base

The Stray Goose detachment experienced many problems in moving from CCK in Taiwan to Nha Trang in Vietnam. Even though frequent wartime name changes and moves of units from one location to another are nothing unusual, they all present various challenges to the people involved. This relocation was complicated by its urgency and the lack of adequate facilities for a unit of our size. The secret nature of its mission, questions about who owned its assets, and who had the ultimate responsibility for directing its operations complicated matters even more.

The SOG in Saigon had its Army Special Forces assets spread throughout Southeast Asia (SEA) and needed daily flights to maintain its logistical pipeline. The First Flight proved to be too small to carry on this daytime load. The Stray Goose C-130s could do much more, but they were based in Taiwan. They could not be fully utilized unless they started operating from a base in Vietnam. Nha Trang Air Base was the obvious choice. It was the home base of the 14th Air Commando Wing, which was co-located with Camp McDermott, which housed the 5th Special Forces Group Airborne. The Special Forces Green Berets conducted covert operations into North Vietnam, Laos, and Cambodia and depended on SOG's airlift support. To support SOGs operations, the air force was obligated to provide maintenance and administrative service for aircraft and crews that worked for this super-secret organization. This would create occasional misunderstandings even among the most dedicated people responsible for commanding their respective services during the Vietnam War.

Personnel of Detachment 1 consisted of about 160 men and four MC-130E(I) aircraft. There were six eleven-man crews, commander, operations officer, mission planner, maintenance officer, and a complement of about ninety maintenance and administrative personnel.[1] The code name for the unit's deployment to SEA was Combat Spear—the name that has been retained to the present day. The target date for the bed-down was September 1966. However, that date slipped because the facilities in Nha Trang were not ready. Only a small number of men and two aircraft began operating from there in September.

Much construction and refurbishing of facilities had to be done by the incoming personnel. The unit's first arrivals were directed to a vacant two-story building that was to be their new home. They spent their first night sleeping on the floor. The next morning, they borrowed a green truck from the 5th Special Forces at Camp McDermott and drove it to an air force warehouse that had beds, mattresses, metal wall lockers, desks and chairs, electric fans, and other basic things they needed. It was a day of moving in. No one at the warehouse stopped them. No one kept any records of what was being loaded on the truck and no one signed for anything. They even got air conditioners for the upstairs rooms. On the next day an air force truck with supply people arrived with beds and

This 1968 photograph shows the US Army Camp McDermott with the Air Base and the city of Nha Trang in the background. (Wikipedia photo)

bedding. Since they already had beds, they accepted everything else. They scrounged around for tools and carpentry supplies to fix up the building for those who were coming later. They made good use of the truck they named "Green Elephant." They liked it so much they kept it as a crew transport until the air force provided vans for that purpose.[2]

They never returned the Green Elephant to its army owners. It remained the unit's borrowed truck used primarily to haul potable water until Anh Hoa Hotel ceased to be the BOQ during the Nha Trang Air Base draw down and eventual closing. The army people who let the first comers borrow it either forgot about it or they rotated out of Camp McDermott and there was no one left who remembered the favor to the air force guys. Some of the Green Berets had short three-month temporary duty tours and just kept returning for more after some time back home at Fort Bragg. That is where they got to know the Stray Goose crews and sympathized with them when they arrived at Nha Trang with almost nothing but their Blackbirds, as the aircraft were known to the Special Forces Green Berets.

Once the other aircraft and crews arrived, they lived in congested quarters. Officer crew members occupied the large upstairs windowless rooms with air conditioning; the rooms had bunk beds. Downstairs building space with open ceiling cross ventilation was occupied by enlisted crew members and crew chiefs. Sleeping under those conditions was difficult for crews that had to fly at night and sleep during the day. Other enlisted members occupied limited space in the administration and operations building, and some maintenance men crowded in with other base maintenance personnel. The commander and operations officer lived in a downtown hotel. They had assigned cars for transportation. Because the upstairs barracks-type space was too small for thirty-eight men, field grade officers (lieutenant colonels and majors) were quartered as guests at the First Flight's beachfront villa. Company grade officers (captains and lieutenants) were allowed to move downtown at their own expense. Most of them bedded down at a very decent motel called Nautique. Security for the downtown living and widely dispersed officers was nonexistent. On several occasions the local chief of police, who knew the French motel owners and who also befriended some of the officers, warned them to stay on base because he expected Vietcong activity in that part of town.[3]

Secrecy and the protection of detachment's aircraft presented a considerable problem for the limited flight line space. Four Stray Goose C-130s required a designated secure area, which also needed as-yet-unconstructed revetments to shield the planes from mortar attacks. This space was normally marked off by red lines that warned visitors not to cross into the area unless they had security badges authorizing them to be near or in the aircraft. Armed guards watched over the aircraft around the clock. The guards would challenge all intruders. Inadvertent ones would be escorted away and those who ignored the challenge could be fired upon. So, the host base had to give up much of its precious tarmac space to a new incoming tenant whose home wing was based at CCK in Taiwan. This created unavoidable animosities against the perceived prima donna status of the new Stray Goose unit.

Things were also not very congenial at the base's social level. Normally, when a unit moves to another base, it gets an appropriate welcome. Friendships are formed quickly and people work together and support one another. They normally share in a common mission. It was not like that in this case. We had members of a new unit coming in who needed everything for a bed-down and insisted on priority to get what they had to have. It was difficult for its members to be appropriately secretive about their mission and to keep a low profile even with individuals they knew from prior assignments. Their old acquaintances would often comment that so and so had changed since he got assigned to that privileged unit.

However, there was one thing that has not changed from one war to another. No one ever has enough of the needed "stuff." Everything is in short supply. Some units have more of the "stuff" than others. Some ingenious soldiers trade and barter for the "stuff" they need. Some just take it and develop a pretty good knack for appropriating somebody else's "stuff." They even build an enviable reputation for their can-do talents. They rationalize that it is not really stealing. Whatever they acquired belonged to the government and it remained as that government's "stuff." It simply changed hands. Besides, the new owners could make better use of it than those who couldn't even figure out where it went. The Stray Goose detachment had talented individuals who did very well in obtaining everything they needed for the creature comforts of their troops.

The men of Detachment 1 were ingenious doers who kept busy to self-improve their living conditions. They insulated the upstairs walls to increase the efficiency of air conditioning. Some acquired electric fans and refrigerators. Personal radios, tape players, and TVs were available but not practical in such a close living environment. It was like a step back to basic training, keeping one's stuff in metal wall lockers and bedside footlockers. However, the enlisted crew members never stopped improving their living quarters. Sustained improvements continued until their unit left Nha Trang during the US forces draw down. One inspector general (IG) team that conducted inspection of base facilities reported that our unit's enlisted barracks were the best they had seen in Vietnam and that they were probably the best ones of any base in the Southeast Asia.[4]

Command Accommodations

While the men of Detachment 1 rose to the occasion and did their role in the bed down of personnel and aircraft, their presence in the war zone generated some control concerns at the command levels above them. Very few high level officers at the Seventh Air Force in Saigon, which was responsible for all air force assets in Vietnam, were briefed on SOG's operations. There was a natural resentment when SOG could go directly to air force units like the First Flight with its UWC-123s and the newly arrived Stray Goose with MC-130E Combat Talons and bypass the normal channels within the Seventh Air Force. The commander of the Seventh Air Force, Lt. Gen. William W. "Spike" Momyer, was also the deputy commander for air operations under Gen. William C. Westmoreland who commanded the MACV and was the top military officer in charge of the US war effort. We were not fully aware of Momyer's views on special operations, but we soon learned that our aircraft and activities did not fit into his vision of a modern all-jet-aircraft air force. The problem that kept us out of the Seventh Air Force command channels had to be resolved at the highest air force level. Thus, on 26 October 1967, a Memorandum of Understanding between the air force chief of staff and the commanders of the Seventh Air Force and SOG established the office of Deputy Commander for Special Operations (DCSO) under the 14th Air Commando Wing at Nha Trang. The new DCSO was given operational control of First Fight's UWC 123s and Detachment 1, 314th TAW's MC-130Es. He was also given tactical control of the 20th Special Operations Squadron with its UH-1 gunships that had already operated under the Nha Trang wing's command in executing missions for the SOG. This is how it is recorded in the Combat Talon history book, *The Praetorian STARShip* by Colonel Jerry Thigpen:

> As a result of this MOU, OPCON of Combat Talon and Heavy Hook flowed from SOG through the DCSO directly to the units themselves, effectively placing an intermediate organization between SOG and the unit commanders. Through the 14th SOW, the DCSO was also

> responsible for all administration and supervision of assigned personnel, including (1) flying safety, (2) adherence to AF regulations, directives and policy, and (3) performance of such other functions normally associated with service responsibility.[5]

There were many changes in the names of units referred to in this book. The MOU referred to our unit as Detachment 1 of the 314th TAW (Tactical Airlift Wing) because shortly before, on 1 August 1967, the wing's name was changed from the Troop Carrier Wing to the Tactical Airlift Wing. Also note that the 14th Wing from Nha Trang is referred to as the 14th SOW (Special Operations Wing). At the time of the MOU it was still called the 14th ACW (Air Commando Wing). Its name was not changed to the Special Operations Wing until 1 August 1968.[6]

The 14th ACW commander at that time was Col. John M. Patton. His first DCSO was Col. David C. Collins who did not assume that position until 2 March 1968. The Memorandum of Understanding did not resolve all the operational problems, but it was well received by the affected units. The First Flight invited Colonel Collins to live in their facility on the beach. He was ready to accept, but his boss, Colonel Patton, nixed the idea. He wanted his deputy to be quartered on the base. The addition of a new deputy to the wing staff impacted his overall authority even though it did not change his before Col. John M. Patton operational control over the two SOG units. That might have relieved Colonel Patton of some command's anomalies and headaches. Even though up to that time he was responsible for the safety of the aircraft and the crews, he was not in on the missions flown by the C-123s and the C-130s. He needed an escort to enter the guarded aircraft area, and he definitely did not have the need to know what kind of electronic countermeasures we had behind the curtain inside of the aircraft. When he came unescorted to check out the First Flight's living quarters on the beach, the Nung guards would not let him pass through the gate. He had to wait until a member of the unit came out to escort him in.[7] It was awkward and unusual to have a wing commander who was not fully involved in the wartime operations of his subordinate units because he did not have the need to know.

The command relationship with the wing improved a few days after Colonel Collins assumed his official duties. On 15 March 1968, Detachment 1 of the 314th TAW was renamed the 15th Air Commando Squadron (ACS) and transferred with all of its assets to its new Nha Trang Air Base parent 14th ACW. That made things much better, at least on the new command lines displayed on paper. The distant parent wing at CCK in Taiwan was now out of the picture, and our newly named squadron and our new contact DCSO became a part of the same wing.

Our new DCSO's immediate background was in the Tactical Air Command. He had flown airlift C-130s, and served as both squadron operations officer and squadron commander. As a lieutenant colonel, he became the chief of the Supporting Systems Branch in the command's Doctrine Division. He authored an article on "Doctrine Development for the Employment of Tactical Air Forces" in which he dwelled on the tedious process involved in lengthy back-and-forth coordination between the tactical air and ground forces. All aspects of support for the ground forces had to be scrutinized meticulously and eventual mutual agreements had to be clearly documented for use in joint operations.[8] With such doctrinal credentials he must have been interested in Lieutenant General Momyer's views on accommodating special operations with their modified obsolescent aircraft into the modern-day air force. Now as a new deputy commander for special operations in the 14th ACW, he was at the application level of concepts he dealt with at the doctrinal command level. In his new assignment he was to improve the coordination with the SOG in Saigon, while his wing did everything imaginable with more than ten types of obsolescent aircraft modified for special operations that had nothing to do with that secret organization. Some of the wing's squadrons were located at other air bases at Phan Rang, Pleiku, and Tuy Hoa. Their operations included close and direct air support, interdiction, combat airlift, aerial resupply, visual and photographic reconnaissance, unconventional warfare, counterinsurgency operations, psychological warfare with leaflet dropping and aerial broadcasting, forward air control operations and escort, search and rescue, defoliation operations, flare drops, civic actions, and humanitarian actions. Surely, his wing commander, Colonel Patton, would use him in conducting pressing non-SOG operations.

The SOG tasking and operations did not change at all because of his addition to the wing's staff. Perhaps it was felt at the commander's level, but we, in mission planning, did not notice any difference. He would come to our planning room at First Flight every time we planned a new mission and then would come to the final mission briefing with the crew, and he often joined us to see the aircraft take off. Our post-mission debriefings could hardly be called as such. Nothing unusual ever happened. The only incident that merited any debriefing and follow up was when we were pursued by an interceptor outside of Haiphong Harbor, as I described. The rest could be summarized as, "Flown as planned without an incident." Enemy reaction was always as anticipated, and the EWOs had recordings of all signals received from enemy defenses. On his visits to our planning room we learned that Colonel Collins began his career as a navigator and that he had flown missions in B-29s over Japan. That explained his curiosity in some of our mission planning details. He flew on some of our daytime shuttle flights and got well acquainted with our terrain following operations.

Anh Hoa Hotel

The most welcome relief for the detachment came when it was allowed to rent a downtown hotel that could be turned into bachelor officers' quarters (BOQ), open mess (dining facility), and rooftop officers' club. Maj. Howard Reeve, aircraft commander of the SG-5 crew, was tabbed by the detachment commander, Lt. Col. Donald Britton, to coordinate the bedding down of all officers in one place. Some officers, who had been searching for a suitable facility for a while, came upon a hotel called Anh Hoa. Its owner showed some interest, so Major Reeve and one US Army lieutenant colonel from Camp McDermott, who was the focal point for leasing local facilities to military personnel, began negotiating with the hotel owner. He was hesitant at first because he was considering turning

This is how Anh Hoa Hotel looked like when it was acquired by the detachment. One of the diesel generators is still sitting at the entrance. (Photo by James L. C. "Les" Smith)

it into a brothel. After several talks, the owner was persuaded, realizing that he would not have to invest any money into a new business and that it would be much simpler to just collect monthly rent. The Americans were willing to rent it just as it was.[9] It needed a lot of work to make it functional, but it provided the detachment with an ideal solution to the billeting problem. It had a forty-man bed-down capacity. That was exactly the number they needed. The detachment had thirty-six officer crew members, a commander, an operations officer, a mission planner, and a maintenance officer.

The first thing that had to be done was to make the building secure. The bottom floor of this three-story hotel had street-side store-like windows and doors. These glass walls were replaced with plywood studded walls with cutouts for four window-size air conditioners. Walk through connections between the bottom floor rooms were also sealed off. That turned the room on the right into a dining room and the ones on the left into dormitory rooms for eight occupants. Next, the sidewalk in front of the building was closed off by a wall stacked with interlaced sandbags that reached up to the bottom of the high-capacity air conditioning units. Concertina wire coils were stretched along the base and top of the wall to prevent anyone from climbing over the sandbags. Two armed guards pro-

Two of the vigilant Nung guards posted at their stations. Protective sandbags are stacked under the air conditioning units of the dining room. (Photo by John F. Lewis)

vided round-the-clock security. Besides the few Vietnamese citizens who worked in the hotel, only the resident crew members and their escorted guests were allowed past the guarded gate into the building. The menacing presence of the guards caused the pedestrians to cross over and walk on the opposite side of the street.

The guards were Vietnamese citizens of Chinese heritage from the 5th Special Forces Nung Security Platoon. The Nung are members of a Vietnamese-Chinese minority group with a reputation as fierce fighters. They served in a variety of roles with the US Army Special Forces and were trustworthy; they frequently were used as reliable camp guards.

Past the gate was a corridor that led to the back courtyard. The corridor itself was normally full of parked vehicles, including a jeep and a former ammunition carrier truck (Green Elephant) with a hitched water trailer tank for potable water that had to be trucked in from the base. Past that, toward the northeast corner of the courtyard, was a shed for two diesel-powered generators that provided electricity for the hotel. The courtyard was secure from intruders. The two story building on the right went all the way to the corner by the generators. The two story building on the left also went all the way to the northwest corner of the courtyard. Neither of the neighboring buildings had windows or openings facing the hotel backyard. The backside was enclosed by a high wall with concertina wire on top. Beyond that was the back neighbor's garden, which was accessible only through the building that faced the next street.

Going to the left from the entrance corridor was a tiled walkway that went between the back of the hotel and the kitchen all the way to the left-hand neighbor's wall. From this walkway one could enter the dining room, the zigzagging stairwell to the upper floor rooms, and the large dormitory rooms that we called Hog Heaven. In a nook under the stairway was the building's only telephone and a pigeonhole rack for incoming mail. On the right-hand side of the walkway was the kitchen, and beside it, just outside of Hog Heaven, were cement washbasins where the maids hand washed and scrubbed our laundry the old-fashioned way, using only cold water. Across from Hog Heaven, next to the neighbor's wall, was a hotel storage room with extra tables, chairs, wall lockers, and other accumulated items.

Overhead the walkway were four crosswalks from the second- and third-floor rooms to the bathrooms that were above the kitchen. Each floor had four bathrooms with toilets and showers. On top of the upper bathrooms were two cement water tanks. One was for storing city water for the bathrooms and the other for potable water for the kitchen.

Each floor had sixteen single-occupant rooms that were accessed from four parallel hallways. Each hallway served four rooms. Front rooms faced the street and those were the only ones that had windows. None of the upper floor rooms had air conditioning. They had only ceiling cross ventilation provided by about two-and-a-half-foot-wide openings near the ceiling that were framed with mosquito netting. This way the air could circulate from one room to another as well as from the hallway to each room. Noise carried from one room to the next, but the ventilation was functional. Any mosquitos that got in through the open doors would be food for the numerous geckos that made themselves at home on the walls and ceilings.

Obviously, the choicest rooms were the ones that faced the street. Next were the rooms on the courtyard side of the hallway because they would get more fresh air coming in from the outside. The least desirable were the two four-man Hog Heaven rooms, even though they had air conditioning. Rooms were assigned by rank. Consequently, lieutenant colonels and senior majors got the street side rooms. I had enough time in grade as a major to get a courtyard side room on the second floor. Lieutenants and junior captains lived in the Hog Heaven.

The most used facility was the hotel's roof. It had a beautiful view of the city and the surrounding hills. That is where the bar, tables for entertainment, and beach-type lounge chairs for sunning or just loafing around were. We had a ping pong table and pool table that were in almost con-

View of the Buddha hill from the hotel roof. Buildings on the side of the hill became a temporary stronghold of the Vietcong during the Tet Offensive in 1968. (Photo by James L. C. "Les" Smith)

tinuous use. The bar was self-served during the day. In the evenings two sisters, Ann and Susan, served as barmaids. They could serve us drinks, or a person could just help himself. There was no pay for the drink service. No money was exchanged. We had a book ledger in which each officer had his own page. All we had to do is make a hash mark in a column for a 5, 10, 15, 20, or 25 cent drink. Soft drinks went for 5 cents. Cheap beer brands were 10 centers. Popular beer brands cost 15 cents, and some foreign imports 20 cents. Mixed drinks went for a quarter. Designated club officer would add up the hash marks at the end of each month and we would pay him by check or MPCs. We had another ledger in the dining room that was for bottles of wine. These varied in cost from $2 to $5 and more. Because of the occasional wine bottles I bought for the whole table, my monthly bar bill would be almost $15.

MPCs were our currency. It was money printed for the use of forces in the Southeast Asia war zone in order to avoid profiteering by black market trading in US dollars. MPCs were colorful and about the size of "monopoly money." Just about every year they printed a different looking batch for each paper denomination. Local currency was piasters. We could exchange them for MPCs, or MPCs for piasters at the base bank. The Vietnamese were not allowed to do so. We could also get US dollars if we were on orders to fly out of Vietnam to Taiwan or the Philippines.

The first six crews that came to Nha Trang might have had a difficult time in getting settled there, but both the airmen and officers were blessed with men among them who had many talents. Instead of usual soldier griping, they rolled up their sleeves and did things to improve their environment. Among the officers was Jean Lesieutre, a French born and educated captain, EWO on SG-4 crew who turned out to be at the right place and the right time to expedite things. His French background opened up many doors for him in Vietnam with French-speaking officials. He learned from the Officers' Club manager on base that it would be possible for the detachment to establish an officers' mess and bar at the hotel they were about to rent. He helped the detachment set up a commissary account in Saigon for needed groceries.

The hotel's kitchen had not been used for some time, so it had to be redesigned and furnished with appropriate equipment. Captains Guenon and Mattingly designed it and other ingenious members procured stoves, refrigerators, freezers, kitchenware, and tableware. Meanwhile, electrically savvy officers converted the hotel to handle standard US electricity that was produced by two acquired diesel powered generators. Then they needed a cook. This is how Lesieutre handled that:

> I contacted the Chief of Police and asked his help to find indigenous personnel to run the Mess. He said to me that very day that I was in luck as he could recommend a very talented chef. He arranged for me to meet him that very day. I was impressed with "Charlie" and he told me that he and his family could provide all the maids, waiters and cooks for our need. They were all relatives. I asked the Police Chief to vouch for the necessary security background and he replied that it would be done with no problem.[10]

The dining room was pretty basic. It had ordinary tables, with tablecloths, which could be rearranged easily to accommodate four to twelve people. The dinnerware and silverware was also ordinary. There was no special lighting and the walls did not have any decorations. But the food was terrific. As soon as we arrived in August 1967, the operations officer, Lieutenant Colonel Hines, wrote letters to all state governors requesting small state flags to display on the dining room walls. The governors responded promptly and we soon had dining room walls full of flags. We had two Vietnamese waiters that worked during lunch and dinner. They did the dish washing and assisted the two Chinese cooks in the kitchen.

Our Vietnamese/Chinese cooks were also Nung. Charlie, the senior cook, was an excellent chef with prior experience in hotels and restaurants. His sous-chef was also excellent, but, in their cultural custom, he deferred to Charlie with everything that anyone requested of him. He had to get Charlie's nod of approval before he reached into the refrigerator to get a requested item. The kitchen had everything a kitchen should have except an automatic dishwasher. It was air conditioned and, where needed, well ventilated. We had two commercial size stoves with twelve burners, two big multichambered ovens, and refrigerators and freezers that lined the whole courtyard walkway wall. The designated mess steward bought groceries at the commissary in Saigon. His shopping trips were coordinated with SOG. They gave us longer scheduled ground times at Tan Son Nhut Air Base and also provided us with a truck and a driver to bring the groceries to the aircraft. The groceries were stored in a big pantry at the entrance to the dining room. We were a nonprofit military

Dining room scene with members of the S-05 crew. *Left to right*: John Lewis, Charlie Claxton, Pat Watson, Hugh McCormick, waiter Mr. Tuy, Bob Rosser, John Gargus, and Tom Hines. (Photo by Hugh McCormick)

dining facility. Salaries of cooks and waiters were covered by the air force and we paid only for the cost of food. The steward would calculate each officer's monthly cost based on the number of days he was present in the hotel. In my one-year stay there my monthly cost fluctuated between $45 and $49. That was incredibly cheap living.

Not long after our arrival I witnessed a site that resulted in a quick hotel improvement. I was on the roof just killing time when I saw Walt Pine, aircraft commander of S-03, come by in his swimsuit with a bath towel over his shoulder and a bar of soap in his hand. Seeing my puzzled look, he told me that it was time for his hot shower. That was strange because we did not have hot water in the bathrooms. He pointed to the moving storm cloud that would soon give us a dose of daily rain. When it began to pour he stepped under a downspout of rain draining from the tin roof of the bar. He was soaping himself up and enjoying the rainwater that turned hot from the tropical heat absorbed by the corrugated tin metal of the roof. I tried this the next day when a similar cloud brought more rain.

After that I learned that we had some abandoned French-style gas water heaters in the storage room. When the time came for the S-05 crew to serve as a rotating hotel duty crew, I went to the storage room across from Hog Heaven with Karl Wiegand. We found six of those dust-covered heaters; they were still in French-labeled boxes. We opened one of them and found written installation instructions. Karl asked me if I could translate them. They were simple enough. I had hand-written translations of them in no time. The older waiter, Mr. Tuy, spoke French and told me that he had a plumber friend who could install them for us for a modest price. Instructions were simple enough, so I told him that we have crew members who could probably do that. Someone came by and commented that we would need metric size fittings to do the job. Well, the hotel was built with French metric measurements and appropriate fittings were all there in the boxes. The aircraft commander of the S-05 crew, Bob Rosser, said he could do the job. All he needed was some tools and pipe dope. In about two days he showed up with more plumbing "stuff" than he needed for the job. He was the best scrounger we had. He was from Tennessee, and he could always find somebody from that state who would give him everything for free or for a couple of double shot drinks at the club on base or at Camp McDermott.

Several amateur plumbers pitched in, and we had hot water in three bathrooms on each floor. It was amazing! Each heater worked perfectly the first time it was activated. Hot water output was almost instantaneous. The heater would fire up as soon as the water began moving through it. The plumbing geniuses installed them in such a way that they could be activated by either the shower or the bathroom sink hot water knobs. Mr. Tuy, who observed the work from a respectful distance, was amazed at what the American officers could do.

The next improvement was the enclosure and air conditioning of the rooftop bar. Scrounging and trading for San Miguel beer, we acquired building materials from the Green Berets at Camp McDermott. We found out that there were many carpenters among us. Most pitched in by building studded plywood walls with cutouts for electrical outlets and a very large window-type air conditioner that turned up just in time for measuring its proper space on the already standing walls. We used Styrofoam padding from aircraft flares used by the C-47 Magic Dragon gunships to insulate the walls. Large rectangular blocks of Styrofoam fitted perfectly between the precisely spaced 2 × 4 × 8 pinewood studs. It was the best structural improvement made to the hotel. Only one flaw was never properly resolved. Normal bar lighting, air conditioning, beverage storing refrigerators, ice making machine, and a TV put a heavy load on the existing hotel wiring. Circuit breakers would pop very often.

Perhaps now is the best time to describe how we came to have such a nice bar. All our guests would say that it was the best one they ever visited while in Vietnam. It didn't just happen. It took a lot of good luck and work.

The first Anh Hoa bar manager was Capt. Art Heaphy. He hoped to follow up on what Captain Lesieutre accomplished with the Officers' Club manager when it came to getting the Anh Hoa dining started. He wanted to create a beverage account for the bar. The Officers' Club was not interested in getting involved. So, Heaphy went to the NCO (Noncommissioned Officer) Club. There he found a sympathetic ear from the sergeant in charge who was interested in what the C-130s could do for his establishment with the frequent flights to Clark Air Base. Heaphy's SG-1 crew was about to go to Clark for scheduled Fulton Recovery and electronic warfare training with F-102 interceptors. The NCO Club manager claimed to have an account with his counterpart there who could help him to get bar supplies. He gave Art enough cash to buy one pallet-full of cases of Seagram's liquors and two pallets of cases of San Miguel beer. Heaphy started a long-lasting purchasing account relationship that continued even after its creators departed for other assignments. No one recalls who made similar arrangements with the liquor supply outlet at CCK in Taiwan. It was most likely one of the Stray Goose NCOs who were equally gifted at obtaining "stuff." Consequently, getting everything a well-stocked bar should have was no problem.[11]

Shortly after the officers settled at Anh Hoa, SOG tasked the detachment to pick up two Opel sedans at Tachikawa Air Base in Japan and fly them to Saigon. What ensued is best described by Jean Lesieutre, EWO of the SG-4 crew.

> All went well, until the Tachikawa's Base Commander decided that we were unlawfully smuggling the sedans into Vietnam, and ordered that we stand down, and would not allow us to continue loading until he could verify the legality of our mission. When he insisted to come aboard the aircraft, he was told by Captain Phil Yoder, our aircraft commander, that he would not be able to look into the classified curtained off compartment. That evidently reinforced his suspicion that we were really smuggling those cars and wanted to know what was in there. Knowing this would take some time to resolve, we took off for the officers club. There the club manager found out that we were stationed in Vietnam and asked if there was anything he could help us with. We told him about our hotel Officers Club in Nah Trang and our need for bar furniture, mainly tables and chairs.

> In a matter of minutes he said he believed he had all we could use, as they had just recently renovated the club. It was cooperation of the highest level. He took us to the warehouse where all the club old furniture was stored, and told us if we had room in our C-130 he would have it delivered to us on the ramp. True to his word he did just that. We came back with a 20 foot long bar and all the furniture we could use. From that day on this ended up as the best Mess and Bar in the country.[12]

Even though the rooftop had many military visitors, it was quite exclusive. No one could just walk in to see how we lived. Our classified mission shielded us from curious walk-ins. A visitor to our hotel had to be escorted in by one of us. We would either walk in with our guests or be summoned by someone to come to the gate guards who would hold them there until someone could vouch for them. We never had a written policy on bringing female friends into the hotel. There was a general understanding that not only the commanders but also most of us did not want such presence. Security was the overriding consideration here. There were many female spies who gleaned information from American soldiers. We

Inside view of the rooftop bar at Christmas time with our two sister barmaids Ann and Sue. (Photo by Dow Rogers)

could not afford that. The other consideration was a moral one. We were all married and had many children back at home. On several occasions we had Vietnamese officers and their wives for dinner and drinks at the rooftop. All enjoyed our hospitality.

I remember only one incident when Tom Hines got upset with one of the First Flight's officers who showed up at the gate with a female companion. It was awkward for the guy who invited him to send him away, so he escorted them to the rooftop. The visit did not turn out well. Tom Hines made an appropriate follow-up with the First Flight.

I was indirectly involved in one unwelcomed female event. We had civilian technical representatives for radar, ECM system, Fulton Recovery gear, and Loran-C. Since they were a part of the Stray Goose project, they had access to the hotel. The Loran-C tech rep would tell me every now and then that he had a girl who was a "knock out" and that I should meet her someday. Well, that day came unexpectedly. He showed up with her at the rooftop. She was an attractive girl who spoke acceptable English and was a good pool player. I think that she won every game she played and became the main attraction of the evening. She looked provocative in the roof lights. She wore what hundreds of other Vietnamese girls wore during the day: a long white gown-style dress, panties, and a bra. Her two undergarments were of a darker shade than the opaque gown. That feature stood out in the roof lights, to the delight of the pool players as she bent over the table to make her shots.

Tom Hines came to the roof when they were about to leave, but he immediately came after me. I told him that I did not invite them. Then he directed me to tell my friend that he could not bring his girlfriend to the hotel again. Because Tom and I were good friends, I asked him to tell the tech rep what needed to be said. I told Tom that if I did it as he asked, I'd lose my friendship with the guy. He understood and took care of it himself. We never saw the young lady again.

The treasured ice-making machine had a story that can finally be told. A still anonymous crew member spotted it unattended on Tan Son Nhut's tarmac. The forklift operator who was loading our cargo for up country destinations was told to load up the palletized machine as well. It was put to immediate use in the bar and its shapely ice cubes were enjoyed by all. A few days later, base operations officials from Ton Son Nhut queried all aircraft they had on record transiting through there on the days they thought the machine disappeared. We learned that the ice maker's intended destination was General Westmoreland's headquarters.

We can also tell the incredible story about how we acquired a jeep. The Green Beret neighbors from across the street used several jeeps for transportation. They lived in a much smaller two story structure that used to be a restaurant; it had several rooms and a rooftop that they turned into a bar. We called their place "Fort Courage" after the popular comedy sitcom *F Troop*. One day we noticed that they stopped using one of their jeeps. It stayed in the same place all the time. Closer examination revealed that all of its tires were flat, ruptured by a grenade that must have exploded beneath the vehicle. It wouldn't have been possible to have that happen where it sat, because it was only about 30 feet from the Anh Hoa gate guards. We concluded that some of the troops made a visit to a place where they shouldn't have been and someone tossed a grenade under their jeep. Not wanting to be caught in that location, they drove the jeep home where it sat for days. They obviously did not need it because they were going about without it and we needed it more than they did. So the inevitable thing happened.

Our ingenious procurers towed the jeep to the First Flight's maintenance compound on the north side of the base where they fitted it with new tires and changed its color scheme from olive drab green to Stray Goose dark jungle green. They also changed the ragged seat upholstery, which would have been a dead giveaway for anyone who would look down upon it from the Fort Courage roof. Now our new jeep got parked right across the street about 30 feet from where we found it. It sat in front of the two Nung guards, facing down the street in the opposite direction. Our neighbors never caught on. None of them came even close to examine the new vehicle. The menacing guards kept everyone, Vietnamese and Americans, away from our side of the street.

I don't remember who was responsible for acquiring the shuffleboard table. I believe that it came from some outfit at Camp McDermott. They had it just sitting there, unused, because they did not have enough space in any of their buildings where it would fit in. Because of its length, it had to be delivered in a borrowed truck. It fitted perfectly in the barroom along the wall opposite the bar. Getting the heavy board up to the bar was difficult. It was too heavy to be passed from hand to hand up the side of the second- and third-floor walkways. One slip of the hand could have caused it to drop to the ground and sustain irreparable damage. Here we got some help from the loadmasters. They put up wooden support beams between the base of one of the water tanks and sawhorse supports on the roof. They mounted pulleys on the support beams, and the way they connected the pulley system, hoisting of the shuffleboard table became a snap. Once perfectly leveled in place the shuffleboard became the major play attraction on the roof.

The most extensive improvement was to get our own water supply that would make us completely independent of the city's utilities. I remember very well how this came about. Our operations officer, Tom Hines, got upset when he learned that the officer who paid our monthly water bill directly to an agent at the business office would always pay the agent a few extra piasters as a customary tip. This practice began just after we leased the hotel. One day, water stopped flowing through the pipes and all assumed that this was some kind of a plumbing problem. But soon the officers learned that the water was turned off on purpose to extract a bribe from the new occupants of the hotel. Once the water department official responsible for the shutoff received satisfactory compensation, he had the water flow to the hotel restored. Hines vowed that we would no longer pay a bribe to this official.

Just at that time Hines ran into a couple of Australian officers who depended on our shuttle transport to go from one Green Beret camp to another where they drilled water wells, not just for the troops, but also for the natives as part of their civil action program. He met them on one of the flights and invited them to the club. The story about how we paid for our water came up. Before we knew it, the Aussies agreed to drill a well for us in the backyard. That was done within about a week's time. Included in this gift from the Aussies was a water purification package with all needed equipment, minus the chemicals, which we could get on the base. They tested the water for several days and then declared it up to our drinking standards. The amateur plumbers made all the necessary plumbing connections and turned off the city water supply. All went well for us, but we learned from our chef, Charlie, about the neighborhood problem we created. He informed us that an employee at the city's water office turned off the water main that supplied the neighborhood. That affected "Fort Courage" across the street and our neighbors on the left who were a mixture of army officers and military contractors. This was in retaliation against us with the hope that because the other Americans were also affected, we would continue using the city water. Our commander, Lt. Col.

Dow Rogers, complained through official channels and the neighborhood water supply was restored. We kept pumping water from our brand new well.

Maj. Charlie Claxton was the S-05 crew's third pilot. His ambition was to inherit the dining room steward's job from Capt. Gerald Van Buren who was on the S-01 crew that was the next one to complete its tour of duty. He was diligent and started to inventory everything in the pantry. He wasn't discouraged by the fact that the cooks and Van Buren's shopping list never equaled what we purchased at the commissary in Saigon. Much of that had to do with the generosity we showed our enlisted crew members. They had their own shopping list as well, but part of our groceries were misdirected for their use. By the time we arrived in Nha Trang the enlisted crew members had remodeled the upstairs of the building vacated by the officers. They ended up with rooms for five enlisted members of each crew; the rooms had air conditioning, a TV, a cooking stove, and a refrigerator/freezer for food and drinks. Their setup was the envy of all army and air force soldiers who served in Nha Trang. All enlisted crew members could eat free at all hours in the mess hall, but it was nice to be able to prepare a gourmet meal in one's crew room.

We never suspected that our employees could be taking some of the food with them. Charlie, the cook, prided himself on keeping the pantry

Enchilada cooks Charlie Claxton and John Gargus. (Photo by John Gargus)

locked up. He probably never let anyone on his kitchen staff have the key, so none could go into the pantry alone. On the other hand, anyone on the daily duty crew could get the key and retrieve from the pantry such barroom things as peanuts, potato chips, olives, maraschino cherries, pickles, or anything else. On one occasion I surprised my maid while she was cleaning my room. She was startled and in the process knocked down an apple that I had on the table for several days. She picked it up and started to wipe it with a cloth that wasn't clean. I assured her that all was okay and then gave her the apple to keep. Late that afternoon, someone called me and said that the gate guard was holding up my maid for some reason. When I got to the gate I learned that the guard suspected her of stealing the apple I gave her. After my assurances, she was free to go. That showed me that the Nung guards not only kept unauthorized people out, they also made sure that none of our "stuff" was carried out.

Charlie Claxton and I developed pretty good relationship with Charlie the cook. His English was not very good. He understood it quite well but did not speak much. Around me he preferred to answer in French. That also worked out pretty well. At one time I asked him if he could fix us a

Typical early morning scene in the hotel backyard. Maids are doing laundry. (Photo by Dow Rogers)

Spanish omelet. He was not familiar with it and wanted to know what went into it. Once I told him, he assured me that there would be no problem. However, when we got his Spanish version of the omelet it was more like a western omelet with onions, peppers, and tomatoes, ingredients that were just lightly sautéed in a Chinese-style wok. I told him that he had the ingredients all right, but that he needed to cook them for a long time. I went to the kitchen with him and thinly sliced the onions, green peppers, and tomatoes. Of course he understood the julienne style of slicing vegetables. My preference was to slow cook the vegetables at least two hours, or until the mixture got pasty. That encounter cemented our future relationship. On the day of our next combat mission I asked him to make a batch of Spanish sauce that would be enough for six omelets. When we returned to the hotel after four in the morning, I found the prepared mix in the refrigerator. With Charlie Claxton's help we had six Spanish omelets ready in no time. That started a precedent. After that we always had Spanish omelets after nighttime missions. Because other officers started asking for Spanish omelets for breakfast, Charlie made sure that there was some mix always ready in his vegetable refrigerator.

I introduced Charlie to another dish that was unknown to him. I made my second trip to the Saigon commissary when Jerry Van Buren flew with our crew on a day shuttle flight so that he could introduce Charlie Claxton to the facility. While Jerry and Charlie looked for things on their list, I browsed around and ran across large tin cans of Old El Paso enchilada sauce. I seized two of them immediately and started looking for corn tortillas. I found them and put ten packages in the shopping cart. That was 120 tortillas. Next I found some hot dried chili peppers. I was going to make enchiladas once we got home.

Charlie had no idea how to proceed with the preparation. All he needed to do was watch us go at it. Claxton and I had two other curious helpers who liked enchiladas and wanted to learn how to make them. We tasked Charlie's sous-chef to dice onions into a large bowl and shred sharp cheddar cheese into another large bowl. They also made a very good hot sauce in a blender by pureeing tomatoes with hot peppers from the commissary. We browned several pounds of hamburger meat mixed with some finely chopped onions, and when properly seasoned and done we mixed in several handfuls of grated cheese. Then we greased two large pans to use for baking the enchiladas in the oven. Next, I handled the most delicate part of the process myself. I heated up cooking oil in a twelve-inch frying pan and began dipping corn tortillas into the oil, turning them over until they became soft enough to be able to roll the hamburger mixture into them. If they were cooked too long, they would become brittle and hard to roll. Claxton's task was to dip the softened tortillas into another twelve-inch pan that contained simmering enchilada sauce. He handled them with tongs one by one and placed them on the worktable where our two other helpers spooned hamburger mixture on the overheated tortillas and rolled them up like cigars. They stacked the filled-up tortillas next to each other on the baking pan. They laid them side by side in two rows, filling the pan completely with forty-eight of them. Altogether we used up ten packs of tortillas. Once done, we spread the leftover hamburger mix, cheddar cheese, and onions over the top of enchiladas. The final touch was sprinkling the leftover enchilada sauce over the top of everything. After baking for thirty-five minutes at 350 degrees they were ready to be served. The resultant meal was a huge success. I don't recall how many diners we had that night, but the pan was left clean and some would have eaten even more.

By popular request, we had to repeat the experience. This time we had Charlie cook up enough Spanish rice and Mexican pinto beans to go with the two trays of enchiladas. That made it a more complete Mexican meal. Charlie did not get to participate in the second cooking because I had so many volunteers who wanted to help and learn. Soon the officers began to invite friends to the Anh Hoa Mexican dinners. I was forewarned by the invitations so we increased our production to three trays or 144 enchiladas. That would always leave some left over. However, they would disappear the next morning because the officers would order them with their breakfast eggs.

Periodic enchilada cooking continued until we departed from Vietnam. Kitchen staff took over the complete process even though there were plenty of volunteers who wanted to participate. When my wife heard about our enchilada cooking, she sent me a Mexican *molcajete* (mortar made from hollowed-out lava rock used for grinding chili peppers) and very hot small chili peppers picked from the bushes in her parents' yard. I enjoyed grinding down the peppers with salt and tomatoes for a very good homemade hot sauce.

My wife envied the quality of food we enjoyed at Anh Hoa. She reminded me often that at home she and the children would eat a lot of hot dogs, beans, and macaroni and cheese. As far as our children were concerned, they ate very well because that is exactly what they liked. Our youngest twins were one-year-olds and just past their Gerber baby food meals. The older children were still very young. They did not yet have the dexterity to handle a steak with knife and fork. Besides macaroni and cheese, they loved hamburgers and meat loaf. They could handle a chicken drumstick. But I got my wife's point. We were eating very well, and she could not go to a restaurant with four kids to get the type of meal I was having every day.

5

Realities of War

Mortar Attack

By November 1967, my S-05 fellow crew members and I became accustomed to what promised to be a pretty comfortable setting for our one-year tour in Vietnam. But that was not to be. We were awakened to the reality of war on 25 November when the Vietcong mortar attack destroyed one of our precious aircraft. We heard several distant explosions and concluded that it was another hit-and-run mortar attack on the air base or at Camp McDermott. During the night we learned something different.

Aircraft #64–0563 received a near direct mortar round and was completely destroyed. The plane parked next to it sustained major structural damage that required it to be flown back to the States for repairs. The other two had only shrapnel holes that could be repaired at Nha Trang. We were lucky that we did not lose the entire crew that was scheduled to fly it that night. When the crew members started their routine preflight checks, the word came down from a runner dispatched by the First Flight's operations office that the night's mission was canceled. Tom Hines was going to fly with the crew, so as soon as he got the cancellation word through the mission planner Major Thompson, he jumped into the jeep and went to the First Flight's operations on the north (Vietnamese) side of the base to make a secure telephone call to SOG in Saigon to find out what was happening. Meanwhile, the crew went to our operations office to return their combat gear and retrieve all personal items and identification documents that they could not take on flights over North Vietnam. Before Hines got out of his jeep at First Flight, he heard several incoming explosions and

Composite of USAF photos shows the destroyed Combat Talon #64–0563. Impact point of one mortar round can be seen in the right-hand photo. (Composite of USAF photos by John Gargus)

saw a big ball of fire from the area he had just departed. He raced back and saw one aircraft already gone and the other three being moved away from the intense fire. There was no doubt that we would have lost many lives had the mission not been canceled.

One aircraft, which was closest to the one in flames, was taxied away by maintenance personnel, who, in their haste, failed to reset the engine oil circuit breakers before starting the engines. This caused the engines to run without oil and burn up. They had to be replaced. The most seriously damaged aircraft had to be flown back to the United States for more extensive repairs. We did not fly for almost two weeks.

The commanders used this unexpected down time to give all crews some relief. Those of us who opted to go somewhere out of the country were issued permissive temporary duty orders that authorized us to fly on any US aircraft. Many of us opted to go to Bangkok, Thailand, for a few days. We all hated the loss of our aircraft, but we appreciated the unexpected opportunity to be away from the war in Vietnam.

Mission of Destroyed 64–0563 Remains a Mystery

I became curious about the mission of this aircraft when I started writing this book. I learned that none of my still living contacts remembered which crew had been scheduled to fly it. I questioned crew members from S-02 through S-06 and they all claimed that it was some other crew. The only two members from the S-01 crew, both of them loadmasters, separated from the service and could not be found through the air force locator service back in 1997. David Fitzwater, the destroyed aircraft's crew chief, and other enlisted maintenance personnel who moved the three Blackbirds away from the burning aircraft did not remember which crew was involved in the aircraft's ground aborted mission. The only conclusion remains that it was Major Day's S-01 crew that escaped a possible disaster that night and then met its fate one month later.

I was unable to learn anything about that night's mission either. Lt. Col. Dow Rogers, who was the unit's commander at that time, does not remember its mission. He attended all combat mission briefings, but there were so many of them that he cannot be expected to remember the details for each one. Members of other crews did not have the need to know what kind of mission was to be flown. The crew chief would have had the best clue for that because it was his aircraft, and he had to be there when its cargo was loaded or off-loaded. He was the last person to leave and lock the aircraft before it received a direct mortar hit.

Normally, if a mission with infiltrators was aborted, a secure van would wait there to remove such team without any contact with maintenance personnel who would be around the aircraft. An aborted cargo resupply mission would have required off-loading of the cargo by the First Flight. It would take several days to make arrangements for a new time on target for such a flight, and the aircraft could not just sit there with its clandestine cargo on board. A bogus, diversionary cargo drop mission could fly on the following night because there would be no precise prearranged delivery time for it. In any case, each cargo resupply would contain explosives and ammunition. Because there were no secondary explosions while the aircraft burned to the ground, no such cargo could have been on board. A leaflet drop mission could also fly on the following night, and the millions of tightly packed and boxed leaflets could be left secured on the aircraft. Again, there was no evidence in the ashes that the aircraft had a leaflet cargo on board. No one has yet stepped forward to confirm which crew was scheduled to fly that night and no one knows what kind of clandestine mission was aborted. I hope that someone who reads this book served either in the First Flight as cargo loader or at SOG during this time frame and will remember unknown details about this destroyed C-130's mission.

Civil Action Program

Because of our security-imposed low profile in the community, the first arrivers did not have a civil action program whose intent was to build amicable relationships with the locals. However, some of our members were eager to do something for an orphanage. What harm to our secretive image could come from assistance to an orphanage? There were several of them in town and some of our enlisted men befriended an American lady who was assisting one of them with support she received from her church's congregation back at home. Our commanders considered this and picked me to be the civil action officer for our unit. That came about because Tom Hines and I knew about the civil action from the Air Force Reserve Officer Training Corps (AFROTC) curriculum at Texas A&M where we advocated its merits. I contacted the wing's civil action officer and I did not learn much from him because he was too curious about who we were. We were not yet part of the 14th ACW. He introduced me to his Vietnamese counterpart who did not show any curiosity about our detachment's existence. He told me that every American wanted to help the orphans and that they already had a sufficient number of benefactors. He was interested in doing something for the needy military families. When he found out that we already had a contact with a Roman Catholic orphanage on the north side of Nha Trang, he informed me that this orphanage was located in an unsafe neighborhood with suspected Vietcong sympathies. Nevertheless, he was happy to have an organization that was willing to assist the local community.

We recruited our wives to help us in this civil action effort. They rose to the occasion and exceeded all our expectations. Several collection centers for candy, toys, and clothing opened up in different parts of the country. My wife started one in Bryan, Texas, where she received support from the Kiwanis and the chamber of commerce. Other wives did likewise with the Rotary Clubs, Knights of Columbus, and other men's clubs in their towns. Karl Wiegand's wife, Mona, became the chief coordinator of this charitable effort, which turned out to be larger than we expected. Donating organizations covered the cost of packaging and shipping to Pope Air Force Base, from where the goods were flown to Nha Trang in a Tactical Air Command's airlift C-130 that was rotated to Vietnam.

We were amazed by the amount of goods we received. We filled the whole upstairs room of the headquarters building with boxes stacked on top of each other. Since I was the unit civil action officer, I was in charge of sorting the goods. Initially, I had more helpers than I needed. But, by the time I got things organized, I was down to only three or four helpers. That was about all I needed. As always, some were just curious about what kind of "stuff" we received, and others found the working conditions too uncomfortable. It was very hot and dusty up there. I wore only a swimsuit during the hours I spent sorting the goods. We had more toys, sweets, and children's clothes than we could use in that one orphanage. So we came up with two more places where we could distribute the Christmas items. Some of our crew members befriended one young English-speaking priest at the cathedral who helped us to organize a Christmas party for the Boy and Girl Scouts who were affiliated with his church. We then offered our First Flight colleagues help with the Christmas party they planned for the Vietnamese members. That was a big help because we had too much adult clothing in our boxes. This development pleased my Vietnamese civil action contact. It was exactly what he had in mind, but not necessarily only during a religious holiday celebration. Thereafter our sorting was easier. All adult items, some toys, and plenty of sweets went into boxes that were taken off our hands immediately. The First Flight people sorted their goods and prepared appropriate packages for individual families. Our task was to separate things for the orphanage and for the scouts. Scouts needed only sweets and toys. The orphanage got all the rest, which included a huge supply of all kinds of children's clothing.

Christmas at the Orphanage

The orphanage project proved to be very successful. Not everyone came to the presentation of gifts because we didn't have enough vehicles to transport all those who wanted to attend. The children were surprised. They must not have been properly informed about what to expect from us. They were mostly war orphans who must have had their own impressions or memories of American soldiers. The operating priest was surprised as well. He did not anticipate so many toys, sweets, and clothes. The clothing was admired by the girls and they pretended to put on some of the pretty dresses. Those would be sorted and distributed later on by the orphanage staff. They also set aside most of the candy and sweets. But all the toys were gone in a hurry. We learned from the staff that none of the children had their own personal toys. The toys at the orphanage were shared by everyone. It must have been a unique experience for some of them to select a toy they could claim as their very own. Some of the toys were not familiar to them. They didn't know that plastic bats and baseball-like balls and gloves went together. They were also puzzled by the crisscrossed jacks and red rubber balls. Some of the airmen showed a few girls how to play jacks. That attracted attention and amused them a lot. We also brought containers of Kool-Aid that was served in paper cups. Nuns who ran the kitchen welcomed all the Kool-Aid packages we gave them. They received dozens of them, in all available fruit flavors. We also gave them many pounds of chocolate. Bon-bon style chocolate melted in its boxes, forming a messy slab of chocolate and its various flavored fillings. We were

Detachment commander Lt. Col. Dow Rogers talks to children at the orphanage. (Photo by Dow Rogers)

going to throw those chocolate boxes away, but the orphanage lady said that they could use the hardened slabs from the boxes in their kitchen. Consequently, many pounds of this once melted and solidified chocolate ended up in baked cakes and cookies for the orphans. Separately wrapped Hershey bars, Milky Ways, Baby Ruths, Snickers, and many other candies that remained within their wraps during repeated meltdowns were distributed with other candy.

Christmas at the First Flight

Only the top officers and few airmen attended the Christmas party for the Vietnamese members and employees of the First Flight. All but the candy was neatly packaged in Christmas wrapping paper by the Americans of the First Flight and addressed to individual families. They were delighted. Most of us did not stay for the food and drinks that followed. It was always intended to be their in-house party.

Christmas Party at the Cathedral

The party at the cathedral was also a huge success. We scheduled it to occur on Christmas Day following the daytime mass. The number of boys and girls of all ages in their scout uniforms surprised us. Almost everyone from our detachment came. That included the airmen from the base and officers from Anh Hoa. We coordinated this one with our civil action counterparts and I invited their chief, who I knew was a Roman Catholic. He brought several of his officers with him and the appearance was that they were also Christians. Charlie Claxton was dressed up as Santa Claus. We didn't have any elves to assist him with several bags of toys, but he got plenty of help from others. Gift distribution was random yet pretty orderly for the large group of Boy and Girl Scouts. Candy distribution became chaotic. The scouts respected Santa Claus and waited for their turn. That wasn't the case with his helpers who decided to distribute candy and chocolates. We noticed that the number of children in street clothes grew. It started with ones who were obviously dressed for church and came out to the fence-enclosed courtyard of the cathedral after the mass, but we soon realized that we had children coming over the fence to join in.

The airmen organized a sack race, which was followed by some scout-originated games. We all had fun until the last game. They called it a human

Operations Officer Tom Hines, Charlie Claxton as Santa Claus, and a Vietnamese civil action officer at the cathedral Christmas party. Below is the elbow-to-elbow crowd that crashed in on our Boy and Girl Scouts party from the surrounding streets. (Composite by John Gargus; photos by Dow Rogers)

chariot race. Six men laced their arms together and the driver jumped on the shoulders of the man in the middle. They formed two chariots to race against each other. None of the men had participated in such a race before, so as could be expected, feet got tangled up and both human chariots collapsed—to the delight of onlookers. The crowd encouraged a restart, but we gave it up. Several men sustained bruises from their fall and we could not risk a disabling injury in a crew member.

Mission Directive

As soon as we returned to the hotel, Maj. Roy Thompson, our mission planner and intelligence officer, came to me to tell me that we had a fragmentary order for a combat mission waiting for us at the First Flight's operations office. Roy's end of tour was approaching and he was not going to be replaced by another planner because our personnel manning document was being downsized. I volunteered to replace him, and my S-05 crew's EWO, 1st Lt. John Lewis, volunteered to assume Roy's intelligence officer duties. We left immediately to see what this Christmas Day frag order had for us.

The frag order called for an unusual combat mission. (Frag order is a shorter term for a military fragmentary order that directs implementation of a mission without complete and routine details on how such task should be executed. In our case, it gave us only the aircraft load, target area, and the time to execute. The how to do it details were up to us.) It directed us to execute two airdrops deep inside of North Vietnam. The first one was to be a high altitude leaflet drop on a north-northeast heading just west of the Red River and the second one a low-level resupply drop on a southerly heading just west of the Black River on the other side of the mountains. We positioned ourselves in front of a large-scale classified wall chart with numerous circles of various diameters and colors that depicted locations of known enemy defenses. We traced a probable inbound and outbound route with our fingers and concluded that the mission was a feasible one. The only possible threat to our aircraft would come during the "short look," the leaflet drop, when the Blackbird would be in close proximity to the Yen Bai Air Base and its MIG interceptors, or from any other Hanoi area base that had MIGs on night alert. Otherwise, everything else looked good. We would be able to lay out a flight path that would be clear of lethal ranges of all known surface to air missiles and anti-aircraft artillery.

This interesting mission was scheduled for the night of the 28/29 December. We briefed our commander and operations officer about our tasking and joined everyone on the roof where our own Christmas Day festivities were just kicking off. Our Christmas party Santa Claus, Charlie Claxton, had shed his red suit and put on a kitchen apron to supervise the lavish meal that was being prepared. Charlie had just taken over the kitchen stewardship from Gerald Van Buren. We had plentiful appetizers and several courses that pleased everyone. Then most of us went to our rooms to write or tape letters to our families. Timewise, we were half a day ahead of our families at home. It was early Christmas morning there, and our children were experiencing happy moments opening their gifts and thinking of their fathers who were not present to share their joy. We were all young then and we all had two to five young ones. My twin daughters were born in December of the previous year, so this was the first Christmas that would have any meaning for them.

Early next morning, we went to the First Flight's operations room to obtain the latest known positions of North Vietnamese air defenses. Because this was the first mission planning experience for me and for John Lewis, we spent a lot of time in front of the large wall-mounted chart that was a mosaic of individual joint operational graphic air charts. Their scale was 1 to 250,000. The giant mosaic was covered by a clinging sheet of plastic on which were grease-penciled circles of different colors and sizes that represented locations and lethal ranges of all known SAM sites and AAA batteries, as well as locations of the enemy's air bases. We were looking at the most formidable active air defenses of modern warfare. This frightful air order-of-battle chart was kept current by the First Flight intelligence officer. It was a sobering sight to see it all depicted in one chart. On our prior missions we had copies of only those air order-of-battle charts that affected our route of flight. Once Lewis obtained geographical coordinates for all enemy defenses that would impact our flight, we went to the mission planning room next door to lay out the route for the crew that would fly this mission.

S-01 Crew

The mission was assigned to the S-01 crew. It was their turn to fly it. There were some questions about whether they should be skipped over because their aircraft commander, Maj. Dick Day, and loadmaster, airman first class (A1C) Lino Licudan, were on duty not including flying (DNIF) and two other crew members were not at Nha Trang at that time. Lt. Col. Don Fisher, navigator, was on his rest and recuperation (R&R) leave in Hawaii, where he met with his family. We expected him to come back that day. The other, also a loadmaster, SSgt. Earl Pechuman, departed that morning for CCK with the S-03 crew. He switched positions with SSgt. Ed Darcy, who planned to save some money by remaining in Nha Trang. This mission gave the first pilot, Capt. Edwin Osborne, an opportunity to move up to the crew's aircraft commander's slot and for Capt. Gerald Van Buren from the second to the first pilot's slot. Maj. Charlie Claxton, who had missed the last mission with our S-05 crew, was tabbed to fly as the second pilot. Replacements were needed for one navigator, Lt. Col. Don Fisher, should he fail to return in time from Hawaii, and for A1C Licudan who was DNIF. I volunteered to take Fisher's navigator's slot. I would have been the most convenient substitution because I was already involved in the mission's flight planning and could replace him up to the predeparture crew rest time. Sgt. Jim Williams from the S-02 crew volunteered to take Licudan's slot. Don Fisher returned from Hawaii that evening and expressed his eagerness to fly with his crew. So the mission crew was complete even though it had three substitutes.

Mission Planning

The flight planning progress was slow. We used the standard high altitude flight plan from Nha Trang to Channel 108, Skyline TACAN (tactical aid to navigation) in north central Laos. From there we flight-planned a never-before-flown closed loop terrain following route to our target locations in North Vietnam with return to the Skyline TACAN. The return home from that point was again at normal high altitude. We chose our low-level turning points very carefully. We had some good ones from prior missions that crew members confirmed as visible at moonlight or distinguishable by radar. We examined new ones from the angles our aircraft would close in on them and what kind of surrounding terrain they would have to negotiate after turning to new headings. Once the route penetrated into the heavily defended Black and Red River basins, we had to keep the route away from the menacing lethal ranges of SAMs and AAA. These lethal ranges were depicted by circles drawn from the geographical coordinates Lewis obtained from the First Flight's intelligence files. We calculated the locations of the before "short look" acceleration and climb up point and the length of the leaflet drop line. The postdrop recovery turning point needed to be clear so that the aircraft could resume terrain following at 1,000 feet to the next drop, which would take place on a southerly heading on the other side of the highest mountains of Vietnam.

The second drop consisted of two resupply bundles. It was what SOG called a "notional" resupply drop. There was no one on the ground to receive the bundles. Their purpose was to deceive the enemy into thinking that there was a team of agents operating in that vicinity. The drop should be detectable by the people on the ground, or by the early warning radar at Na San. We learned from intelligence sources that the North Vietnamese expended a lot of time and effort after notional airdrops in combing through the suspected areas looking for infiltrated agents that did not exist.

The resupply packages were prepared by SOG personnel at their closely guarded South Vietnamese Air Base at Long Thanh. That is where they trained the agents for infiltration into North of the DMZ. The First Flight's C-123s would bring the packages to Nha Trang and store them in their secured warehouse until the mission time. The First Flight's riggers would help our loadmasters to anchor their pallets to the floor board rollers in the aircraft. We did not know where the leaflets were printed, or what was on them, but the same people delivered them to our aircraft and assisted us in loading them on board.

All bogus resupply bundles were very carefully designed for the specific region of each drop zone. To give them credibility, they contained items that intended to implicate some local or regional Communist Party members as collaborators with the insurgents. All phantom teams had names. As we learned much later, our nonexistent team was called "Mikado."[1] There were also some resupply bundles that were booby trapped, set to explode during unpacking. We didn't yet know if the resupplies of this mission were of this nature. Roy Thompson told us that if that was their designed intent, we would be informed before the flight. He said that when such cargo was on board the aircraft, one of the SOG persons would fly in the back with the loadmasters. We did not yet have the need to know about the kind of resupply bundles we would be delivering.

Once we were satisfied that we had a route that would avoid detection by the early warning radars until the aircraft reached the necessary climb to a drop altitude in the Red and Black River basins, and that we kept it at safe distances from the SAMs and AAAs, we prepared a teletype flight plan message for SOG. This message provided them with geographic coordinates of all turning points and the length of each flight leg in time. Someone there would review it and if they had any concerns about the route, they would question us on it.

We had more than normal lead time between the frag order and the mission. Normally we would get the tasking in the morning, flight plan the route, and have everything ready for the crew on the next day. The crew would then rest during the day and fly that night. Here we had the frag order on Monday 25 December and the mission would not go until the following Thursday. Consequently, instead of working with the crew that afternoon, we scheduled it for Wednesday morning. That would give Don Fisher plenty of time to rest up from his Hawaiian R&R.

Mission Planning with the Crew

The next day's work with the crew was routine. The three navigators and Maj. Charlie Claxton used the flight planners' chart to copy the information they needed on their personal charts. Lt. Col. Don Fisher was going to fly in the radar navigator's seat, so he needed more flight plan paperwork than the others. That included the flight plan log with times between turning points down to a half minute. Since he had the only desktop in the cockpit, he would be in charge of all the paperwork as well as notes that he would make throughout the flight. He would be isolated behind a heavy curtain to ensure that none of his navigator's console lights filtered into the cockpit. Capt. Gordie Wenaas, who would do the map reading during the terrain following part of the mission, needed only a carefully folded 1 to 250,000 scale chart that he could hold in one hand. In his other hand he would hold an Aldus lamp that would illuminate his chart with dim amber light that would not hamper his night vision and would not cause a cockpit glare. The third navigator, Capt. Frank Parker, was the EWO. He would be in the back against the cockpit wall, sitting next to the radio operator SSgt. Gean Clapper. They would be behind a heavy curtain as well. The curtain was there primarily to isolate the classified electronic countermeasures (ECM) equipment from non-crew members, but on a night mission inside the enemy air space the curtain protected their night vision from other aircraft lights. Charlie Claxton, who was flying as the third pilot, would do the map reading from behind Jerry Van Buren, the first pilot, who would fly the low level part of the mission in the left seat. Ed Osborne would fly his first combat mission as an aircraft commander, from the right seat in front of standing map reading navigator Wenaas. TSgt. Jack McCrary was the cockpit flight engineer. His elevated seat was between the two pilots and just behind the aircraft throttles. The other flight engineer was SSgt. Wayne Eckley. He was going to work in the back of the aircraft with the two loadmasters, Sgt. Jim Williams and SSgt. Ed Darcy.

I don't recall any serious questions about the route we designed. They all accepted it and went around preparing their individual charts. Osborne had some concerns over the two airdrops. His first one was about what to do with the leaflets if the drop had to be abandoned or curtailed. The answer was that if the leaflet drop did not occur for some reason, the mission would be aborted. If the EWO warned about a possible SAM lock on during the "short look," the loadmasters were to jettison all the boxes and close the ramp before the aircraft could dive toward the ground on EWO's call. If evasive action became necessary during the leaflet drop sequence, then the remaining boxes should be jettisoned while still on the planned airdrop track. If that could not be done safely and the ramp door had to be closed immediately, the rest of the mission would have to be aborted. The leaflets could not be dropped outside of the programmed track because their content was designed to fit the population of that region of the country. Consequently, if there were any boxes left on the rollers, the second drop resupply bundles, which were located deeper inside the aircraft, could not be delivered either. On this mission there was only one escape heading. The aircraft could not turn around and reverse its course through the high threat area. It would have to proceed on its flight planned terrain following track. Because the highest mountains in Vietnam were just to the left of the leaflet drop track, the aircraft would have to follow the flight planned route toward the Chinese buffer zone and then turn westward around the mountain range and just follow the planned route toward the second drop and then on to Laos.

Osborne's second question was about the terrain following flight after the leaflet drop. His loadmasters needed a relatively level flight to roll the two resupply bundles to the rear of the aircraft. They could not do it safely during an aggressive up and down roller-coaster terrain following flight. We looked at the flight legs that headed the aircraft northwest toward the China border. They were north of the highest elevations of North Vietnam and the terrain below would be relatively level. In any case, this area was safe. It was away from the enemy's defenses, so the crew could fly at a fixed minimum safe altitude during the cargo repositioning.

Lewis and Parker were off to the side mulling over their charts, making sure that none of the air order of battle information was omitted on the chart Parker would use during the mission. He would be targeted by a multitude of SAM and AAA radars while in the Red and Black River basins. Depending on the strength of the wind, the drop could be from as high as 30,000 feet on a northerly track that was between 65 and 70 miles from the heart of Hanoi. All defenses west of Hanoi would be alerted. Millions of residents in the Hanoi area would find the leaflets littering their neighborhood at first daylight. The nearest air base with MIG interceptors, Yen Bai, would be only 30 miles away from the projected end of the airdrop. If they were on night alert, they could be on our tail as quickly as five minutes after takeoff. It wasn't just the terrain following that allowed us to fly through the enemy air space, hopefully, undetected. It was the up-to-date ECM equipment and the skills of the EWOs that kept us out of trouble. Hopefully, they detected enemy's intentions and identified the type of threat to our aircraft early enough for us to take evasive actions and get out of the lethal range of the enemy weapons.

We all appreciated the work of the EWOs. They didn't have much in-flight work during daytime shuttle missions, but they kept us out of trouble at night when we were in hostile air space. We learned that Maj. Cecil Clark, EWO from the SG-1 crew, was dispatched to SOG on a temporary duty to enlighten the officials there on the capabilities of our ECM equipment and of our terrain following radar system. He convinced them that they should give us only the locations of the drop zones and times on target. We would do the rest. That worked very well. This is how Lt. Col. John Drohan, another EWO from that first group, remembers it:

> I believe everyone in that first deployed group will tell you that we owed a great deal of thanks to our Chief EWO, then Major Cecil Clark, who was sent to Headquarters MAC-V in Saigon as Plans Officer. Cecil insured that all of our missions were flown to keep the aircraft covert and safe, by avoiding all SAM rings and AAA lethal ranges. Many of the original Army plans did not take this into account. Cecil made it clear: "Tell us where you want us to go and we will plan the route." I always think of Cecil as the Grandfather of Combat Talon EWOs. May he rest in peace.[2]

Cecil Clark shuttled back and forth from Saigon to Nha Trang and flew all combat missions that were assigned to his crew. He did us a lot of good and was responsible for the diligence with which the First Flight intelligence officers began to maintain the air order-of-battle wall chart. He wasn't very popular with some SOG officials who had entirely different backgrounds. Some of them had spent hours hidden under jungle foliage monitoring the Ho Chi Minh trail, looking into the eyeballs of the infiltrating enemy, suffering from multiple insect bites, and unable to sneeze without risking a bayonet slash or an AK-47 bullet in the head. And here was Cecil Clark, the guy who insisted on keeping the precious air force planes miles away from any enemy threat. Cecil Clark was replaced by a dedicated Plans and Intelligence officer. He was Maj. Roy Thompson who did not have Stray Goose crew member training. He was a navigator assigned to the detachment's staff. This dedicated planning assignment lasted only during his one-year tour of duty in Vietnam. Because of this manning reduction, mission planning duties were passed on to me and John Lewis.

I experienced similar problems in my many years as a planner with my US Army colleagues. Their information on enemy disposition in target areas was amazingly detailed. They could circle locations of their barracks on a map and have the names of their divisions, brigades, down to the number and nickname of each company. But even though they knew what kind of anti-aircraft weapons they possessed, they would not have the exact geographical coordinates of their radars and gun and missile

The approximate route of the 29 December mission. (Computer scan of North Vietnam's map with route overprint by John Gargus)

placements. We could care less what the name of this or that regiment or company was. We just wanted to ensure our safe distance from them on our routes of flight.

Once we finished reviewing our flight planning work, we collected all charts and mission-related papers and ensured that they were properly stamped as TOP SECRET documents. We locked them up in the safe and returned to the hotel. Any crew member who remembered that he might have forgotten something or had some questions about the work already done could return to the mission planning room with one of the mission planners. It did not happen this time.

Mission Briefing and Departure

The next day's mission briefing was a whole crew affair attended by the commander and operations officer. This was the first time the enlisted crew members learned about the target area. All five—two engineers, two loadmasters, and the radio operator—were present on the tarmac late that afternoon when the First Flight's cargo handlers loaded the aircraft. Major Thompson started the briefing using a chart-filled easel. He briefed the weather. Lieutenant Colonel Fisher followed him with the route of flight and the two planned airdrops. Then the EWO, Captain Parker, briefed everyone on the threats they could encounter along the route of flight. Finally, it was the aircraft commander Captain Osborne's turn to brief the crew assignments and to emphasize the need for safety, especially during the repositioning of the resupply packages to the rear of the aircraft. Colonels Rogers and Hines had some questions about everyone being properly prepared for the mission with all personal affairs in order and then wished the crew good luck.

After that we, the three flight planners, "sanitized" the crew. We collected all their personal effects: identification cards, family photographs, and even jewelry. We placed everything into individual plastic bags and saved them for their return. Each crew member was left only with his dog tags and Geneva Convention card as identifying documents. That was the standard procedure for all combat missions.

The crew departed in a crew van and we remained behind to secure everything in the safe and lock up the building. When we caught up with the crew, they were already on board, running their predeparture checklists. I walked the length of the aircraft looking at the cardboard boxes full of leaflets and the two palletized resupply bundles. Both were relatively small, about 5 feet high, fitting the base of each pallet. I waved to everyone I passed without realizing that I was the last one off the aircraft. Jim Williams stepped behind me to pull up the crew door as soon as I stepped out on the pavement. We witnessed an orderly engine start and watched them taxi out in Romeo "Charley," aircraft #64–0547 to the end of the runway. It was already thirty minutes into the next day—29 December—when we observed their takeoff and watched them disappear into the darkness over the South China Sea.

We returned to the hotel to get some sleep. Thompson and I planned to return to our detachment's operations room about three hours later. That is where we had one radio operator listening for periodic aircraft progress reports from our crews on all nighttime combat missions. Before bedding down I went to the rooftop bar to tell those still there that the flight had departed without any problems. I noted that the picture frame with our caricature Stray Goose mascot with a combat spear in its mouth was turned upside down. That was our custom. On days when we had a combat mission someone would turn the picture frame upside down to indicate that the Stray Goose would fly that night. An upside-down mascot always prompted many good luck toasts from those at the bar on those nights.

Mission Following

I went to sleep in my clothes to be instantly ready when Roy Thompson came to get me. We joined SSgt. Harry Yates from the S-05 crew who was on flight following duty that night. He offered us some strong coffee and informed us that the flight was progressing normally. He monitored a special high frequency (HF) radio over which Gean Clapper transmitted coded mission progress reports whenever the aircraft reached a predetermined in route turning point. This radio station, in an unknown location, broadcasted continuous Morse code letter "V" at regular intervals. The airborne operator monitored the same frequency and at proper moments would insert a two-letter Morse code signal, which would let us know which point of the route was reached and gave us the status of the mission's progress. This was such a short burst of transmitted energy that the enemy, who was sure to monitor the same frequency, would not have enough time to zero in his direction finders to locate the position of the aircraft. These transmissions were the only breaks in radio silence allowed during combat missions.

From the last received two Morse code letters inserted after the monotonous "di di di dahs," we knew that the aircraft had to be at high altitude dropping leaflets. We would get the next two-letter code after the aircraft reached its post drop turning point, where it would resume terrain following. That report came on time. So, the first drop was successful and there was no evasive action taken by the crew while at high altitude. Then again, just as we expected at 0430, Clapper sent another two-letter code message informing us that they were headed south toward the resupply bundle drop zone. The next report would be after that drop just before their planned exit from North Vietnam.

Lost Contact with the Aircraft

As we waited for that word, we imagined what must have been happening in the aircraft as the crew readied for the slow-down and the drop. Roy talked about some other diversionary and unusual drops that he had been involved in. The call was late. Staff Sergeant Yates checked with us to see if he had the anticipated next reporting time correct. It was correct. We waited and waited. There was no interruption in the Morse code monotony. Something had gone wrong. Naturally, the first thing we suspected was that Clapper had problems with his on board HF radio. We knew that once outside of North Vietnam, heading toward the Laotian Skyline TACAN, the pilots would be free to communicate on other frequencies to let us know that all was well. That didn't happen either. We returned to the hotel and reported to Dow Rogers and Tom Hines that we had lost preplanned contact with the aircraft after the second drop and that we have not heard any reports from the crew since that time.

The two officers rushed to the operations office and began making calls to all bases in Thailand and Vietnam where our silenced aircraft could have landed. Then when the landing time at Nha Trang went by, they notified SOG. Once the aircraft's fuel exhaustion time went by, the aircraft was declared as downed in an unknown location. Thereafter, the SOG took over all appropriate missing aircraft reports and handled all search efforts. Several F-4 search missions were launched to scan the area between the aircraft's last report and the Skyline TACAN. The weather turned bad so the aircraft could not see anything on the ground. There were no signals from the crew members' survival radios. The beaver tail mounted crash position indicator was also silent. It either malfunctioned or failed to deploy, if and when the aircraft crashed. There were several follow-on flight searches for a large aircraft crash scene, but none produced any results. Finally, on 29 January 1968 the S-01 crew of eleven was declared as missing in action (MIA).

There were many guesses and opinions as to what might have happened. We discounted a loss to enemy action. The aircraft was proceeding normally on its assigned mission after the leaflet drop, which was the most hazardous part of the flight. Enemy attack on the aircraft would have been reported. The enemy had a chance to detect the aircraft by Na San radar, which must have been alerted about the aircraft's escape westward toward Dien Bien Phu. Had this happened, there might have been some forces in the vicinity of the drop zone capable of bringing down a low-flying aircraft with small arms fire. But such an act would have been heralded as a great victory by North Vietnam. The enemy would have learned of the aircraft's fate almost immediately. Even with our low profile, the failure of our aircraft to return to Nha Trang could not be concealed for very long. The enemy should have concluded that the missing aircraft was the one that had dropped several million leaflets over Hanoi. They did not take credit for its disappearance on this mission. But some thought of a more sinister scenario. The enemy had the aircraft and perhaps some members of the crew and they would use them for propaganda purposes. However, as time elapsed, this possibility dissipated. It became obvious that the aircraft must have impacted a mountain in an isolated area sometime after making its last position report. The return of our prisoners of war (POWs) in 1973 confirmed that. The names of the S-01 crew members were not known to any of the returnees.

It was a very sad time at Anh Hoa and at the Nha Trang Air Base. We lost two aircraft in two months and one complete composite crew of eleven airmen. We had everyone's sympathy, yet we were still unable to tell the curious anything about our missions or where we suspected our aircraft was lost. The word on the base was that the crew was presumed downed when their fuel got exhausted. This unreal notion that our aircraft simply ran out of fuel somewhere in Vietnam is something I heard repeated in a 1997 reunion of Nha Trang veterans in Nashville, Tennessee.

Summary Court Officer

I was designated to serve as the summary court officer (SCO) for my dear friend Charlie Claxton on January 3, 1968, by Special Order A-11 issued by the 14th Air Commando Wing. A summary court officer's duty is to assemble all possessions of the deceased or missing in action soldier and ship them to the next of kin with appropriate correspondence. As a good friend of the family, I was the logical person to be named as Charlie's SCO. That became the toughest assignment of my air force career, which continues to trouble me to this day. The necessary restrictions on divulging classified information prevented me from acting in a personal and compassionate way as a family confidant. The same restrictions prevented all eleven SCOs from doing what was proper and comforting during this time of grief. All we could tell the families was that the flight failed to return from a classified nighttime mission and that the whole crew was missing in action. We promised that the search for the aircraft would continue and that the families would be properly informed as soon as there was more news. We could not say that the aircraft was lost over North Vietnam. No one expected that the aircraft crash site would go undiscovered for the next twenty-five years.

Even before my appointment as the SCO for Charlie, I succeeded him as an interim mess officer. My first duty was to force open his metal wall locker in front of two witnesses to retrieve his kitchen and dining room records. They were not there. But I found them in his locked room inside of his secured locker on the day I became his SCO. As an interim mess officer, I had to audit the books with Maj. Barney Dowd, who volunteered to take on the job. We worked together and accomplished the transfer of the mess account to his name. The transfer was an easy chore. Charlie served as our mess officer only for a few days, but he generated a good paper trail when he took over the kitchen accounts from Van Buren. But that was just the beginning. I then made a detailed inventory of everything Charlie left behind. I sorted items that were personal and those that were issued to him just for the duration of his tour of duty in Vietnam. Government issue items had to be returned to the base supply with documented evidence that he was missing in action with his .38 caliber revolver, survival radio, and other crew member items that he had carried on his last flight. There was a requirement to have all laundry items properly cleaned. The hotel maids did not qualify for this task. So I had all his launderable clothing processed at the base at government expense before I packed it for shipment with all other inventoried personal items into an 8-cubic-foot box. The box weighed 163 pounds. I shipped it by Colombia Export Packers to his wife, Pat, in Michigan. I had to document everything I did as the SCO in my personal log and on two air force forms, which I also sent to Pat. The first one was AF Form 1122 that listed all of his personal effects. The second was AF Form 1122a that summarized all his financial affairs. When I received Pat's reply that she received my letter and all of Charlie's things, I thought that my duties as SCO were over. I was wrong.

On 25 June I received a call from a captain in the personnel office that I still owed them one document. Pat did not return signed AF Form 1122, which made her case still open. The fact that she informed me that all was okay was not sufficient. The diligent captain from the personnel office was ready to return to the States, and my file with him had not yet been closed out. So I had to write a letter to Pat to remind her that she owed us a signature. She responded promptly, so at least as the personnel office on base was concerned, Charlie Claxton's MIA case was finally properly documented.

Hotel Bombing

Subdued life at Anh Hoa went on and so did the war. The Vietcong did not leave us at peace. Late one night we were startled from our sleep by a loud explosion that caused the building to shake, knocking out some windows

The sandbag protection for the dining room and Hog Heaven. The truck with the bomb that was directed to explode attempted to park in front of the void spot between the dining room and Hog Heaven. (Photo by John Lewis)

and dislodging air venting wire mesh separators near the ceilings of the rooms. Many of us ran out on the walkways to the bathrooms, where we could smell the results of the explosion. It looked like it happened on the bottom floor of Hog Heaven. But when we saw its occupants come out as well we knew that it had to be the building next door to us. We didn't get the full story about what happened until the next morning.

The Nung guards reported that a big truck stopped in front of the hotel about midway between the dining room and the Hog Heaven. That alerted the guards. One of them ran out to the truck where he saw that its driver turned off the lights as if he intended to park there. He forced the driver at gunpoint back inside the cab. The driver obliged and moved his truck around the corner of the adjoining building into a narrow walk-through alley that connected our street to the one behind us. The guard did not follow him and did not see him stop his truck again and disappear into

The holes made in the outer and inner walls of the house connected to Ahn Hoa Hotel. Destroyed truck was thrown against the building wall on the other side of the narrow alley. (Composite by John Gargus; photos by John Lewis)

the night. After the guard returned to his normal post at our gate the truck blew up, knocking a huge hole into a double brick wall and the inside brick wall of the hallway behind it. That second hole was just one room's length from the wall to Hog Heaven. None of our neighbors were at home that night, so no one got killed. The blast threw the truck against the wall of the building on the opposite side of the alley. Had that bomb gone off in front of the hotel, we would have lost everyone in Hog Heaven, and the floors above might have collapsed as well. The 5-foot sandbag barrier and the plywood wall would not have been sufficient to prevent catastrophic damage to the building. There is no doubt that we were the truck bomber's target that night.

Tet Offensive

At the end of January we had another rude awakening. On 29 January we were on the roof observing Vietnamese New Year, "Tet," celebrations. Vietnamese Tet is like a combination of New Year's Day, Christmas, Easter, and Thanksgiving. It is the Festival of Purity and Renewal. Vietcong and Americans honored this holiday by declaring a pause in the hostilities so that Vietnamese warriors of both sides could spend joyous time with their families. It was like the Fourth of July and New Year's Eve in our part of town. Neighbors up and down the street were shooting off all types of firecrackers, and military outposts were firing tracer bullets that crisscrossed the skies above Nha Trang. In Nha Trang that night, fireworks displays were family affairs. We enjoyed it all and at some time after midnight we even dismissed the sporadic explosions that sounded like incoming ordnance.

A rude awakening came early that morning. There was noise everywhere. We were told that the town was under siege by the Vietcong, who broke the truce at 12:25, just after midnight. The guards reported that about thirty armed Vietcong in civilian attire (mostly in their typical pajama-type dark shirts and pants) sneaked stealthily along both sides of the street past our hotel. Wisely, the guards retreated toward the kitchen and let them all pass to the left. Several blocks farther the Vietcong attacked a provincial compound. Defending troops claimed that they killed all of them. That was the battle report we heard frequently. Presumably all attackers were suicidal and always perished when they confronted better-equipped regular forces. We know that many simply hid their weapons and blended into the population, hoping to fight another day. The guards reported that none of the attackers retreated back along the street.

Soon, almost everyone was on the roof watching several small aircraft and helicopters from the squadrons of the 14th ACW; they were rocketing the houses on the east side of Buddha Hill. There was a small but prominent hill just to the right of the straight line between the hotel and the west side of the Nha Trang Air Base. On top of it was a huge statue of White Buddha. The base of the hill was cluttered with small, humble Vietnamese homes. That is where the Vietcong got surrounded. We could see them as they ran here and there between houses and when they fired into the sky at the rocketing aircraft. Every now and then a helicopter or an OV-10 would approach its target from overhead of the hotel and we could hear the whoosh of the rockets and follow them to their targets. They did not seem to cause a great deal of damage. We are accustomed to seeing on our TVs whole buildings disintegrate after a single rocket burst. These were fired against flimsy structures, and their explosions seldom even lifted up their roofs. The rockets must not have been more potent than regular hand grenades. Some of us had binoculars and we passed them from hand to hand. We saw one man emerge repeatedly from somewhere and position himself against a tree. He would look straight at us. I am sure that some of us even waved to him, but he did not respond. The general conclusion was that he was not Vietnamese. He was definitely

Helicopter gunship firing rockets at Vietcong position on Buddha hill. (Photo by Dow Rogers)

taller; perhaps even a six footer. Those who saw his face when he did not have binoculars against his eyes said that he had non-Asian eyes.

The scene on the roof was bizarre. Clearly, we were out of lethal range of the weapons the Vietcong had. Unconcerned, we were consuming bar drinks, observing the ongoing slow-moving battle, and recording it with our cameras. It seems incredible to me to this day, but some guys even played ping pong and shot pool while this was going on. The commander and operations officer were on the phone a lot getting reports about what was going on. We had only one telephone, at the bottom of the stairway. As far as I know, we had only five pistols and one shotgun for defense. These belonged to Rogers, Hines, Thompson, Gargus, and Lewis. We were the only ones authorized to wear weapons off base for our own security. John Lewis was issued a shotgun so that he could literally ride shotgun in a jeep for the commander and operations officer if they needed to go to the base at night. This also happened on those occasions when the barmaids remained working past curfew and needed a safe ride home. On

Rooftop observers of the attack on Buddha hill. Some are photographing the action and the fires at the base of the hill. (Photo by Dow Rogers)

those occasions I became the designated driver. I don't recall how this practice started, but everyone relied on the two of us, slow beer drinkers, to pull this extra wartime duty. I still can't believe that John and I did this so many times.

The battle scene changed somewhat as the morning progressed. Vietnamese reinforcements came from the site of the night battle and occupied some lower-lying rooftops between us and the Buddha Hill. These snipers quickly reduced the movement of the Vietcong between the houses on the side of the hill. Many shots were fired from our direction against them. Then reinforcements arrived. Two army soldiers were dispatched from the base to defend our rooftop position. Their weapons were M-14s. Perhaps it is a good thing that their rifles did not have the range to tackle Vietcong on the hill that was more than 800 yards away. We were sure that the Vietcong knew of their presence among us because the tall man kept monitoring our surroundings. Just about that time, our neighbors from "Fort Courage" across the street joined the battle. They had only M-15s to begin with, but somehow they came up with a heavier weapon that could reach the hill. They began taking pot shots every time they saw some movement between the houses on the hillside. Their outgoing shells went just past the southwest corner of our hotel. It wasn't long before this new source of firepower was discovered. We heard several pings on top of the barroom roof. The Vietcong began firing at "Fort Courage," and we were in the way just to the left. That thinned our crowd in a hurry. I went to my room to pack my tape recorder and several other things. By that time our leaders had informed us that we were ordered to evacuate our three aircraft to CCK. Our commanders were now debating which three crews would fly the aircraft and who would be going to CCK just for the ride.

Evacuation to CCK

It was already early afternoon when an air force blue bus pulled up to evacuate us. We expedited boarding it and were on our way. Not far from the cathedral was a wall to some building complex and between it and the street was space where a group of people normally congregated and young children played. It could have been a bus stop, but it wasn't marked as such. Our bus stopped right there and what a site it was. Between us and the wall were two rows of dead Vietcong covering the ground. There must have been more than twenty bodies. I did not have my camera ready, but everyone came to my side of the bus to snap pictures. Most of the dead Vietcong had sandals made from rubber tires still on their feet. They were laid on their backs and some of their feet were already lifted off the ground. They appeared to have swollen, pregnant-like bellies. The heat of the tropical sun made their body gasses expand and bloat them up. There were flies all over their faces, especially on those that were bloodied. We saw three women and one child walking from body to body stirring up clouds of disturbed flies as they moved along. I was glad when the bus moved away from that gruesome scene.

Once we got off the bus, we learned that we would be dead-heading, flying as passengers with Major Pine's S-03 crew. But there was a catch. SOG wanted us to stop at Saigon before proceeding on to Taiwan. Our commander, Dow Rogers, was the only officer who stayed behind, manning the detachment's operations office. With him remained all maintenance and administrative personnel, with the exception of the crew chiefs who flew out with their assigned aircraft. Very few enlisted men lived off base in the Nautique Motel. They remained stranded there until the town got cleared of the Vietcong insurgent forces.

Walt Pine took off with a planeload of crew members as soon as he could. Once we reached the traffic pattern over Tan Son Nhut Air Base, we found ourselves in a terrible mixing bowl of overhead aircraft. Combat aircraft that were rocketing, bombing, and strafing Vietcong positions both in and around the city had priority. I was not on a headset, so I cannot attest to the radio chatter that must have been going on. Tan Son Nhut Air Base was surrounded by areas that were under attack, and airborne aircraft were expending their ordnance wherever it was needed. Air traffic controllers would not let us land, so we headed for the open sea and on to Taiwan. I made a brief visit to the overcrowded cockpit from where I could see the fire and smoke over various parts of the city. I could not orient myself during my brief stay, but I was amazed how much of the city was under attack. How could all this be happening? Was the war being lost? Very helpless, we were running away to Taiwan with our three Combat Talons. The fourth one, which had been damaged during the mortar attack, was not yet back from stateside repairs.

Our mood changed as soon as we landed. Reports from Vietnam were optimistic. Saigon was still besieged by thousands of Vietcong, but they had suffered devastating defeats all over the rest of the country.

The BOQ at CCK was full, so we had to stay in a nice downtown hotel. This suited us fine because we were closer to the familiar places we normally patronized. There were two "must go to" restaurants in downtown Taichung. One was a large restaurant that specialized in Mongolian barbeque. The chefs cooked assembled plate of meats and vegetables while diners watched and applauded their skill in frying and stirring with long chopsticks. The other was the Taichung Theater Restaurant, a huge gymnasium-size place with a stage that featured continuous entertainment and round tables with lazy Susans loaded with family-style menu items.

Right across the street in a twenty-story building, the well patronized United Service Organizations (USO) was located on one of the higher floors. On an earlier visit there, I was coming down in one of the elevators during an earthquake that caused some of us to fall to the floor before our descent to the lobby ended. We ran out to the street and watched some of the buildings sway for a while, but other than getting scared, nothing serious happened. The USO was a good gathering place for American soldiers based at CCK, and for those who were transiting through there.

I don't recall how many of us gathered at the USO and how many of those chose to go across the street to the theater restaurant. I think that each one of the five crews was represented in our group. As soon as we entered, the maître d' recognized some of us and became very accommodating. He asked us to wait a while so that he could get us the best table. Then we noticed that a large group of people who had celebrated something at the largest table in front of the stage was being relocated to other empty tables at some distance from the stage. Soon the maître d' came smiling and invited us to be his guests at the table that had been vacated just for us. I felt embarrassed as we filed past the tables to where we were being seated. Everyone in the place must have realized what kind of preference was being shown by the establishment to the American soldiers.

As always, the food was plentiful and great. The entertainment went on without a stop yet people hardly paid any attention. They came to eat. We watched the usual acrobatic and magician's acts and had no idea what the comedians were saying. A few people would laugh and few applauded when acts ended. A few of our jokers decided to have some fun at our table. So when a comedian said something that only a few laughed at, they began to laugh aloud, and when someone applauded politely, they burst out in applause. Obviously, our table attracted much attention and the people began to respond to the comedian who realized that he had aroused his audience. Then we all applauded at appropriate times, not knowing what was being said. The comedian came to the edge of the stage by our table and we think he joked with us, and when he pointed to our table, the whole place applauded.

What happened next was even more entertaining. A skinny guy in shabby clothes came on the stage with a banjo. He also acknowledged our table and began strumming American banjo music for our benefit. He was great, but once he began singing, his English became unintelligible. When he came to "I came from Alabama . . ." our joking companions, who had already had enough wine, stood up and joined him "with a banjo on my knee" . . . and much more. The place erupted in applause when that tune ended. The banjo player was delighted. Then he went into "California here I come . . ." and most of us joined in. When that was over, the banjo player pointed at our table and we got a standing ovation. Once he was off the stage, he came to our table and proceeded to shake hands with all of us. His spoken English was better than his singing English. After he left us, we noticed that people who were leaving made it a point to walk by our table, make eye contact with us, and bow in appreciation. Among those who bowed were members of the party that had been evicted from their table to make room for us.

Return to Nha Trang

We returned to Nha Trang after two nights at CCK. We flew in three aircraft and brought with us more San Miguel beer than ever. John Lewis and I managed to talk base supply out of two washers and dryers for our laundry. At that time we were still a detachment of the 314th Tactical Airlift Wing. We didn't become a permanent part of Nha Trang's 14th Air Commando Wing until 15 March of that year when our name also changed to the 15th Air Commando Squadron (ACS). That was when our umbilical cord to the wing at CCK was severed. We acquired a new parent after that. But when we came to CCK for shelter from the Vietcong's Tet attack, we were still treated by the 314th TAW as orphans that needed parental help. At least that was our pitch to those who were privileged to participate in the war from afar. By giving us "stuff" they felt like they were contributing to the war effort.

We were greeted by our commander, Lt. Col. Dow Rogers, upon our return home. He was glad to see us. Along with him were Maj. Dick Day and Capt. Pat Watson, who had returned from R&R in Hawaii on the day we left for CCK. We were of the opinion that our temporary escape to CCK was not necessary, but our commander assured us that sporadic fighting was still going on after we left and that the air base came under mortar attack, which he had endured in a nearby shelter. After the shooting at Nha Trang ended, Pat Watson arranged for a jeep to bring him to the hotel to find out if things were in order. The loyal guards were glad to see him. He then walked from room to room, noting that things appeared just the way we left them. However, there was no electricity. Electrical power died when the generator ran out of diesel fuel. The absence of electrical power resulted in the only collateral loss to our unit. All refrigerated food in the kitchen refrigerators was spoiled.[3] Day and Watson restarted the power generator, so when we came back home, things were quite normal. We had plenty of cold beer and beverages in the bar and plenty of ice. The cooks and maids were back as if nothing had happened. We had plenty of canned food in the pantry to eat until the lost meats and other perishables were replaced. The first day's duty crew brought in a full bag of mail, which had accumulated during our time away. All normal flight scheduling resumed.

What transpired in Nha Trang during the Vietcong attack on the city is described by Jerry Thigpen in his *The Praetorian STARShip* book:

> At 12:35 A.M. on Tuesday, 30 January, the Tet offensive of 1968 kicked off in South Vietnam on the outskirts of Nha Trang City. The initial attack was on the Vietnamese Naval Training Center, but due to confusion by the attackers, an all out push to capture the city did not occur until four hours later. Within 28 hours of the initial attack, Vietcong enemy forces had been beaten, and the city was declared clear by the South Vietnamese security forces. The attempt to capture Nha Trang was a costly one for the Vietcong. According to official South Vietnamese records, of an initial force of 800 soldiers attacking the city, 377 were killed, 77 were captured, and one surrendered. Eighty eight South Vietnamese troops were killed, and 220 were wounded in action, 32 civilians were killed and 187 wounded with 600 homes destroyed. Other than a few bullet holes, the Anh Hoa Hotel escaped unscathed.[4]

All the maintenance troops that remained behind and were quartered on the base were safe. There were a few alarms sounded that sent them to the fortified shelters, but they were never exposed to direct enemy attack. A few of our members were among those who lived in the beachside Motel Nautique. They were stranded there during the fighting without any way to defend themselves. MSgt. Mel Hendrickson, chief of the avionics section, was one of them. He and Sgt. Henry Harrison worked late and missed the last bus to town. It was 5 miles to the motel, the night was nice, so they decided to walk all the way. When they got to the motel, the celebrating fireworks were already deafening, and the gate to the motel was already shut. They had to bang on the gate for a long time before they were heard and allowed to come in. After a few drinks they went to sleep only to be awakened by a couple of their friends who had realized that Nha Trang was under attack. This is how Hendrickson describes it in his unpublished memoir.

> We all sat there in the darkness theorizing what was going on and what we should do. We had no means with which to defend ourselves so we decided to cool it till daylight. I had visions of the Viet Cong kicking down our door and slaughtering us like caged animals. It was great relief to see the first rays of light come creeping across the South China Sea.
>
> With the dawn we mustered the courage to creep outside to investigate. The fighting had subsided and only a random burst of gunfire broke the stillness. Through the iron gates we could see numerous bodies lying in the streets, a machine gun riddled vehicle had come to an abrupt stop against a lamppost, the occupants blood spattered bodies sprawled lifeless inside. It was like a horrible scene from a war movie, only much more vivid.[5]

That was not all. They were stranded behind the walls of their motel complex until the third day.

> We could only pray that our side would get to us first. Throughout the day air strikes bombarded enemy positions within the city. During the night parachute flares lit up the sky with an eerie orange like glow as the fighting continued through a thousand eternities. On the third day we could distinguish the shouts of American voices amid the noise of the battle. The aircraft strikes had been replaced by armored personnel carriers with machine guns mopping up the remnants of enemy resistance. It was the most beautiful and welcomed sight in the world when that olive drab Army bus, escorted by two armored personnel carriers, pulled up to the gate. We climbed aboard, eagerly anticipating the reunion with our comrades at the base.[6]

Post-Tet Events

After the Vietcong Tet offensive things returned to normal. The SO-7 crew came in to replace the lost S-01 with our fourth, now repaired, aircraft. We were back to full strength. The only crisis we experienced after that was the siege of Khe Sanh. We had daily missions flying through there bringing out wounded for treatment at a field hospital at Hue Phu Bai. That was the only time the aircraft I was on received a bullet hole; the bullet struck the fuel tank between the third and fourth engine. We discovered it upon landing at Hue Phu Bai. Fuel was leaking from the very bottom of the tank. Flight engineer Mort Ellis stuck a pencil-size stick in the hole, which reduced the fuel loss to a slow drip. The pilots burned off this tank's fuel before we landed at our next stop at Da Nang. Other crews were caught on the ground at Khe Sanh during sporadic shelling of the field by the North Vietnamese regulars that infested the surrounding hills. Soon after that, SOG let us know that Khe Sanh would be off our daily itinerary because our aircraft were too expensive for the routine flying we were doing to support the troops there.

As our unit's mission planner I was learning more and more about SOG and its role in the war. I made only couple of visits to the headquarters in Saigon but they did not turn out to be very enlightening. Most of the officers I met there were US Army guys, and it was obvious that they felt that I did not have a need to know about many things. One distressing thing I picked up was the fact that out of all the teams that were infiltrated into North Vietnam, they had only three trustworthy ones on the ground. I wanted to know more about that. They told me that most had been captured and were no longer in touch with SOG. Some were considered as compromised. I wanted to have that explained in plain English, but all I got was that they had problems with them and that some might have had double agents among them. It was true that some teams were completely wiped out, as if the North Vietnamese had known when and where they were going to be inserted.

Mole in the Chain of Command in Saigon

Most of my feedback on our unit's performance came from the SOG air force liaison officer who would come to spend a night with us at Anh Hoa. He partied with the troops. Once he revealed to us that they received a request for Fulton Recovery System exfiltration of one member of a team which was suspected to be compromised. Their request was denied. He more or less assured us that they would never risk one of our crews for a Fulton pickup of a man from any team. They had alternate and obviously more elaborate means for getting people out of North Vietnam.

The liaison officer told us an interesting story about another team that did not go anywhere. Team members were carefully recruited, often with some ties to the area or region of the country where they would be air-dropped. Their integrity had to be impeccable. Their training was intensive and detailed. Some would operate in isolation from the population, others could blend in with the locals. Some had specific targets to destroy and were to create suspicion and distrust of the local communist authorities. Before going on a mission, some were given special favors. One such favor was given to a man who wanted a day in Saigon. He was escorted by two bodyguards who went with him everywhere. On one busy street corner he jumped in front of a moving bus and ran across the street. The moving bus prevented his guards from giving immediate pursuit. Once the bus passed, he was nowhere to be seen. This wasn't just a loss of one man. His whole team became useless. They trained together and knew everything about one another. Their mission was over even before it began. The rest of the team members could not be released to wherever they came from because they had learned too much. They became a tremendous liability and were held in isolation like prisoners of war. What do you do with good men like that? Risk having them train with another team?

It wasn't until the summer of 1971 when the suspicions about having a mole somewhere in the upper echelons of command were confirmed. He was Huynh Van Trong, an assistant to the most trusted political assistant to President Thieu. This man was authorized to see everything going up channel to the president. He had a personal radio operator who transmitted appropriate messages to Hanoi and to selected North Vietnamese commands.[7]

Change of Command at SOG

We received a new boss at SOG early in 1968. Col. Steve Cavanaugh replaced Col. Jack Singlaub. We did not realize it at that time, but we were also transitioning from one SOG operation to another. We had lost one aircraft on a bogus resupply drop to a phantom team named Mikado. It was a part of eighteen phantom team locations throughout the North. It was called Operation Oodles.[8] This operation was successful because it convinced Hanoi that we had more teams operating inside their homeland than they were aware of. Resupply cargo and the accompanying documentation was very convincing. Specific target areas were identified as well as some local communist officials who could be counted upon if a team got into trouble.

The follow-on, and somewhat overlapping, operation was Operation Borden. It involved training and infiltrating real teams that were recruited from the North Vietnamese prisoners of war captured in South Vietnam or Laos. American agents would do preliminary recruitment of these likely turncoats before they were turned over to the South Vietnamese authorities. They were very carefully evaluated. Those who passed were retained for training and those who failed reverted to their POW status in South Vietnamese custody. Each Borden "ringer" was groomed through weeks of training at Camp Long Thanh to absorb information from casual chats with his pseudo teammates. This included closely held information on agent identities, code names, plans, secret rendezvous sites, and so on. Even washouts were put to good use by being fed carefully orchestrated disinformation before being transferred to POW camps. The bottom line, according to Colonel Cavanaugh, was "to implant in their minds the idea that we had effective teams working up North; that there was a strong underground and this underground was being resupplied and that we were sending these people up there as couriers with further instructions as to what to do, and how to implement operations." A recurring theme was that assassination plots were afoot against senior military and government officials with the connivance of North Vietnamese Communist Party members.[9]

Visit to Long Thanh

Even though I had landed at Long Thanh with my crew on many occasions, I was able to spend time on the ground only once. It was a moment I anticipated for some time. We stopped at Tan Son Nhut to pick up several SOG officials, including the air force liaison officer. He told me that I would get a rare opportunity to sit in on some of the meetings about current happenings and future plans. Wow! That was exciting. We were scheduled to fly the delegation back to Saigon that afternoon, and in the meantime our crew would fly around the flagpole and perform several paratrooper training jumps. That was just great. I excused myself from my crew and stayed on the ground. I have no idea why John Lewis was not asked to join us at the meeting. He served as our intelligence officer.

After we met some local officers, one Saigon officer told me that I could not accompany them inside the conference room. What was about to be discussed was internal planning and it was not meant for my outsider ears. I was disappointed, but I realized that those were the rules of the game. Now I had some time on my hands. It was too late to rejoin my crew, so I decided to watch the airdrops. They were parachuting right over the runway.

Even before the aircraft's first pass, I noticed that there were two Vietnamese soldiers not far from me looking at the sky just like I was. I thought that they were there to watch the show. When our eyes met, I acknowledged their presence as if I wanted to talk. They kept their distance and did not leave. I had a feeling that they were there to watch me. They were armed. So was I. But my .38 was hidden under my loose-fitting jungle fatigue shirt. The bulge gave my weapon away. It occurred to me that they might not have been used to seeing American officers who were armed. They stuck around me during all the aircraft passes and in between when I sat down on a crate in the shade of a tree.

It must have been during the last airdrop pass with the last load of troops when I witnessed a most unusual sight. These combat training jumps were made with full gear that probably weighed as much as the slight Vietnamese paratroopers. The very last jumper was different. He didn't have any combat gear on. Most likely he was one of the administrative types and this was his jump for pay, or just for sport. He was not coming down as fast as the others. In fact, he just seemed to hang up there. It was a hot day without any wind and there must have been a pretty good updraft from the hot runway and from the sandy terrain around the field. All the paratroopers were already on the ground gathering their chutes while he was still up there. He would come down some but then his body was lifted up even higher. Those heavy-laden paratroopers who were already moving off toward the buildings noticed that he was still floating above them. They dropped their chutes and began shouting at him and laughing. I am sure they were giving him all kinds of instructions. He was struggling with his risers, pulling them here and there with limited success. It was indeed a funny sight. He did inch down somewhat, but his descent did not increase until a slight wind started blowing in the direction where I was standing—now surrounded by many onlookers. He floated overhead still at about 200 feet, and as soon as he came over the green foliage at the edge of the jungle, the updraft subsided and he descended into the tree line. I am sure that this incident would have been funnier had I understood any of the comments and shouts that his parachute jump generated.

Interesting Special Operations Missions

It was unfortunate that I was not allowed to participate in the meeting that was going on inside of the building, but I got enough stories about some of the Operation Borden that we mission-planned later. Debriefings of our loadmasters were very interesting. There was one where the team stood up ready to jump off the ramp on the navigator's green light, when an accompanying SOG jumpmaster stopped the second man and had everyone sit back down. That must have been a double agent who was headed for a rude awakening when the authorities could not locate his team buddies. Another one was with two jumpmasters who let only two men jump, and one of the jumpmasters had a drawn pistol when these exited. Our loadmasters were there just to open and close the ramp. SOG jumpmasters did not communicate with them, and all team members whose jumps were unexpectedly aborted just sat there in silence like mummies with their faces covered with camouflage paint. The men who picked them up in a windowless van after our aircraft landed were also silent. Who knows, maybe they also didn't have the need to know what happened and why.

There is no doubt that we infiltrated some double agents on some of the teams. SOG was well aware of that and took proper precautions to protect our aircraft from inflight sabotage. Colonel Singlaub was well aware of losses caused by inflight double agents. Back in 1952, when he, as a major, conducted similar operations in Korea, one of the double agents threw a hand grenade inside the C-46 before jumping out. This caused a loss of one aircraft and its entire crew.[10] Consequently, infiltrating team members were not allowed to carry grenades, could not visit the cockpit, and were closely supervised (guarded) by armed SOG jumpmasters.

We had one really extreme case on which we were prebriefed because it required special rigging and cooperation from the loadmasters. It was a team of five agents that were destined to one southern region of North Vietnam. Only the first man, the team leader, would be allowed to jump. The rest would be quickly ushered aside so that the loadmasters could release four loads specially rigged from overhead rails. These loads consisted of huge blocks of ice concealed in dark plastic bags with trays to catch the melting ice water. The plastic cover and container with melted ice water blew off in the slip stream and four parachutes, each supporting a huge block of ice imbedded with human blood, deployed following the team leader with just a slight delay. The real drop zone was in a jungle, just past the suitable drop zone where the entire team thought they would land safely. I was curious about how this one materialized, but we never got the feedback. The air force warrant officer from the First Flight was responsible for attaching the parachute harnesses to the frozen ice blocks and for designing plastic bags to catch the melting ice water during the hot and humid low-level ride. He told me that keeping the ice from melting was his toughest part of that mission.

We had only one problem with SOG on one of our resupply missions for a team called Red Dragon. It was located north of Hanoi a little over 200 yards outside of the 20-mile buffer zone with China. From the terrain following aspect, the best drop zone approach was flying from the south to north with a left-hand escape turn to the west. That is how we proposed to fly it. We received a message from SOG to change the approach to the opposite direction, which would have us dropping on an easterly heading with a right-hand escape to the south toward Hanoi. They were correct in claiming that our proposed drop would carry the aircraft into the forbidden buffer zone during the post drop turn to the westerly heading. It was a very nit-picking point that illustrated the silliness of our ceding 20 miles of air space for fear that we would come closer to China than this self-imposed distance from their border. We had these buffer zones in Europe during the Cold War and we chose to deny ourselves a similar corridor of air space with China fearing that our flying closer than that would provoke them into activating their defenses, which could menace our aircraft. So it was forbidden to enter that air space. Many pilots had flown into that forbidden zone and had jeopardized their flying careers. In this case we did not have intelligence information on locations of Chinese radar. They probably did not have any along the border with Vietnam. We were sure that the mountains would mask our terrain following approach from the Vietnamese radar. That applied even more so for the very distant Red Crown radar on the Yankee Station in the Gulf of Tonkin that would have been the only US radar to detect our entry into the forbidden buffer zone. Our mission was a clandestine one. We were confident that we could carry it out without being detected. That is why we had all the necessary navigational and electromagnetic countermeasure systems on board. We changed the drop zone approach for this mission in order to comply with the established rules of engagement.

Fulton Recoveries

During the summer of 1968 we began a series to demonstrate Fulton Recoveries for air crews that risked getting shot down in a hostile environment. We were picking up volunteers from all the bases in Thailand and the Philippines. The odd thing about this program was that while we were trying to demonstrate how safely a Fulton Recovery could be performed, the air force command channels did not allow any volunteer fighter pilots and crew members to be picked up. The inside word was that it wasn't worth the risk. Consequently, we ended up picking up mostly eager life support airmen who were servicing ejection seats and repacking aircrew parachutes. Many of these recoveries were two-man pickups. I was on two of them. The first one was flown by Maj. Paul Lausier at Udorn Royal Thai Air Force Base (RTAFB) and the other at Takhli RTAFB by Maj. Harry Kempe.

My third live Fulton Recovery was the most unusual one. Somehow, Lt. Col. Tom Hines, who had replaced Lt. Col. Dow Rogers as our squadron commander, succeeded in getting an exception from the restriction on pickups of aircrew members. He arranged to be picked up by Lt. Col.

Change of command Fulton Recovery System pickup of Tom Hines by Russ Bunn, the incoming commander of the 15th SOS. (Composite of USAF photos by John Gargus)

Russell Bunn as a part of a unique change of command ritual. Bunn was succeeding him as the new squadron commander. Hines scheduled me to be the crew navigator for that memorable event. As soon as he freed himself from the pickup suit and harness, he came to the front of the aircraft, where Bunn passed him the command of the aircraft. Hines made the landing. He thus earned the distinction of landing a C-130 aircraft that took off without him. That distinction did not last very long. Less than one year later another outgoing squadron commander, Lt. Col. John Kummer, accomplished the same feat by getting picked up by his replacement, Lt. Col. John Newell.

Visit to Japan

John Lewis and I took advantage of a rare opportunity to visit the Pacific ELINT (electronic intelligence) Center at Fuchu in Japan. That was where all the electronic intelligence data recorded by our reconnaissance aircraft in Vietnam was processed and made usable by those who had to challenge the North Vietnamese air defenses. John thought that he had entered into an electronic heaven. I did not have his EWO background, so I was overwhelmed by the discussions he had with various staff members. Nevertheless, I got the big picture and gained more respect for the challenges of electronic warfare. I listened to many recordings of different radar signals. About all I retained was that each one had its own distinct sound, but I could not identify them by name. It was too much to absorb in one show-and-tell session staged for my benefit. But it did make me a better planner. Experience like that was priceless. It had a lot to do with my being paired up in mission planning for the Son Tay raid in 1970 with none other than the master Stray Goose EWO Cecil Clark. John Lewis and I connected again in Germany in the Combat Arrow's 7th Special Operations Squadron. I was the chief of plans and John became my electronic intelligence officer. John had a remarkable career in that field. Later, as a lieutenant colonel, he commanded the 6990th Electronic Security Group in Kadena, Okinawa.[11]

Together, we learned a lot about the enemy's capability to detect and track our aircraft as well as about the effectiveness of our aircraft in a hostile environment. It was very consoling to me personally. My concerns over getting captured alive by the communist forces no longer concerned me. I believed that any loss of aircraft on any of our flight planned routes would be due to an unforeseen accident.

It was great to be a flight planner. It had some ups and downs, but the best part was that what we planned we carried out. Many planners spend hours writing plans that go out of their offices to someone else and they never get feedback on how things turned out. Security must be practiced everywhere, and the need to know is a good way to protect the product and to limit the number of participants. That certainly kept our unit out of the loop on many things we did. However, we had the satisfaction that the flight plans we generated for the missions we were assigned represented our best efforts.

6

Daddy Is Coming Home!

Post-Vietnam Combat Talons and Special Operations

Because this book's story does not end until 2015, it is necessary to fill in the time span with major Combat Talon events that took place after the end of the Vietnam War. More than three full decades went by before the families of the S-01 crew members received the remains of their loved ones. In the meantime, the Combat Talons received timely modifications that kept them up to date with advances in technology. Special operations experienced ups and downs during this time until the air force established the Special Operations Command as a separate major air command on 20 May 1990.

Once our crew's tour in Vietnam ended in August 1968, we went our separate ways to various follow-on assignments. I ended with an assignment to Combat Knife's Detachment 2 of the 1st Special Operations Wing (SOW) at Pope Air Force Base as a terrain following radar navigator instructor. There I instructed Vietnam-bound crews and participated in flight testing and instructing of Mod 70 radar and navigation systems, which had replaced the original equipment of the Stray Goose project aircraft. This renovation included new forward looking infrared (FLIR) and inertial navigation systems tied to a dual antenna mapping and terrain following radars that were designed specifically for the Combat Talons. The modification was followed by strengthening of the ramp section that allowed it to be lowered for airdrops at normal operating air speeds. Then, when the 7th SOS at Ramstein Air Base in Germany began receiving its newly modified Mod 70 Talons, I was reassigned to that European Combat Arrow unit. Consequently, I ended up serving in all three Combat Talon units, as predicted by the colonel at the AFMPC when I volunteered for the Stray Goose program in 1966. I spent eight years in special operations assignments.

When the war in Vietnam ended, the history of the special operations began to repeat itself. Special operations assets were no longer needed. Experienced and battle tested commandos were dispersed throughout the commands and their obsolescent flying machines began to disappear from the air force inventory. The ongoing Cold War needed only a few of the most technologically advanced aircraft. This preserved the Combat Talons, Spectre and Spooky gunships, and the Jolly Green Giant helicopters.

As time went by, Combat Talons kept up with the advances in technology, receiving timely systems modifications. They also kept changing their unit names and home base locations. In Southeast Asia, the Combat Spear unit had its name changed from the 15th SOS to the 90th SOS in 1970 and was relocated from Nha Trang to Kadena Air Base in Japan in 1972. This move caused the unit's name to change to the 1st SOS. The squadron was relocated to Clark Air Base in the Philippines in 1981 and returned back to Kadena Air Base in 1993. At home in the United States at Pope Air Force Base, North Carolina, Combat Knife Detachment-2 of the 318th Air Commando Squadron (ACS) became Detachment 2 of the 1st SOW in 1968 and then in 1971 its name was changed to the 318th SOS. This squadron moved to Hurlburt Field in Florida in 1974, where it merged with the 8th SOS. The Combat Arrow unit in Germany was more stable. Its only name change simply dropped its commando affiliation when it went from the 7th ACS to the 7th SOS. Its geographical relocations were from Ramstein AB to Rhein Main Air Base in 1973 and then to Royal Air Force Alconbury, England, in 1992. Without a name change, the 7th SOS was moved once more to RAF Mildenhall.

There were many growing pains involving special operations units at higher echelons of the air force. Tactical Air Command passed its special operations assets to the Military Airlift Command (MAC) on 1 March 1983. A giant step forward was made in 1987 when MAC's 23rd Air Force moved to Hurlburt Field and gained control of the Stateside, Pacific, and European Combat Talons by placing them under those three theater MAC wings. That opened the way to the final step when the Air Force Special Operations Command (AFSOC) became a major air command.

> Establishment of AFSOC on 20 May 1990 was a memorable event for Air Commandos of all ages. Finally, after forty-seven years of ad hoc existence that was marked by repeated activation, deactivation, and shuffling of special operations units among various Air Force major commands, they were grouped into a major command of their own. With it came clearly defined role in the US military doctrine to provide readily deployable unconventional warfare forces for the regional commands. AFSOC's commanders would be three-star generals. The sustainability of their new command would no longer be a worrisome problem because under the equally new budgetary process they would not have to compete with other Air Force commands for scarce resources. They would receive their share of resources to forge a well-trained and well-equipped special operations air force that could support all challenges to the US national interests in joint military operations, not only in war but also in peace and in all levels of conflict in between, at "any time, any place."[1]

Throughout that time, the numbers of Combat Talon veterans grew steadily. Many retired and purchased homes in the Hurlburt Field area where they once served. The Air Commando Association established a Hall of Fame for memorable achievers in special operations, and the community dedicated Memorial Air Park at the entrance to Hurlburt Field where special operations aircraft are displayed. Reunions of the Air Commando Association and of various special operations units became well-attended annual events. There the veterans and active duty airmen from Eglin-Hurlburt bases remember and laud accomplishments of their units and individuals who had distinguished themselves.

It is proper to highlight a few of these: 1st Lt. James L. Hobson Jr. came to Nha Trang as a young pilot on the S-07 crew that replaced the lost S-01 crew. He stayed on with the Combat Talons and became the commander of the 8th SOS. In 1984 he won the prestigious MacKay Trophy for the most meritorious flight of that year during the Operation Urgent Fury in Grenada. Then in 1994, as a major general, he became the commander of the AFSOC. A group MacKay trophy was awarded to one 7th SOS crew for their heroic rescue of fifty-six people from the Republic of Congo in 1997. The most accomplished Combat Talon veteran to this date must be Gen. Norton Alan "Norty" Schwartz. He became the nineteenth chief of staff of the air force in 2008 and was the first without experience as either a fighter or a bomber pilot. His background was in special operations, where he flew MC-130 Combat Talon I and Combat Talon II aircraft and MH-53 Pave Low III and Pave Low IV, as well as MH-60 Black Hawk and Pave Hawk special operations helicopters.

After my retirement from the air force in 1983, I frequently attended reunions with Combat Talon veterans who were members of the Air Commando Association, Stray Goose International, 7th SOS Association, and Nha Trang Reunion Association. The loss of the S-01 crew would always come up in conversations. We learned that reunion attendees did not have contact with the families of the lost crew members and that there was no news from the active Combat Talon units about the discovery of the crash site.

Search for Information about the Lost S-01 Crew

Meanwhile, other people were interested in the fate of the crew. One was retired MSgt. Charles Timms, who had served in our administration office at Nha Trang at the time of the aircraft loss. He organized the Nha Trang Reunion Association for all army and air force veterans who had been stationed there. I attended their 1995 reunion in Dallas, Texas, where I reconnected with retired Lt. Col. Dow Rogers, who was our commanding officer in 1967. He brought an Associated Press article, "MIA Team Finds Human Remains in Indochina," which was published in the *Columbus Dispatch* in October 1993. This article covered the efforts of the Joint Task Force–Final Accounting (JTF-FA) teams in Southeast Asia and cited various statistical data on their past and recent excavations. It contained the following sentence: "One planned excavation was of a site in the northwest where a cargo plane carrying several Americans crashed on a remote mountain peak."[2]

Timms, Rogers, and I discussed this with other attendees, questioning whether this could be a reference to our lost aircraft. The general area was correct, but the article did not specify the type of aircraft and the number of Americans involved. We all knew there were other transport aircraft, such as C-47s and Caribous, that flew in that part of Vietnam earlier in the war. The South Vietnamese flew C-47s there as well. We agreed that this was not our aircraft. Our aircraft tragedy represented the largest single aircraft loss of life in that war. It wasn't just "several Americans." Certainly, our C-130 aircraft's discovery would have warranted more than just one sentence. We were all wrong. It turned out to be our aircraft.

Master Sergeant Timms showed us the results of his quest for information on the S-01 crew. Hoping to learn something new, he requested information from the Air Force Military Personnel Center (AFMPC) on the status of the MIA crew members through the Freedom of Information Act (FOIA). The AFMPC reply of 12 October 1993 gave vital statistics for each crew member with an identical description of the incident. It did not reveal that the aircraft crash site was discovered one year before that. It stated that each individual was declared missing in action (MIA) as of the time of the aircraft's "estimated fuel exhaustion." The curious thing about these eleven documents was that only eight crew members had their MIA status changed by the Department of the Air Force to killed in action (KIA) on 27 April 1978. Three crew members were reclassified from MIA to KIA respectively on 24 June 1977, 29 August 1977, and on 8 June 1978. How could this be if they all perished in the same aircraft on the same day?[3]

The other individual who made it his quest to find out about the fate of the crew was Gene Kremin. He was a good friend of radio operator Gean Clapper. He made a 1992 New Year's Eve resolution that he would find out something about his lost friend. He began by calling several air force agencies without getting any clues. He went to the Lockheed Corporation, which built the missing aircraft; he requested that aircraft number's history. All he learned was that the aircraft had been lost somewhere in Vietnam in 1967. He also spoke with a Lockheed representative at Hurlburt Field in Florida and did not learn anything more. He tried the C-130 System Program Office at Robins Air Force Base in Georgia. This did not provide any information on the lost aircraft either. Someone referred him to a lawyer at Kirtland Air Force Base in New Mexico for help in finding an agency that should know. From there he was referred to the Historical Research Agency at Maxwell Air Force Base in Alabama. There was nothing there. Then, in mid-1997, he wrote to Lee Hess and the commander of the USAF Special Operations Command Maj. Gen. James Hobson. Lee Hess called him back without giving him any news. Hobson was about to retire and did not get his letter.

Finally, Kremin resorted to the Internet, where he searched for the aircraft number and for all crew member names. That finally produced results. He located the JTF-FA teletype message of 23 November 1992 at the Library of Congress; it contained a detailed report from the survey team that explored the site of the crash. During his search process Kremin also located our former commander, Dow Rogers, who informed him that I was writing a story about the S-01 mission; Rogers referred Kremin to me.

Plans for the S-01 Memorial

Earlier in 1997, I learned from now retired Col. John Lewis, who participated in mission planning for that fateful flight, that the special operations community at Fort Walton Beach was making plans to dedicate a memorial to the lost S-01crew at the Hurlburt Field's Memorial Air Park. Lee Hess's Stray Goose International was spearheading this effort. The Air Force's Special Operations Command, headed by soon to retire Maj. Gen. Jim Hobson, gave this effort its blessing. Stray Goose International planned to locate the families of the crew members and have them participate in the dedication ceremony scheduled for the following year. That presented me with an opportunity to break the long-lasting summary court officer restriction on information about this crew's mission and share the story with all the families. I agreed to write a detailed account about the mission of their lost airmen. By that time the activities of the Studies and Observations Group, which directed our clandestine missions, had been written about in historical accounts of the Vietnam War. So, with John Lewis and Roy Thompson refreshing my memory, I began writing. Unfortunately, Roy, who introduced Lewis and me to mission planning starting with that flight, passed away before he had an opportunity to read the first draft of my story.

The story was already finished when I learned from Gene Kremin that the aircraft's crash site had been located almost five years earlier. I had to rewrite the last pages by adding information I was able to gather from copies of two JTF-FA teletype messages I received from Kremin. These dealt with the recovery teams that excavated the crash site in October 1992 and again one year later in October 1993. My story was published in a booklet for the families and attendees of the memorial dedication that took place at Hurlburt Field Air Park on 12 July 1998. The story was also printed in the Air Commando Association newsletter and in Colonel Thigpen's book *The Praetorian STARShip: The Untold Story of the Combat Talon*. Its full text is included in appendix A.

Crash Site Survey Team Leader

One unexpected opportunity to expand my story came too late because I had already written the story and the text was out of my hands. I attended a joint reunion of former Vietnam prisoners of war and Son Tay raiders in Dallas, Texas, in March 1998. This was when the prisoners celebrated their twenty-fifth year of freedom. Mr. Ross Perot hosted us at his ranch and then at a very moving banquet at the Morton H. Meyerson Symphony Center in Dallas. On the last day of this gathering I overheard one attendee talk about excavating for human remains in North Vietnam. I joined the group and I was stunned. This man was talking about recovering the remains from our aircraft. I interrupted him and we identified ourselves to each other. He was army Col. Jack Donovan who was still on active duty. He first visited the crash site in March 1993 to determine if an additional excavation of the site for human remains should be undertaken. The group that conducted the first survey in 1992 recommended that further excavations should not be made because of the site's remoteness and the hazardous conditions on the rocky slopes of the mountain. Then, he, as a lieutenant colonel, who commanded Detachment 2 in Hanoi, recommended a new excavation with a team that would be better prepared for the conditions of this hazardous site. That resulted in the final site excavation that lasted from 24 October to 8 November 1993.

It was great encountering Donovan. We kept in touch while he was still on active duty, and I learned a lot from him about the crash site. At that time his name and those of the other JTF-FA members who conducted excavations were still redacted from the official messages that were released to the public. This was necessary to protect them from direct contact with people such as me who were curious about specific recoveries and sought information outside official channels. Donovan showed me his personal photographs of the crash site that showed the treacherous terrain they had to cope with during the excavation. The terrain was very rocky, with many loose boulders, some of which were loosened by the aircraft's impact. These boulders and other rocks had to be secured in place or removed so that they would not tumble down the slope onto team members working below. The recovery team had to string ropes across the numerous crevasses to assist them in crossing from one side of the site to the other. There was very little topsoil on the steep hillside. Decaying jungle vegetation and some dirt was trapped in crevasses and at the roots of trees. Stories of some natives burying the bodies of crew members on this site have to be suspected. Obviously they did not bring with them any digging tools. Their burial must have consisted of placing the bodies in crevasses and covering them with rocks and available loose soil. Because Donovan was still on active duty at Fort Polk in Louisiana at the time of the memorial dedication, I invited him to the ceremony. He was not able to attend. I did not mention my encounter with him in my story to the families and promised Donovan that I would not release his documents and photographs without his permission. Unfortunately, I lost contact with him over the years, however, most of the photographs and documents on this case, including his fax message recommending a more extensive repeat excavation of the site in 1993, were provided to me by the Joint POW/MIA Accounting Command (JPAC) through the Freedom of Information Act.

Memorial Dedication

The S-01 Memorial dedication ceremony at Hurlburt Field Air Park took place on 12 July 1998. It was a moving event attended by nine of the eleven families and many special operations veterans who make their homes in the Florida Panhandle. Retired Col. John Lewis delivered a tear-jerking speech based on our story. Families of the crew members were appreciative of the event; however, not only they, but all the rest of the attendees, had the same question. Why is it taking so long for the people in Hawaii to finish their identification work? At that time, we believed that remains of eight crew members were already positively identified. This came about because we concluded from the teletype messages that eight sets of remains turned in by the natives represented eight individuals. We did not yet have the information about how few remains there were and what their condition was. Everyone wanted to know how soon the families would receive the remains of their dear ones for proper funerals.

Composite photo of the S-01 memorial pedestal and a flyby by a lone Combat Talon. (Photo courtesy of Lee Hess)

COMBAT TALON AIRCREW S-01

Lost During Combat Mission into North Vietnam
29 December 1967

Lieutenant Colonel Donald E. Fisher - Navigator
Major Charles P. Claxton - Pilot
Captain Edwin N. Osborne, Jr. Aircraft Commander
Captain Frank C. Parker III – Electronic Warfare Officer
Captain Gerald G. VanBuren - Pilot
Captain Gordon J. Wenaas - Navigator
Technical Sergeant Jack McCrary – Flight Engineer
Staff Sergeant Gean P. Clapper – Radio Operator
Staff Sergeant Edward J. Darcy - Loadmaster
Staff Sergeant Wayne A. Eckley - Flight Engineer
Sergeant James R. Williams – Loadmaster

They Made The Ultimate Sacrifice
For God And Country
There Is No Higher Calling

Dedicated: 12 July 1998
By
Stray Goose International

Memorial brass plaque mounted on a pedestal in the Hurlburt Memorial Air Park. (Photo composite by John Gargus)

We received many thanks from families and ceremony attendees. Steve, the son of flight engineer Jack McCrary, sent us the following e-mail:

> I felt great when I left that service and your heart felt story was a big part of that. Again, I want to thank you for all you have done for the family members of the lost crew members of S-01.[4]

I also received a nice letter from Frank Parker's wife, Suzanne:

> People talk about this bringing closure for us, but I have to tell you that the history you and John Lewis wrote gave me the piece of the puzzle I needed for closure and for that I will always be grateful.[5]

Suzanne M. Parker, wife of Frank C Parker III, lays a rose on the plaque that holds her husband's name. (Scan of a photo by MSgt. Kevin Hoeth from the 16th SOWg Commando newspaper)

After the dedication ceremony, I continued to receive many questions from my Combat Talon friends about the slow recovery and identification of remains. The story I authored made me the focal point for seeking more information on this process. Since I was also concerned about it, I planned a vacation to Hawaii and asked Maj. Gen. James Hobson, now a former commander of AFSOC, if he had any contacts there who could introduce me to the proper agencies. He put me in touch with Brig. Gen. Jack Holbein at Special Operations Command, Pacific (SOCPAC), at Camp Smith in Honolulu. This was on 5 March 2000. Holbein was a Combat Talon navigator who remembered me as an instructor from Pope AFB. We began exchanging e-mails and he arranged for me to meet the right people: US Army Brig. Gen. Henry B. Axson, commander of JTF-FA, also at Camp Smith, who was responsible for crash site recoveries in Southeast Asia, and US Army Col. David J. Pagano at the Central Identification Laboratory, Hawaii (CILHI), located at Hickam Air Force Base, who did positive identification of recovered remains.

Visit to the Special Operations Command

I arrived in Hawaii with my wife on 24 May and met with Air Force Brigadier General Holbein. He was most helpful. I gave him copies of my S-01 story and he made sure that the copies preceded our arrival by giving them to the other offices we visited on the island. He was puzzled why the SOCPAC, which he commanded, had not been made aware of the crash site discovery back in 1992. A teletype message from Detachment 1 in Bangkok on 23 November 1992 addressed to the JTF-FA was transmitted as information, not only to the Commander in Chief in the Pacific (CINCPAC), but also to the chief's liaison officer in the Pentagon.[6] It addressed the discovery of the aircraft, which represented the loss of the largest special operations crew of the Vietnam War. Yet no one forwarded the news to his level at SOCPAC. This went on repeatedly with all other subsequent teletype messages that were addressed to the same commands and agencies. The oddest thing about this matter was the fact that one could see the task force offices from Holbein's building, and that is from where the S-01 crew's recovery teams operated. It was not the task force's responsibility to communicate with everybody connected with the aircraft loss. A teletype message from Detachment 1 in Bangkok accomplished that by informing all upper echelons of appropriate commands and governmental agencies. Obviously, there was no information flowing downward to the units that were even closer to the tragedy. The successor to the Combat Spear unit from Nha Trang was now based in Kadena, Okinawa, under the name of 1st Special Operations Squadron, but it still operated under Brigadier General Holbein, who commanded the Special Operations Command in the Pacific.

Visit to JTF-FA

Army Brigadier General Axson was not available to meet us, but he ensured us that we would receive a good reception wherever we went. Lieutenant Colonel Childress became our escort officer. He introduced us to the staff, where we received a detailed briefing on their function and on how their deployed teams conducted excavations at the aircraft's crash site. Staff members had many questions about my story and were glad that they could talk to someone who had so much information about what to them was just a difficult recovery operation for a crash with a big loss of lives in a remote jungle of Vietnam. Interviewing me brought their work closer to home.

I asked why the recovery of the remains was taking so long. Their explanation was that even though their team closed the crash site in November 1993, both our officials and Vietnamese officials kept receiving periodic reports either from or about people who claimed to have knowledge of a crash site in the same province and professed to have knowledge about some human and other aircraft remains. They were obligated to follow up all such leads, which required locating and interviewing these individuals. This took up a lot of their time and, in this case, did not produce anything more than what they already had. They showed us many photographs of the crash site and of various articles that were recovered. There were no photographs of human remains. They told us that we would see the crew remains later in the identification laboratory at Hickam AFB.

Visit to the Central Identification Laboratory

On the next day we went to the Central Identification Laboratory where we met with Army Col. David J. Pagano. Two navy families who came to see the remains of their relatives joined us. We received a good briefing on how the lab conducted identification of the remains they received from the task force. After the briefing, the navy families continued their escorted tour of the lab. We were held back for a follow-on meeting with various members of the staff who were interested in my story. They wanted to question me about some crew members and other aircraft configuration details.

Several new staff members joined us, filling up the available conference table chairs. They informed us that the identification of our crew's remains was completed as of the tenth of March. This was only five days after Major General Hobson put me in touch with Brigadier General Holbein, who then approached Brigadier General Axson. I commented that this was a fast response to a high level inquiry. However, Colonel Pagano assured me that this case had been waiting for closure for a long time and that its time had finally come. Documentation I received from them through the Freedom of Information Act showed a paper trail that gave a clear indication that they had reviewed all recovered remains, materials, and pertinent evidence leading to closing of the case early in 2000.

Staff members of the laboratory were eager to talk with someone who knew all the people aboard and had information about the flight. They took notes and made references to their tablets with diagrams of the crash site. Their main interest was my story's description of where each individual should have been in the aircraft at the time of the crash. They were correlating the recovered remains with crew positions inside of the aircraft. They wanted to know if the aircraft had any explosives on board and of what type they could have been. I assured them that all resupply bundles contained some explosives and other armaments, but that we never knew the exact content of any of them. One forensic staffer asked if the aircraft was equipped with a chaff dispenser. He volunteered that a recovered bone fragment contained tiny slivers that could be from chaff. I pointed to the right side of the EWO's position and I even used Captain Parker's name. He nodded with satisfaction and thanked me for confirming his suspicion.

Once we finished in the conference room, we proceeded to the lab to see the remains. They informed us that normally only the family members of the deceased had access to the room we were about to enter. They asked me not to use my camera. The room was the size of a high school cafeteria. Instead of tables it had many rows of hospital type gurneys. About one-third held skeletal bones carefully arranged on white sheets. We stopped not far from the door and I looked around for the gurneys that had the most bones on them. Our escorting staffer pointed to the gurney right in front of us. "These are the remains of your crew." My knees went weak instantly. On the gurney in front of us were six plastic bags. Five had three to five pieces of bone fragments and the biggest one was about the size of a small couch pillow. It had many small charred bones that together might have weighed about ten pounds. I just could not believe that eleven of my former colleagues could have been reduced to what was in front of us.

The escort went on to explain that the five small plastic bags had remains of the five individuals they were able to identify and that the large bag contained human bones from the crash site that were either too small or too badly burned for DNA testing. They were certain that because they came from that site, they belonged to the rest of the crew. I said that the message we had from the task force stated that eight sets of remains were turned in to the team during the first excavation in 1992. That was true. Local natives turned in eight bags of remains. Each one of the "sets" did not belong to the same person. Also, many of the bones that were turned in were not human. All of the identified human remains, either those turned in by the natives or the ones recovered by our own teams, were here in front of us. They were already sealed and ready for shipment to the Air Force Mortuary Services at Randolph Air Force Base in Texas. On the table were also several blue, about two-inch-thick, loose leaf notebooks. They contained pertinent information that would be handed over to the families along with the remains. I was allowed to leaf through one without noting the name of the crew member. When I asked whose book it was, they informed me apologetically that since I was not a family member I could not have that information. Likewise, they declined to tell us which five crew members had been identified. We learned later from the families that they were Darcy, Eckley, Fisher, Parker, and Williams.

The very next exchange I had with the staff was also tasking. I let them know that I had contact with all the families who knew that I was in Hawaii checking on the recovery and identification process. They pleaded with me not to communicate with anyone until the Mortuary Services could make official contact with them. We understood that bringing my wife and me into the JTF-FA/CILHI loop made us virtual recovery team members. Our contact with the families could create unexpected problems for the official flow of communication with the families. Now we were obliged to sit back and wait.

Air Force Mortuary Services

As soon as we got back to our home in Austin, Texas, I went to Randolph AFB and met with Mr. Garold D. Huey, senior mortuary specialist at the

Air Force Mortuary Services. I explained to him who I was and what we did in Hawaii. He knew that the remains were coming and that he would have to expedite his staff's personal meetings with the families. Since there were eleven, the largest number ever for a single crew, they would all have to be held within a short period of time because of intercommunications between the families. And above all, he wanted me to stay out of the loop and let them handle it all. He appreciated that I came to see him about this development.

Once again I felt like I did when I was assigned summary court officer duty for Charlie Claxton. I could not call his widowed Pat, or anyone else, about what I had learned in Hawaii. However, this time I was comforted by knowing that the situation was well in hand of competent people who knew how to handle the disposition of crew remains properly. They would brief assembled family members and answer their questions.

Personal contacts by the Mortuary Services staff with the families were conducted with utmost dignity and compassion. Here is one response from Wendy, the daughter of loadmaster Ed Darcy:

> I am Edward Darcy's daughter and I wanted to share this with you. My head is still spinning. DADDY IS COMING HOME!!! They are finally releasing the remains. We met with Gary Huey and Art Navarro from Air Force Mortuary Services on Thursday. It was a very long meeting and they gave us a report with pictures of crash site. Wow, very rugged terrain. Of the 11 men, they were able to identify 5. And the biggest miracle of all was they gave Mom his dog tag and Geneva Convention card. I think that it was worth more than 1,000 lbs of gold to her. There is one more family that they needed to meet with. There will be a group burial at Arlington, but I am not sure when. I will let you know.[7]

The Mortuary Services staff concluded their meetings with the families on 7 September. They also arranged for a common grave burial in the Arlington National Cemetery on 15 November 2000. Even though three families opted for private funerals for their lost members, all eleven agreed to this lone casket burial.

Arlington National Cemetery

It was a well-attended funeral on a very cold, breezy morning. Sixty-eight retired Combat Talon veterans, many accompanied by their wives, came from all parts of the country. The 16th Special Operations Wing flew in one Combat Talon aircraft from Hurlburt Field in Florida with many local area retirees. This lone aircraft flew overhead of the group gathered at the gravesite ceremony. Eleven flags were ceremoniously stretched out over the common casket one by one, and then neatly folded in a compact triangle, which was then handed over to a family representative by an air force brigadier general. I was invited to say a few words following the eulogy, which was delivered by the air force chaplain who had conducted the funeral ceremony. I anticipated that moment, so I drafted a short speech during my flight to Washington. I said:

> A long time ago, 12,012 days ago, I saw Jim Williams close the door of your aircraft and then watched your takeoff from Nha Trang on your last mission.
>
> The war ended for you that night, and the long days, months, and years of anguish for your loved ones had just begun. Those of us who were fortunate enough to return to our families from that war could not even comfort your loved ones by telling them what your ultimate sacrifice was all about until two years ago when we met in Florida to dedicate a memorial to your crew.
>
> Now that we are gathered here to pay our final respects to you, we also wish to acknowledge the sacrifice of your families, because the lives of all—from your grandparents, mothers, fathers, brothers,

Patricia Claxton and her granddaughters place single white roses on the S-01 crew casket during the funeral at the Arlington National Cemetery. (Computer scan of a photo by Capt. Carol Kanode from the 16th SOWg Commando newspaper)

sisters, wives, sons, daughters, to grandchildren—were adversely affected as a result of your ultimate sacrifice in the line of duty for our country.

God bless you, your families, and our country, the United States of America!

Their common grave is located in Section 60, Site 7915. Names of the crew members are also engraved on the Vietnam Memorial Wall panels 32E and 33E. Visit them every time you are in Washington.

The gravestone at the common grave of the S-01 crew members at Arlington National Cemetery. (Photo by John Gargus)

Missing Decorations

The funeral should have ended the tragic story of the S-01 crew. It might have gone that way if it had not been for an oversight made by the USAF Mortuary Affairs Office. They prepared shadow boxes with medals that were earned by the deceased crew members. These were presented by the mortuary staff at the reception that followed the funeral at our hotel. Several of us noticed that most of the boxes were missing the Vietnam Service Medal that was awarded to everyone who had served there. The ones that had these medals were in boxes of enlisted crew members who had prior short temporary duty tours in C-130s that took them on flights to Vietnam. What an oversight! Men died in Vietnam, yet they were not credited with the Vietnam Service Medal. Mortuary staffers who were at the funeral were embarrassed by this discovery and made very quick corrections. They provided families with new medal shadow boxes.

7

Crash Site Recovery

No other country in the world devotes as many resources to the recovery of its fallen soldiers as does the United States. We have about 83,000 American soldiers from past conflicts whose bodies have not yet been recovered.[1] Dedicated men and women, in and out of uniform, are determined to bring them home one day. It is a formidable task that may never be accomplished, but we can be assured that the search for those still missing will continue and that the missing will not be forgotten. We can be proud that we care so much for those who made the ultimate sacrifice while serving our country.

Joint POW/MIA Accounting Command (JPAC)

The Joint POW/MIA Accounting Command (JPAC) is responsible for carrying out this global-wide search, recovery, and positive identification of American soldiers. This command's history is still short. It began at the conclusion of the Vietnam War in 1973 with the establishment of the Central Identification Laboratory in Thailand. This laboratory focused its activities on Americans missing in Southeast Asia. Three years later, in 1976, it became the US Army Central Identification Laboratory, Hawaii (CILHI), with responsibility to search for, recover, and identify Americans from all previous wars.

In 1992 the Department of Defense established the Joint Task Force–Final Accounting (JTF-FA) at Camp Smith in Hawaii to augment the CILHI's teams with three supporting detachments located in Bangkok, Thailand; Hanoi, Vietnam; and in Vientiane, Laos. Ten years later, in 2003, the JTF-FA and CILHI were merged into one entity, which became the Joint POW/MIA Accounting Command headquartered at the CIHLI's location at Hickam AFB.[2]

Investigation and Analysis

The co-location of the merged units into one command level organization did not affect the already well-established missions. A good portion of the daily work involves accumulation of personal, medical, and dental files of deceased soldiers whose remains have not yet been recovered and investigation of reports of possible sites for remains of Americans. These are researched for historical events at suspected locations and for names of military units and individuals who might have been involved in military operations there. Reports of confirmed sites are then surveyed by investigative teams (ITs) for possible recovery excavations. ITs consist of four to nine members who possess highly specialized skills in anthropology, languages, medicine, explosive ordinance, and life support. They interface with local authorities in conducting on-site reconnaissance and surveys of the terrain for safety and logistical needs for eventual excavation. They also interview potential witnesses and gather useful information that could assist them in the identification process.[3]

The teams normally travel to the sites in chartered helicopters accompanied by their host nation's counterparts. Very often they face hazardous flying conditions. On 7 April 2001, one such helicopter crashed into a hillside in Vietnam, killing all sixteen men on board. There were seven Americans and nine Vietnamese on this team. Among the Americans were two army lieutenant colonels. One was the outgoing Detachment 2 commander from Hanoi and the other was his incoming replacement.[4]

Recovery of Remains

The next step after the site survey is the recovery of remains. This can last as long as thirty-five to sixty days, depending on the accessibility and condition of the site. Often the recovery phase cannot begin until after satisfactory conclusions of negotiations with property owners of excavation sites, which may involve appropriate compensations. A recovery team can have from ten to fourteen individuals. It has a military team leader and a forensic anthropologist who directs the excavation. Other members include a team sergeant, linguists, a medic, a life support technician, a forensic photographer, a communications specialist, an explosive ordnance disposal technician, and, if needed, even divers or mountain climbers. Very often these team members have to work under difficult conditions far away from distant base camps because the sites can be in remote terrain that will not permit helicopter access. Nevertheless, their work must be diligent and methodical. The anthropologist divides the site into convenient working areas; he sections off the surface into 4 × 4 meter grids with stakes and strings. Each such section is then excavated, and everything unearthed is sifted through 1/4-inch wire screens. This ensures that everything gets looked at and, if needed, documented and packaged for eventual laboratory analysis. It is slow and tedious work that requires hiring local workers who must be trained in this recovery process. All recovered remains and artifacts are transported to Hawaii on board US military aircraft. Upon arrival at Hickam AFB, the JPAC holds an arrival ceremony with a joint service honor guard. This ceremony is attended by senior officers from each service as well as by a variety of active duty personnel and community leaders and representatives.[5]

Identification of Remains

Once the recovered remains and artifacts reach the Central Identification Laboratory they are stored in a secure limited-access area. Forensic anthropologists produce a biological profile from the skeletal remains that includes the sex, race, age, and height of the individual. The anthropologist who is assigned to a case cannot be the same one who participated in the on-site recovery of the remains. This is done to isolate him or her from any bias that could influence his scientific judgment. His judgment should be based only on the examination of the remains assigned to him.

Laboratory scientists use a variety of techniques to identify human remains. Available dental records are valuable because the teeth are durable and survive better than human bones. X-ray photos of prior broken bones are also useful in cases where complete skeletons are available. The most modern technique is DNA analysis. It has seen tremendous advances in recent years and now allows identification of even the smallest pieces of human bones. The laboratory has to obtain DNA samples from close family members to conduct such identifications.

Once the laboratory completes the identification of remains, there is still more paperwork. A carefully composed and reviewed document is prepared for the families; it accompanies the remains, which are sent to the appropriate service mortuary office. That office notifies the next of kin and assists in arranging proper funerals.[6] Some of the JPAC's surveys, excavation recoveries, and positive identifications can take a long time. Some may last several years. On the average, the JPAC completes six identifications every month.[7]

S-01 Crash Site Survey

It was already 1992 when the natives from the remote mountainous Tuan Giao District of Lai Chau Province learned that American teams were searching for aircraft crash sites. Elders of a small Phu Nhung village recalled that there was one such large aircraft site in their area. Some of them had visited it in the past and scavenged the wreckage for salvageable cargo and metal parts. They also knew that airmen who were killed there

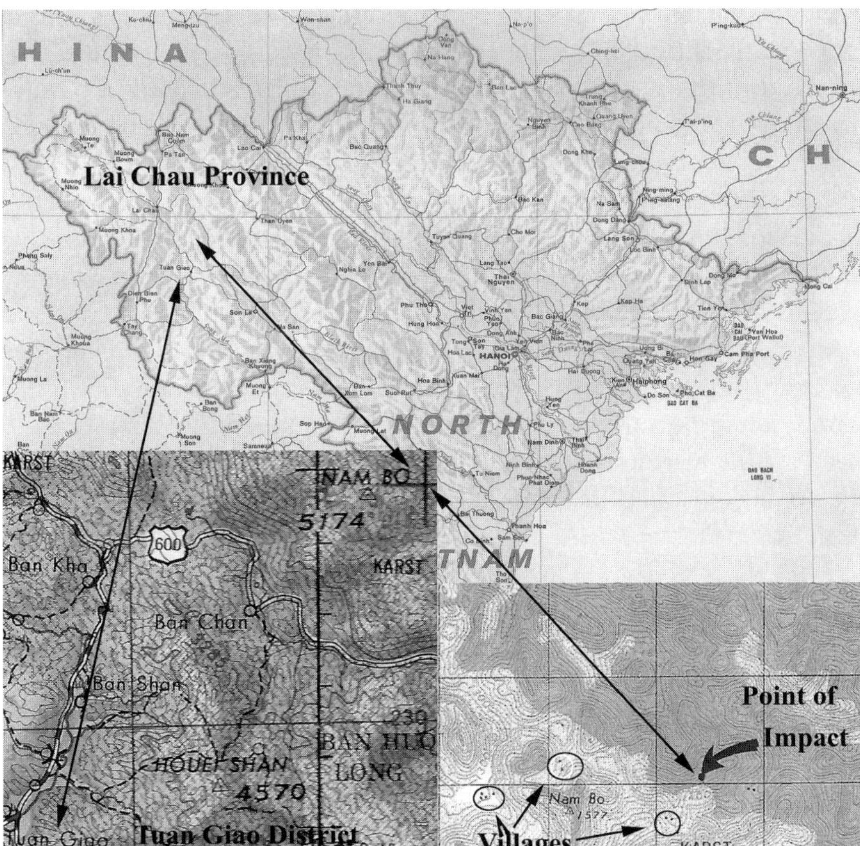

Map of North Vietnam with inserts that show the location of the aircraft's crash site. (Computer scanned composite and overprint by John Gargus)

were buried on that site in various crevasses that had enough topsoil and rocks to cover their broken and burned bodies. Believing that there would be rewards for turning in human remains, they reported the site to the Vietnamese Office for Seeking Missing Personnel (VNOSMP). This office responded by conducting a unilateral investigation and recovery of the site. They searched for human remains in the likeliest spots and dug up broken skeletal remains that they packaged in four bundles. These four sets of remains were turned over to the joint US-Socialist Republic of Vietnam team that arrived to survey the crash site on 29 October 1992.

The first joint JTF-FA and VNOSMP survey team was led by a Captain and had the following seven members on it: five military personnel —medic, life support technician, linguist/analyst, and two mortuary specialists; two US civilians—archaeologist and linguist; and two Vietnamese civilians. The names of the Americans were redacted from all messages made available to the public. This was done to protect their privacy and to shield them from unofficial inquiries that could jeopardize the well-structured recovery and identification process. REFNO 0945 was the reference number assigned for this recovery site.

The joint survey team flew in to the Tuan Giao district headquarters from Hanoi on an MI-8 helicopter. They flew over the reported crash site location and circled the area without locating it. The fly-by gave them a preview of the challenge they would face once on the ground. The site that eluded their view was in a rugged mountainous area. While circling, they looked for a place where their helicopter could make a safe landing. They found none. Spots that appeared to be clear enough for landing were too steep for the helicopter to touch down without having its blades contact the sloping terrain. It became obvious that they would have to travel some

Russian-built MI-8 helicopter used to transport JTF-FA teams to aircraft crash sites. (Wikipedia photo)

distance from wherever there was a convenient road concealed by the jungle that would allow them to come closer to the site.

Once on the ground at the district headquarters, the team learned that the road trip by truck would take about six hours and that it would bring them to about a four-hour walk/climb to the crash site. The American team captain decided to take the truck option. However, after about a forty-five-minute ride, when they arrived at the Phu Nhung village, the driver informed them that they could not go any farther. The rest of the way would have to be done on foot. It would take the team anywhere from seven to eight hours to reach the unseen-from-the-air crash site. Obviously they were not properly equipped and supplied for that kind of demanding operation. They returned to the district headquarters.

The team captain made telephonic contact with the Detachment 2 commander in Hanoi and informed him of their predicament. He also requested that in order to achieve some success from their expedition they should get an approval to see the available sets of remains and be allowed to interview witnesses. He then recommended that they should return to conduct the survey of the crash site on 6 November and be better prepared for the challenging terrain. He also requested that local villagers should be tasked to cut out a usable helicopter landing zone closer to the crash site.

On the following day, 30 October, the weather turned bad. The helicopter could not fly. The team's anthropologist used this time to view and photograph the four sets of remains, and the others interviewed two witnesses.[8]

Crash Site Witnesses

Interview of witnesses is a significant part of JTF-FA's effort to recover human remains and articles from crash sites. Unfortunately, witnesses connected with this crash site proved to be of minimal value. Those who provided references about other potential witnesses caused only delays in bringing the recovery effort to a much earlier conclusion.

The first witness was thirty-six-year-old Mr. Hung from the Phu Nhung village. He was only eleven years old at the time of the crash. He is believed to be the first person to reach the wreckage of the plane that he thought crashed late in 1967 or early in 1968. He claimed that he saw the aircraft crash but he did not remember the time of the day. When questioned on the direction of the flight before the crash, he could not recall it. He saw no parachutes and did not hear any explosions. Later, he heard many aircraft flying around and could not identify what type they were. He claimed that he arrived at the crash site late in the afternoon. He could not get too close to the wreckage because the area around it was still burning. When he was able to get closer, he saw bodies that were badly burned. He could not tell how many bodies there were but he was sure that they were all dead because of the condition of the wreckage and the fire at the site. He claimed that he returned home without taking anything from the site. He said that he went to the crash site only two times and that he knew that the local villagers began going there to take away pieces of wreckage for use in their homes. He said that when he learned in 1991 that the government was trying to locate missing Americans, he reported what he had seen many years ago to the local authorities.[9]

The second witness was Mr. Ly, a sixty-five-year-old resident from the Phu Nhung village. He did not recall the exact date of the aircraft crash. It took him and his companion, whose name he no longer remembered, about six hours to reach the burning wreckage. He could not identify the aircraft type but knew it was American by the clothing of the dead bodies. He could not tell how many bodies there were because the fire was still burning; however, he was sure that everyone was already dead. He reported what he saw to the village authorities, but did not recall when he did that. He returned to the site two more times. He did not take anything away from the site and did not know anyone else who did.[10]

Before the team departed for Hanoi on 31 October 1992, local residents turned over to the district authorities four more sets of remains that they recovered from the crash site. When the team returned on 7 November, they examined and photographed all eight sets of remains. Included among these remains was one Geneva Convention card belonging to Edward J. Darcy and five military identification tags (dog tags) from Gerald G. Van Buren, Donald E. Fisher, James R. Williams, Edwin N. Osborne Jr., and Edward J. Darcy.[11]

The team reinterviewed Mr. Hung, who had testified previously on 30 October. His story was somewhat different from a few days earlier. He now believed that the crash had occurred only about ten years before. Also, he said that he had visited the crash site on three occasions. The first was after the crash when the aircraft was still burning. The second was in 1991 after he learned that his government was looking for missing American remains. He then went to the site looking for graves. He could not find anything that looked like graves. However, he did dig in several places and found several bone fragments in the soil he turned over. He related that there were only a few big pieces of aircraft left behind because the villagers had removed everything they could carry away. He did not know anyone who had carried away aircraft parts or anyone who could have dug up human remains. His third visit was when he escorted the team leader of the Vietnamese Office for Seeking Missing Personnel to the site.[12]

Survey Team at the Crash Site

Finally, a survey team of nine Americans and two Vietnamese reached the site on 8 November. Two new witnesses accompanied the team to the crash site. Both had been there before, where they recovered remains that had already been examined and photographed by the team's anthropologist. They were interviewed by the linguists once they reached the crash site. The first one was Mr. Vang, who was thirty-six years old and lived in the Phu Nhung village. He said that he found some remains in one hole in October 1991. Two other people were on site with him. They stumbled onto the aircraft wreckage while they were out hunting. Knowing that the government was looking for American remains, they began to search for bones. One of his companions found a pair of military boots. He did not

Survey team on its two-and-a-half-hour trek to the crash site from the nearest available helicopter landing zone. (JPAC photo)

know whether his two hunting companions had turned in the remains they found on that day.[13]

The second local resident was thirty-eight-year-old Mr. Nu. He reported that there were seven other people searching for remains when he arrived at the site. The few remains he located came from a single hole. All the people he knew turned the remains they uncovered to the local authorities, just like he did.[14]

It is obvious from the testimony of these witnesses that the local community was well aware of the crash site and that it had many visitors. The visitors scavenged for usable materials and much later returned to excavate for human remains. However, the local authorities turned over only eight sets, or packages, of assorted bone fragments that they received from the area residents.

We determined from the site's geographical coordinates (21–39.80N 103–31.20E) that the aircraft crashed seven and a half minutes after its last reported position. Its ground speed was 230 knots or 265 mph. Its collision against the rocky cliffs at that speed caused its total and instantaneous destruction. No one could have survived such a devastating impact. We don't know how soon after the crash the site was cleared of all recoverable and usable parts and crew member possessions, such as weapons, watches, and strapped-on survival equipment. The team interviewed only two witnesses who showed up at the site on the day of the crash. Neither one admitted taking anything from the scene or doing anything with the bodies. That is highly unlikely. People always take mementoes from the sites of disasters as a proof that they were there. All eleven crew members carried .38 caliber revolvers, radios, and survival packets on their persons. None of those were recovered. Natives had to take them off the dead bodies. It is doubtful that anyone came to the site with the intention to bury the crew. They would have needed digging tools for that. The team did not report any graves or appearances of graves on that rugged terrain. Knowing what the terrain was like, the natives had to cram the bodies in convenient crevasses and cover them with available loose soil, decaying vegetation, and the plentiful rocks of various sizes. Over the years such makeshift burial nooks and crannies were subjected to erosion that grounded down the already crushed bones, which were then washed down the steep hillside. So, when the natives returned there twenty-five years later to search for human remains all they found were a few eroded bone fragments.

There must have been many scavengers that carted away everything that could be used in their homes. How fortunate were those who recovered the cargo restraining chains and clamps, as well as steel cables and all kinds of wiring. Those materials survived in still usable condition in spite of the tremendous crash impact and intense heat from the fire. The whole Phu Nhung village must have known about the unexpected goods that could be salvaged from the wreckage. It was to their advantage to keep such an unexpected cache a secret. They harvested the weapons and uncooked ammunition and kept the crash site concealed from the governmental authorities.

Mr. Dai, who was the district assistant chief, and who participated in the interviews, explained why it took so long for the district, province, and national level officials to learn the aircraft crash location. He stated that the crash happened in an area inhabited by ethnic minorities who were not always in touch with the authorities because of terrain and distance. When the inhabitants informed their local village authorities, no one knew exactly what to do, not only with the information, but also with any remains or identification data that they removed from the site. The American and Vietnamese governments then initiated searches for missing Americans, and government news of this effort began to reach down to the village authorities. They realized that the incident they had been aware of for so long had to be reported to district and province authorities. That was why reports of this incident didn't begin to flow until after November 1991.[15]

First Survey Team Report

The crash site is located 32 miles northeast of Dien Bien Phu at 21–39.80N 103–31.20E. The following quote from the survey team report describes it as follows:

> B. This is an aircraft crash site in extremely rugged and dangerous terrain. The immediate site area is a rocky mountain slope of 30 to 40 degree grade. For some 500 feet below this point and perhaps another 200 feet above, the rocky face angles 60 degrees and more. This, a karst, limestone landscape generally covered by a mixed forest of tropical deciduous and evergreen broadleafs with dense understory of bamboo, bushy shrubs, ferns, vining lianas, and various grasses. The site itself, however, is nearly devoid of vegetation. There

is a noticeable, roughly circular break in the trees where the aircraft plunged through the forest canopy. The surface of the site is largely covered by limestone outcrops and highly unstable areas of scattered rocks. The latter presumably resulting from the impact of the aircraft against the mountain side. Few pockets of humic soil can be found scattered about the crash area, but for the most part this surface horizon has long been eroded downhill once whatever protective ground cover may have existed was destroyed by the crash.

C. Overall, the crash area measures some 16 meters uphill/downhill and 22 meters across the slope. From top to bottom the site falls roughly 10–15 meters and faces a generally north-northwesterly direction. While considerable amount of aircraft wreckage litters the main site area and portions of the steep slope immediately below, no large pieces of wreckage were observed with the exception of what

A landing gear strut and an engine drive shaft are two of the few heavy pieces of aircraft remains that were not carted off by the natives. (JPAC photo)

> appeared to be two struts from the main landing gear and a section of drive shaft from one of the engines. The rest of the larger wreckage appears to have been gradually carted away over the years by local villagers "mining" the site for scrap metal. Presumably these were the same people who more recently recovered the human remains presented to the survey team. There was abundant evidence of fairly recent digging at this site and at least two witnesses were able to confirm locations where they had recovered human remains.[16]

The survey team explored the crash scene terrain carefully and determined that there was no possibility for graves where the crew members could have been buried. They took three test samples from pockets of soil trapped in crevasses that showed evidence of prior, but recent, digging by the natives. The archaeologist was excited by the third sampled spot because in plain view in the disturbed soil was a small tooth fragment that was ignored by the scavengers searching for human remains. The archaeologist's test site description, which was carefully measured and recorded as TE-3, shows the attention the survey team members paid to minute details.

> TE-3 at the top of the crash area where human tooth fragment was found on the surface measured 1 × 1 meter and bottomed on bedrock at 0.2 to 0.3 meters below surface. Again, the matrix here was the same as in TE-1. Material remains recovered from the TE-3 included small cranial vertebral, rib long bone and tooth fragments, all of human origin. In all small bits of human bone ranging from 9 to 32 millimeters in length appear to be widely scattered across the site trapped in small discontinuous pockets of soil surrounded by bedrock outcrops and/or highly unstable scree of shattered limestone.[17]

The survey team was just as meticulous in documenting fragments of equipment excavated along with the bone fragments. Every fragment was numbered, consequently, the below quoted number (2B(3)) refers to the third item in paragraph 2B. Just imagine how much experience this life support specialist had to have to be able to identify such small components of a parachute. This is how he described the recovered material parts in his report:

The ejector snaps and v-rings (2B(3)), (7). (8)) are from the personnel restraint harness or the personnel parachute. The capewell-type releases (2B(4)) attach the aircrew to the parachute canopy There are two releases per parachute assembly. The presence of 14 parachute releases at the crash site indicates seven parachute assemblies. The connector links (2B(5)) are used to connect the riser assembles to the parachute canopy suspension lines. There are four links per parachute assembly. There are 36 connector links seven more than stated in the recovery report, three of which are of a different type, normally installed in personnel parachutes. A total of 33 links represent a minimum of nine parachute assemblies. The accessory rings (2B(9)) attach the crew member to the survival kit. The personnel lowering device and line (2B(10), (11)) are attached to the back of the parachute and are used by aircrew members to lower themselves to the ground in the event of a parachute tree landing.[18]

These small metallic pieces from crew life support equipment were either buried or were overlooked by the scavengers. (JPAC photo)

The survey team concluded that the eight sets of remains turned in by the natives, which were examined and photographed prior to their visits to the site, as well as the tooth and bone fragments excavated at test sample TE-3, were of human origin that needed to be processed by the laboratory in Hawaii. However, the team also concluded that they could not recommend a normal recovery operation at this site because of obvious and serious logistical, operational, and recovery problems. Their full report on this says it all.

> A. Although this crash site has yielded human remains, recovered by both local villagers and the present survey team, further archeological excavations are not recommended. A number of very serious logistical, operational and recovery problems militate against fielding a recovery team at this site. These are:
>
> (1) The terrain both to and at the site is extremely rugged and is considered exceedingly dangerous to even lightly equipped men. Supplying a full-scale recovery team overland would be hazardous even under the best of conditions. Rapidly changing weather conditions typical of these high mountain localities could leave the recovery team isolated for prolonged periods of time.
>
> (2) There is no alternative access to the site other tan overland. The closest acceptable safe landing zone is presently a three to four hour trek from the site. The possibility of finding a closer landing zone appears unlikely at this time.
>
> (3) The availability of a safe base camp area on site is too limited for a full-scale recovery team. To alternatively place camp below the site, on the other hand, would only increase the opportunity for severe mishap in traveling between the camp and the site twice a day—not to mention a minimum of two to three hours lost in transit each day.
>
> (4) The ruggedness and isolation combine to severely hamper the logistical support of this site, especially in terms of the heavy and cumbersome equipment needed to mount a full-scale field recovery.
>
> (5) As already noted, the terrain of the site itself is extremely rugged. However, it is more the large areas of loose, highly unstable scree that make for hazardous working conditions once on the site.

(6) Excavatable matrix from which material remains can be reasonably recovered is limited to small pockets of colluvial soil trapped among the rocky outcrops. These soil areas represent perhaps less than 20 percent of the site as defined by the observable crash area.

(7) Few of these soil pockets have gone unworked by the local villagers, thus further reducing the recovery potential of further archeologically controlled excavation.

(8) The only other, and very problematic, possibility of archeological recovery of significant human remains is to extend into the downhill wash: however, this area is even more precipitous than the immediate crash area and there is the added factor of requiring the recovery team to work below tons of unstable scree.

B. In summary, this site offers only a marginal potential for the recovery of significant human remains beyond what has already been recovered while, at the same time, presents an unacceptably high risk factor. Further archeological recovery is therefore believed to be unwarranted at this time.[19] (See the full text of the 230220Z Nov 92 teletype message in appendix B)

Second Crash Site Survey

It appeared that this report would close the book on REFNO 0945. But that was not to be. The recommendation did not pass the scrutiny of Detachment 2 in Hanoi. This was the biggest crash site of the war in North Vietnam where eleven Americans died. It begged for a more concentrated and better organized recovery effort. The Vietnamese were satisfied with the conclusion of the survey team and were reluctant to go back to the site. Lt. Col. John Donovan, Detachment 2 commander, decided to go to the site himself, survey it again, and if possible, organize another expedition to conduct a thorough excavation. Accompanied by one sergeant, two VNOSMP officers, and two district officials, he visited the site on 29–30 March 1993. He experienced the same difficulties in getting to the site as those who had gone before, but he came up with a different recommendation.

Although this site could be considered for group burial status, recommend a recovery of this site during a future JFA when we have excavation teams operating in the northern portion of Vietnam. Team composition should be as stated in Para 2 and there should be a train-up for the team members of the use of ropes prior to deploying to SRV. The team should be equipped with sleeping pads/mats, much insect repellant, plenty of water, ropes w/snap links for climbing/vertical hauling lines, safety lines, etc., and MREs. It is further recommended that, for the sake of SRVG "approval" at future tech talks, this "team" be part of an 18 man recovery element which would give CJTF the negotiating leverage with his counterpart to say that we want to bring in only three REs however, one of them will be a bit larger than the other two.[20] (See the 221030Z Nov 93 teletype message in Appendix B for detailed listing of recovered items.)

Crash Site Excavation

Lieutenant Colonel Donovan's authoritative recommendation did the job. A large recovery team of twelve Americans and fifteen Vietnamese conducted a comprehensive fifteen-day excavation of the Combat Talon C-130 crash site between 24 October and 8 November 1993. Besides the hazards associated with this steep-slope site, which were described by the first survey team one year earlier, there was another new hazard introduced into the excavation process. That was the large number of people who would be confined to such a small recovery site space. The upper area of the crash site measured 52 feet uphill/downhill and 72 feet across the slope. In the lower areas of downwash the site extended 180 feet downhill for a total vertical fall of some 115 feet.[21]

Before any meaningful work could be done, the site had to be made safe for this large group of men concentrated in such a small boulder and rock strewn place. This required stretching safety ropes laterally at convenient places for hand support when men had to go from left to right across the steep slope and then vertical climbing and rappelling ropes for going up and down, as well as for raising or lowering supplies and equipment. All dislodgeable rocks had to be moved to the sides of the recovery site. It was eventually divided into seventeen areas for excavation. Because of the terrain, it wasn't possible to designate or mark off normal excavation grid units. Each area then became a measurable excavation unit. Many areas were so small and congested that there was almost no room to deposit the sifted soil. In some places working people were elbow to elbow and had to step over each other if they needed to move out of their position for any

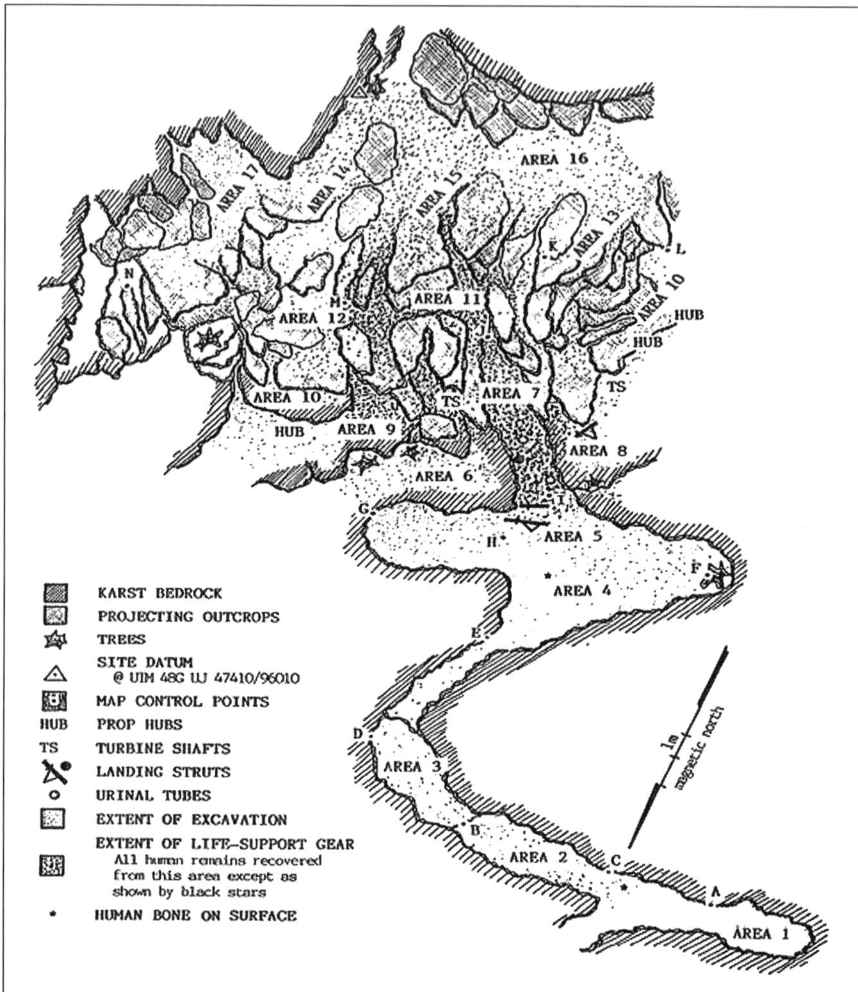

Sketch of the excavation plan shows seventeen areas for excavation and location of some aircraft remains. (JPAC photo)

reason. Taking a toilet break involved work stoppage and a considerable movement away from one's work station.

Excavation inside of each area consisted of removing the top rocks and scraping up the remaining loose soil and debris found underneath them. Everything was sifted through a 1/4-inch mesh and carefully scanned for human remains, personal effects, and aircraft parts. Human remains were small pieces of bones identifiable as being portions of cranium, ribs, vertebra, foot and hand fragments, mandibular pieces, and teeth.

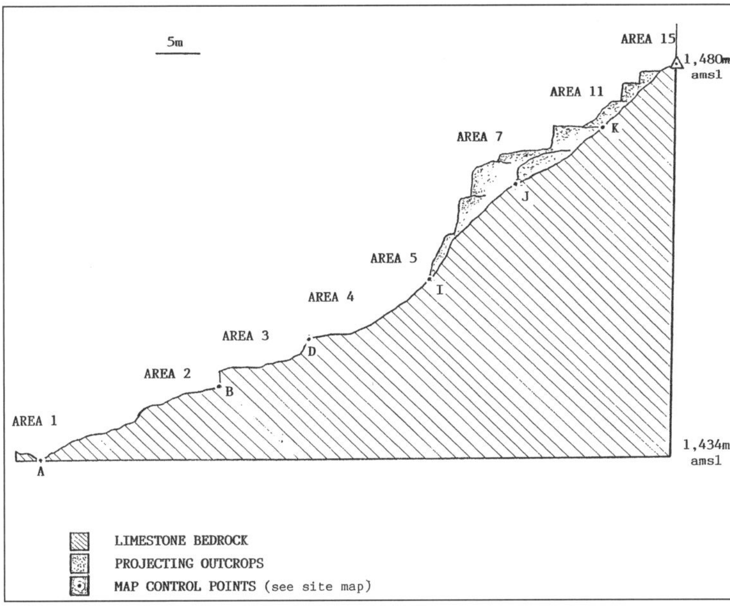

Sketch of the mountain slope shows its steepness and the locations of some excavation areas. (JPAC photo)

Photo of excavation area 11 shows one of the small areas with topsoil where excavations could be accomplished. (JPAC photo)

Excavation moved uphill from area 1, which represented the lower boundary of the site. Upper areas that were adjacent to each other were excavated simultaneously. The distribution of aircraft debris was an indication that the aircraft hit the sloping mountainside straight on, coming to immediate rest. There was no dispersal of aircraft debris above the impact point. Even though they were able to find remnants of only seven parachute fittings, the conclusion was that none of the eleven men exited the aircraft prior to impact.

Top photograph shows the entire team resting just below the aircraft impact point. The lower shows the climbing approach to it. (JPAC photo)

The amount of recovered human remains by this team was very small. There were only 187 pieces of bone and sixteen teeth. Six teeth had identifiable dental restorations. Most of the remains were found in what was still identifiable as the main cabin area of the aircraft. Very few personal effects were recovered. They were uniform buttons, two socks, pieces of expandable watchband, watchband with a buckle, and a casing for a military issue wristwatch. All of these were recovered from the same locations as the human remains. (See the 221030Z Nov 93 teletype message in appendix B for a detailed listing of recovered materials.)

After all those years, it was still possible to delimit the remnants of the rear cargo ramp, the main cabin, and the cockpit. Those aircraft skeletal remains as well as the landing gear struts, engines, and propeller hubs were too heavy to be carted away as salvageable metals. Some were embedded in the crevasses and silted over with eroding soil. They would remain on this remote site perhaps forever.

The CILHI team leader and anthropologist terminated the excavation and closed the REFNO 0945 site at 1100 hours on 8 November 1993.[22] This fifteen-day effort of twenty-seven men produced very little in the recovery of human remains and of identifiable materials. However, it cleared the site of everything larger than 1/4-inch size that was imbedded in excavatable soil. There must have been many human bone fragments even smaller than that. They escaped the eyes of the sifters and will become mountain soil debris that will be eroded to still smaller sizes as they wash down to some muddy river bed.

Remains that were turned in by the local villagers to the Vietnamese authorities and those recovered by the survey team on 29 October through 8 November 1992 were flown on USAF aircraft from Hanoi to CILHI in Hawaii where they were received with proper military honors. Remains that were excavated by the team on 24 October through 8 November 1993 were received in a similar manner on 14 December 1993.[23] The excavation phase of REFNO 0945 was terminated when the team left the crash site, but the positive identification of assembled human remains in the CILHI would become a slow methodical process. The lab received a mixture of several hundred bone fragments that belonged to eleven men. This task would challenge the scientists and technicians of the lab for a long time.

CILHI's Positive Identification

The CILHI was able to identify remains of only five of the eleven crew members. With ranks attained during their MIA status, they were: Col.

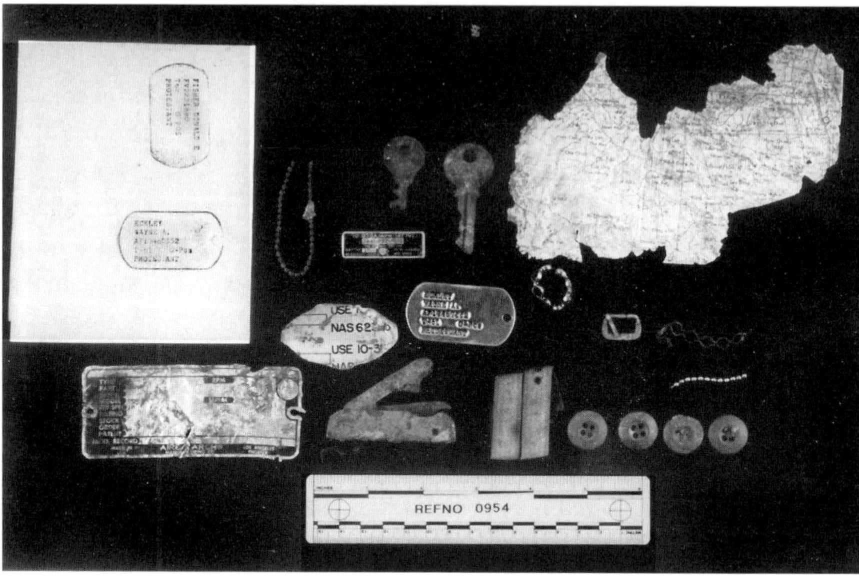

This photo of excavated personal artifacts has an insert that shows a paper rubbing of Lt. Col. Don Fisher's ID tag that was turned in to Detachment 2 in Hanoi. (JPAC photo provided to author by Mrs. Claxton)

Donald Ellis Fisher, Maj. Frank Claveloux Parker III, CMSgt. Edward Joseph Darcy, CMSgt. Wayne Alvin Eckley, and CMSgt. James Randall Williams. Most of the skeletal remains were either too small or too badly burned for positive identification with the technology of that time. Since they all came from the same crash site location, they had to belong to the eleven crew members who perished there. The years took their toll on the remains, which were obviously severely crushed during their high velocity impact against the rocky mountain surface.

CILHI photographs of remains provided to me by Mrs. Charlie Claxton will tell a lot about the task that awaited the scientific and technical forensic staff at the laboratory. DNA technology of that decade was not as advanced as it is today. Today, we see on TV that forensic technicians can use very small pieces of remains to identify a person. As they explained to us during our visit to CILHI in 2000, in the 1990s they had to destroy a sizeable bone fragment for a test to obtain an acceptable DNA match. Most of the recovered bone fragments from the crash were either too small or too badly damaged by fire to be analyzed. Therefore, it is not surprising that their diligent laboratory work succeeded in positively identifying only five of the eleven crew members.

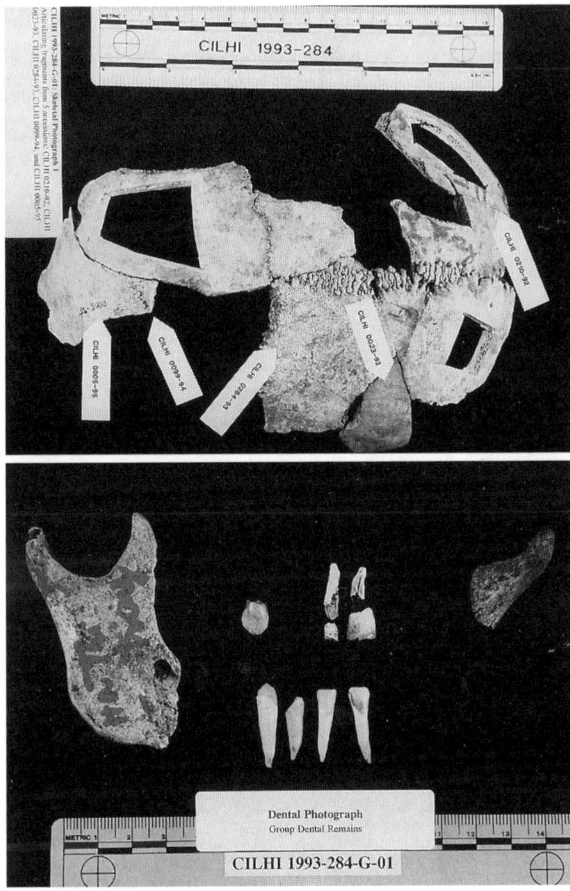

This is a composite photograph of large remains that were of sufficient size for DNA identification with the forensic technology available in the 1990s. Top photograph shows where pieces of bone were cut out. Those cutouts show how much bone material was needed to conduct a DNA analysis. (JPAC photo provided to author by Mrs. Claxton)

This is the conclusion of CILHI's detailed, scientifically technical report:

> Available evidence suggests that (then) Capt. Osborne and his 10-man crew died when their C-130E Hercules crashed on a mountaintop in Lai Chau Province. Analysts at the JTF-FA and DPMO have indicated that there is no evidence to indicate that any of the crew survived the crash. Remains recovered from the crash site, both by Vietnamese sources and through joint US/S.R.V. recoveries, are those of at least five individuals. Dental remains and a dental prosthetic device match the ante mortem dental radiographs and records of CMSgt. Darcy, CMSgt. Eckley, and CMSgt. Williams. Skeletal remains yielded relatively rare mtDNA sequences that match mtDNA obtained from known material relatives of Col. Fisher, Maj. Parker,

> CMSgt. Darcy, CMSgt. Eckley, and CMSgt Williams. Anthropological analysis is supportive. These findings, as well as the material and circumstantial evidence, lead to the reasonable conclusion that the remains of designated CILHI 1993–284 are those associated with REFNO 0945. Laboratory analysis allows for the individual identification of the remains of five of the crewmen; the remaining burned bone fragments can reasonably represent parts of any, or all, of the 11 men manifested on board the aircraft.[24]

Besides the photographs of the bone fragments the final lab report gives specific details for each individual. Just imagine how much time, patience, and dedication it took to identify the below-described bone and teeth fragments from among those that belonged to any one of the eleven men and then assemble them in proper places on the bodies of their owner. This is one for the crew loadmaster Jim Williams:

> CILHI 1993–284-I-05 consists of cranial fragments—including a fragment of right maxilla with three teeth and a fragment of left maxilla with three teeth, five fragments of mandible that articulate to form a single element containing seven teeth, a proximal third of a left humerus, a right tibial midshaft, a relatively intact right fibula, and left tibial fragment. The remains appear to be those of an adult male who experienced perimortem trauma. Dental and mtDNA analysis has associated these with MSgt. James R. Williams, a white male who stood approximately 70 inches tall and was 22 years 9 months old at the time of his loss.[25]

Photographs also show that many of the bone fragments have red ink writings on them. All of these came from the eight sets of remains that were turned in by the natives to the first survey team in 1992. Both the Vietnamese and American linguistic members of the team concluded that these writings and symbols represented names of individuals who either owned or collected them. No one stepped up to claim their ownership.

Interviews of Individuals Who Claimed to Have Information on the Crash Site

The search for witnesses did not end with the termination of the excavation of the site on 8 November 1993. Potential witnesses who had information

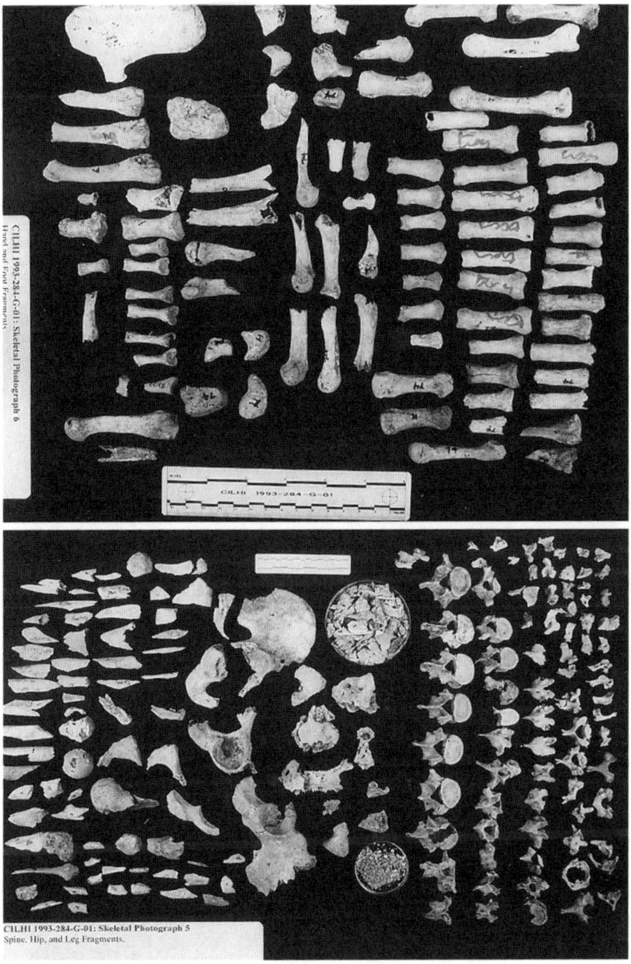

Top photograph shows hand and foot bone fragments that were too small for DNA analysis. Bottom photo shows spine hip and leg fragments. (JPAC photo provided to author by Mrs. Claxton)

about crash sites and human remains kept turning up from various parts of North Vietnam. Some bypassed the Vietnamese channels for reporting suspected sites and contacted the US authorities in Hanoi. Many contacts were made through intermediaries and contained possible ties to the REFNO 0954. Checking on these leads took a lot of time and coordination with the Vietnamese VNOSMP.

One such contact was made on 26 May 1994 by Mr. Dung, a resident of Moc Chou, who provided Detachment 2 with information that appeared to fit REFNO 0954. He brought in three small bone fragments, one small piece of a USAF survival map, and rubbings of identification tags for Wayne A. Eckley and Donald E. Fisher.[26] The follow-up to this contact is documented in detail in a teletype message from the commander of the JTF-FA in Honolulu to the secretary of defense in Washington DC on 17 June 1994. (See the 171102Z teletype message in appendix B.) It shows how vigorously and extensively the JTF-FA followed up on people's reports about missing American airmen. This lead looked very promising, and it was so close to the December 1993 final site excavation that it was worth exploring. Interest was so great on the part of the Vietnamese that an unusually high number joined the investigation team. The team had only two US members from the Hanoi detachment, and two members from the Vietnamese VNOSMP. Then there were fourteen more Vietnamese who represented various provincial, district, and village offices. This joint team had eighteen members who showed up at the home of Mr. Dung on 2 June. He was not there. He had gone to Hanoi to visit his brothers. Most of the team stayed in Moc Chou, and some went to locate Mr. Dung in Hanoi. They found him and brought him back home.

Mr. Dung revealed that a certain Mr. Luong had requested him to intercede on his behalf with the Americans in Hanoi and ask them to come to Son La province to retrieve remains of two US crew members. He said that Mr. Luong knew of other people who had remains of Americans. Mr. Dung led the large team to Mr. Luong's village. Once there, they encountered Mr. Luong's father who was the village Communist Party secretary. His son was working in the fields and the father was puzzled about why he needed to be interviewed because he knew nothing about any remains. As the village's Communist Party leader he should have known about such events in his area. When Mr. Luong came home, he said that he had some acquaintances who knew about an aircraft that crashed and burned and that some had retrieved remains and dog tags from the site. He named the individual who told him about this. However, he himself never saw the remains and he was given only the bone sample and dog tag rubbings that Mr. Dung delivered to the detachment in Hanoi.

During the interview Mr. Dung and Mr. Luong began to argue with each other about some details of their testimony. Vietnamese team leaders intervened and asked Mr. Luong to tell the truth. Mr. Luong then said that he heard that people in Lai Chau province had located remains of seven crew members at a crash site. He also explained about himself that it was common among his people not to give out all information at first but to hold some of it back. He said that it was customary to pass information by word of mouth from one person to another without identifying all of the individuals involved. He insisted that he did not know any more than that. Major Peng, a team representative from the Lai Chau province's Regional Border Defense Force, admitted that Mr. Luong was his cousin and that he "was not a man of good character and was not a respected member of his community." Major Peng also stated that he was aware of the excavation site for REFNO 0954 and that he would personally pursue the matter with people in the Lai Chau crash site area. He believed that he would succeed in recovering all the remains the people had in their possession.[27]

The team concluded that the seven remains in Lai Chau province were the same that had already been turned over to the authorities and passed on to the first recovery team in 1992. The four days' worth of joint effort consumed many man hours and did not produce anything new. It only confirmed the conclusion that not much more can be obtained from the S-01 crash site.[28]

Major Peng of the Son La Regional Border Defense Force came through on his promise to recover reported remains in possession of people in the area under his authority. His troops confiscated additional remains and Wayne A. Eckley's ID tag from the natives who lived in the vicinity of the crash site. These were delivered to the CILHI on 14 February 1995.[29]

The JTF-FA report on the investigation of Mr. Dung's and Mr. Luong's claims has a clear statement about the US and SRV policies about not providing any rewards or favors in exchange for information about, or for return of, remains of US servicemen. Lieutenant Colonel Khoi, joint investigating team member from the Ministry of Defense, explained that when remains prove to be those of US servicemen, the government could reimburse Vietnamese citizens reasonable sums of money for such things as labor, transportation, and storage costs. He emphasized that the mission of the investigating team was a humanitarian one. There were no hidden or unofficial programs for rewards. The Vietnamese members of the joint teams operated under strict directives of the government of Vietnam.[30]

Over the following five years, the JTF-FA personnel responded to many reports from individuals that hinted of a possible connection to REFNO 0945. Most had the same common denominator. People who had remains or knew of aircraft crashes were looking for compensation and relied on questionable intermediaries to deal with authorities. Stories of intermediaries changed between what they reported to the US authorities and what they said when questioned by joint investigation teams. This may be due to a cultural trait or intimidating fear of the Vietnamese interviewers. It is also probable that the informants backed off from their claims once they learned that the hearsay stories about payments for reports leading to a recovery of American servicemen were not true.

In January 1998 Mr. Anh, a retired schoolteacher from Hanoi, provided the detachment with a paper copy of Donald E. Fisher's ID tag and a half-inch fragment of human bone. He claimed that he had the actual ID tag and a complete set of remains. When he was interviewed by a joint team on 26 June, his story changed. He related that when he attended a wedding in Thuan Chau district of Son La province, he learned that local residents had remains of an American soldier. He met with some of the residents and saw several large pieces of bone, part of a skull and a dog tag. The people who had the remains claimed that they bought them from a native H'mong who found the remains in the mountains. They asked Mr. Anh to intercede for them with US authorities in Hanoi. They had the remains for about eight months and expected some compensation for them.[31]

Mr. Anh's information paralleled that of Mrs. Ha, an import and export specialist for the Ministry of Trade. She had contacted the detachment a year before in August 1997 and presented a rubbing of a dog tag. She claimed that her close friends had the actual ID tag and a skull in their Hanoi home. They asked her to intercede with the US authorities on their behalf. When a joint team interviewed her, she altered her story. She related that she kept having dreams about a man who would ask her to assist him with American remains. This dream finally came true. She claimed that there was a Vietnamese man in his forties whom she met in a café. He gave her one ID tag rubbing and told her that he also had a skull. He did not give her his name and said that he would contact her later after she had approached the US authorities. She never saw him after that first meeting.[32]

Both Mr. Anh and Mrs. Ha presented the same rubbing of Donald E. Fisher's ID tag to the detachment.[33] They denied knowing each other. The investigative team concluded that these two individuals were unreliable because they could not lead them to others who supposedly had the original ID tag and the skull. In addition, the final report of the team stated that on 25 July, Detachment 2 informed the investigative team that a certified anthropologist, who examined the bone fragment provided by Mr. Anh, determined it to be of mongoloid origin. Detachment 2 returned the bone fragment to Mr. Anh.[34] This was the last investigation of information with a trail leading to the REFNO 0945 crash site.

8

Official Information Sources

The omission of Vietnam Service Medals from some of the shadow boxes given to the families by the Mortuary Services staff caused me to think about some other things that might have been overlooked by other agencies dealing with the aircraft loss. Why wasn't the special operations chain of command involved in the notification process when the aircraft crash site was discovered? Why was the crew's missing in action status changed to killed in action on different dates? Were the families properly notified and kept informed about the recovery and identification of crew remains? Why did the process take so long?

Vietnam Service Medals

I maintained contact with Mr. Garold Huey at the Air Force Mortuary Services after my visit to Hawaii. I was impatient with the time it was taking them to complete their work in making personal visits to each family. Nevertheless, I did as I promised him. I avoided contacting the families until their work was done. Their office was just outside of Randolph AFB, which was only one hour away from my home in Austin, Texas. I visited them several times and saw them prepare the blue notebooks they were assembling for presentation to the families. They researched each crew member's source documents, including personnel record folders and documents dealing with the aircraft loss from the air force and from the JPAC in Hawaii. They were all young men and women who had not served in

Vietnam, but had proper respect for those who had. I know that they did their best in extracting information for the shadow boxes from the documents available to them. If there was no record of a crew member having received the Vietnam Service Medal, they did not order one for his shadow box. The error occurred somewhere in the wing's personnel office in Vietnam where the personnel records for the crew were closed out as missing in action and forwarded up channel to some other air force personnel office. Most likely it was in the administration office of our detachment where documentation needed to be generated about each MIA member's Vietnam service. Such documentation should also have included information about any other decorations each individual had earned up to the time of his loss to the unit. Each one must have had partial credits toward the Air Medal, which was based on the number of aircraft sorties flown in Southeast Asia. Someone within the Mortuary Services who was much older and who had earned his own Vietnam Service Medal would have caught the omission and corrected the error.

Notification Process

My quest for information about why no one notified the Air Force Special Operations Command at Hurlburt Field and the 1st SOS at Kadena, Okinawa, about the crash site discovery in 1992 was frustrating. I saw it as another embarrassing oversight because the Combat Talon community at Hurlburt Field was planning a memorial for the crew, without being aware that the aircraft's crash site had already been discovered and excavated.

My search for information started with the teletype messages generated by Detachment 1 of the Joint Task Force–Full Accounting in Bangkok, Thailand. They were sent to the headquarters at Camp Smith in Hawaii for further action and were addressed only as information messages to the following top government offices: Secretary of Defense, Secretary of State, Defense Intelligence Agency, Central Intelligence Agency, National Security Council, and CINCPAC and his information office in Washington DC. Apparently, none of these had an obligation to disseminate the information down to neither the AFSOC at Hurlburt Field or to any of its subordinate operational units. However, there was a 3 December 1992 letter from the JTF-FA to the headquarters of the Air Force Military Personnel Center at Randolph AFB in Texas with attention to its subordinate office dealing with missing persons (DPMCB). Its subject was: Detailed Report of Survey Associated with REFNO 0954. It forwarded the text of the teletype message generated in Bangkok, Thailand, by the commander of Detachment 1 on 23 November 1992 at 0220Z. This letter stated that the information was provided for the release to the next of kin.[1]

Consequently, the JTF-FA had the responsibility to inform the air force personnel office that handled the communications with the missing in action family members but had no direct obligation to inform operational units that incurred personnel losses. Nor did it have the responsibility to maintain contact with families of individuals whose remains they were recovering. That was done through the personnel centers at all the military service branches. It is interesting that the personnel office for the missing persons that then notified the families and maintained communications with them was the same one that did not volunteer the crash site discovery information to Master Sergeant Timms in responding to his Freedom of Information Act request about the change of crew status from missing in action to killed in action. The date of that response was 12 October 1993, one year after the confirmation of the crash site discovery. Obviously, the staffers in this office were not all-knowing and focused only on the requests and questions they were tasked to answer.

We know that the agency responsible for the missing in action airmen was the same one that is now called the Air Force Missing Persons Branch. This agency has changed its name and its identifying office acronym several times during the span of its involvement with the S-01 crew. Just as subordinate agencies of other major commands, it was called at different times an Agency, Directorate, Branch, Division and Office of, or Office for, and so on. However, its mission, quoted below, has remained the same.

> The branch serves as the liaison between government agencies and Air Force POW/MIA family members. Branch personnel administer the Air Force hostile and non-hostile missing persons program, and serve as a liaison between the Air Force, the US government and the next of kin of all unaccounted for Air Force Personnel.
>
> The Air Force Missing Persons Branch at AFPC collects, evaluates and disseminates to next of kin and other interested government agencies all information and reports concerning aircraft crash and grave site investigations or excavations, live sightings and refugee interviews.
>
> They operate hand in hand with the Office of the Assistant Secretary of Defense, International Security Affairs/Defense Prisoner of

> War/Missing Personnel Office, Joint POW/MIA Accounting Command, Armed Forces DNA Laboratory, the Life Science Equipment Laboratory, the US Air Force Mortuary Affairs Division, the Joint Personnel Recovery Agency, and the Central Intelligence Agency. They also maintain contact with family organizations such as the National League of POW/MIA Families and the Coalition of Families of Korean and Cold War POW/MIAs. These Air Force personnel respond to casualty-related congressional and other high-level inquiries, and write advisories for the Air Force Board for Correction of Military Records.
>
> The branch office serves as the focal point of contact for the next of kin of unaccounted-for service members from the Korean War, Cold War and the Vietnam Conflict, in addition to any current day operations. They maintain contact with about 3,500 family members. They have maintained contact with families of unaccounted-for Airmen over the years since the Korean War.[2]

There is no specific mention in this mission statement about notifying the unit of the deceased. There are only references to maintaining liaison with the air force and with interested government agencies. That may be a stretch, but its language could also mean to include the unit and command to which an MIA or KIA person had been assigned. Who should initiate this communication liaison? Apparently it should be the losing individual's unit or command. If anyone had a question about an MIA or KIA status of a person, the above-referenced personnel office should be the place to go for information.

I questioned the air force operational units that should have known about the crash site discovery. My first effort was directed at the AFSOC at Hurlburt Field. Because of what transpired with the memorial dedication, I was well aware that the command did not know anything. But I did not want any stones unturned. I received assistance from Mr. Herb Mason, the command's historian. He could not locate any evidence that his command was notified by any agency that had received the 1992 crash site discovery message from the JFT-FA.

The successor organization to the aircraft's losing unit, which eventually relocated to Kadena Air Base, Okinawa, was also uninformed. I rationalized that the omission of this unit from the notification chain could be explained by the fact that the original Nha Trang unit, Detachment 1 of the 314 TAW, changed its name to the 15th ACS in March 1968, then to 15th SOS in August 1968, and to the 90th SOS in October 1970. Finally, it became the 1st SOS in March 1972. Not only that, during the drawdown of the US forces, the unit moved out of Nha Trang to Cam Ranh Bay and after the war to Kadena, Okinawa, Japan, in 1972. From there it moved to Clark Air Base in the Philippines in 1981 and then back to Kadena in 1993, where it became a squadron of the 353rd Special Operations Group. I made contact with Mr. Fred Schramm, the group's historian. His search of documents from the crash discovery period did not turn up any evidence that the JTF-FA message on REFNO 0954 trickled down to that command.

My telephone inquiries with people at the personnel center about who on the operational level should have been notified about the crash site discovery were fruitless. I was sure that some office in that command had that responsibility. However, no one I talked with knew about such office. They all directed me to my starting point in the office that was responsible for maintaining contact with the next of kin. Everyone I spoke with assured me that their office must have done everything in accordance with their responsibilities. My questions were too specific. I understood that no one I talked with could just go to a computer and call up the information I needed. Several of them suggested that I should use the Freedom of Information Act (FOIA) route to obtain my answers. So, I did just that.

I sent an FOIA request to the office dealing with missing persons (DP-MCB) asking about the post-crash-site discovery notification process. I was specific in asking about who within their domain was responsible for notifying losing units upon discovery and excavations of crash sites, and which command units had been thus notified. I was astonished by the replies I received.

Whoever was assigned the task to respond to my freedom of information request completely misunderstood what I wanted. The only logical explanation is that this person believed that I was asking about the notification process in the year 2000 when the excavated remains of the crew were delivered to the Mortuary Services, because my first four questions were forwarded to that agency for their answer.[3] Since I dealt with the Mortuary Services staff in person, I was well aware what their responsibilities were. Nevertheless, they responded to each question, and the sum of it was that their responsibilities were to communicate only with the next of kin and that the only command they needed to notify was the Defense

POW-Missing Personnel Office about the next of kin's acceptance of the identified remains from the Central Identification Laboratory.[4]

It is obvious that there was a foul-up in communication between the two offices. I was seeking information on the notification process that followed the discovery of the crash site after 1992. The information I was provided dealt with the information process once the recovered and identified remains were ready for interment. Not only that, I was lucky to get the reply to my questions because the reply letter was addressed to me at someone else's address in Studio City, California. Fortunately, its envelope had my proper address for my home in Nevada. I am convinced that I would have received different answers had I specified dates for each time period pertaining to my questions. Likewise, I am convinced that those who provided the answers felt that they were addressing my questions properly.

I was not yet ready to give up. I went back to the same missing personnel office explaining that I was after the notification process following the crash site discovery. I wanted to learn about the air force's responsibility for notifying the losing command and its subordinate units of this crash site discovery. Then I received the following short, evasive, and bureaucratic response:

> In accordance with the DOD FOIA guidelines this request does not specifically request any type of record, but rather deals with asking questions about casualty notification process after the recovery of REFNO 0954. FOIA is not a forum for answering questions but a means to provide the public with government records; unless records exist which may answer your questions. On 31 August 2005 we released a number of documents which we felt would answer your questions. We also advised you should contact the Air Force Services Agency's Mortuary Affairs office: that office is responsible for notification and should be able to either answer your questions or provide any additional records which may answer your request. Without knowing what specific "records" you desire we are unable to respond to this request.[5]

Very plainly, they pointed out that I was fishing for information and that their obligation was only to provide me with documents that I could positively identify by addressees and dates. Not only that, this response was signed by the same civil service GS-12 who referred my first questions to the Mortuary Affairs office. That person also sent me back to that same office for further answers to my questions. So once again, that same person ignored my specific request about what was the air force's responsibility, if any, to report the crash site discovery to the losing unit or its major command.

That reply caused me to give up further search. I concluded that the agencies involved with casualty matters followed proper protocol in dealing with the families and did not have the same obligation to direct the discovery information to the unit and command that owned the lost aircraft. The time lapse erodes relationships between the units and the families of its lost members. Personnel reassignments ensure complete changeover of members in two to three years; even sooner in Vietnam where a one-year tour of duty was the norm. A unit's mission goes on and there is no requirement for it to maintain contact with the next of kin of men who once served in it and were lost in combat. That responsibility shifts wisely to a more permanent agency at a higher military personnel level that is staffed just for that purpose. That is exactly what happened in this case. We were all reassigned from our unit at Nha Trang within a year and the Missing Persons Branch office at Randolph AFB became responsible for dealing with the families, providing them information on the status of their missing in action relatives. Those of us who served as their commanders and summary court officers lost contact with the families because we were never good sources for the information they wanted. They wanted to know what the crew was doing when the aircraft went down so that they could appreciate the sacrifices of their men. Unfortunately, their Stray Goose crew member friends could not say anything appropriate to comfort them. In time, this resulted in lost contact with them. Because of that, the families did not inform us about the crash site discovery when they learned about it through the established channels. They also believed that once the crash site was discovered, the losing unit and command were notified and that we were in the communication loop.

To understand what transpired with the flow of information, we need to place ourselves inside of the agencies handling the crash site information at their point in time. To us, the crash site discovery was a significant event we anticipated for twenty-five years. To the Detachment 1 at Bangkok, which broke the news in the teletype message to numerous agencies, it was just part of their normal work. The crash site did not make news at home. Big news stories of that day involved a three-man race for the presidency of the United States between Bush, Clinton, and Perot. One year later there was another teletype report about the crash site excavation. That one did not make the national news either, but a story about JTF-FA work in Southeast Asia surfaced in Bangkok, Thailand, when a JTF-FA spokesman, Lt. Col. David Fredrikson, briefed news reporters about their recovery activities in Southeast Asia. No doubt he gave some details about the S-01 crash site, but his comments were reduced to the Associated Press article, "MIA Team Finds Human Remains in Indochina," which was published on inside pages of several newspapers back home. This story is worth reprinting here because it illustrates how the discovery of the aircraft's site was hidden within its general text.

> US specialists searching for Americans missing from the Vietnam War found human remains in all three Indochinese countries while digging at crash sites and a graveyard, a spokesman said yesterday.
>
> If an anthropologist determines the remains found in Vietnam, Laos, and Cambodia could be Americans, they will be sent to US Army laboratories in Honolulu for analysis, Lt. Col. David Fredrikson said.
>
> Plane wreckage and pieces of uniforms also were found, he said.
>
> More than 200 American specialists are working in Indochina and neighboring Thailand to account for American prisoners of war and those missing in action. Besides excavations, they are studying archive materials and interviewing people who witnessed incidents in which Americans turned up missing.
>
> A total of 2,248 Americans are missing from the war, which ended in a 1975 Communist defeat of US backed South Vietnam.
>
> Remains were found this week in both Vietnam and Laos, said Fredrikson, chief spokesman for the Honolulu-based military unit conducting the MIA search.
>
> He said the latest remains found in Vietnam were unearthed during excavations at two plane crash sites. A total of 21 Americans are missing from the crashes at the sites.
>
> The latest search in Vietnam began Oct. 21. US officials said seven teams of investigators were fanning out over 19 provinces for a month—the most ever for a single project—to investigate as many as 143 MIA cases.

> One planned excavation was of a site in the northwest where a cargo plane carrying several Americans crashed on a remote mountain peak. In an earlier search, three sets of remains were found.
>
> The remains in Laos were found at a plane crash site and a graveyard in the southern provinces of Saravane and Xekong. Another crash site will be excavated later.
>
> The three-week Laos project began Oct. 19. The teams are investigating six priority cases and up to 17 other cases if time permits.
>
> Most of those missing in Laos were airmen shot down while bombing Laotian Communist insurgents or the Ho Chi Minh Trail.
>
> Earlier this month, remains also were found in Cambodia.[6]

Lt. Col. Dow Rogers brought this article to the 1995 Nha Trang Reunion Association meeting in Dallas, Texas. We scrutinized its content and did not connect it to our aircraft. Again, we were blinded by our conception about how big our aircraft loss was. It was the biggest loss of American lives involving one single aircraft in North Vietnam, so we expected a clearer and bigger story than that single obscured paragraph. With what we now know, the underlined paragraph clearly refers to our aircraft. We now know that there were two excavations one year apart and that "several Americans" were our eleven crew members. The first one resulted in four, not three sets of remains. The second one brought in four more sets that were collected by the natives. The 1993 recovery team excavated few more additional remains. It is unfortunate that so many years after the Vietnam War our media did not pay more attention to the events in that part of the world. We had bigger news with the fall of the Iron Curtain, break-up of the Soviet Union, Iraq War to liberate Kuwait, and the historic presidential elections at home.

Why didn't someone, from all the agencies that received the JTF-FA teletype messages, focus on the importance of this crash site and notify someone within the special operations community? Again, let's put ourselves into the proper time period. The recovery and identification were happening in the 1990s. Junior staffers at these agencies who are normally tasked to sort incoming mail and messages were probably in elementary school or high school during the Vietnam War. Since there was no news coverage of the loss when it occurred, how would these relatively young people connect to the loss of this one aircraft? Only someone who had served in Vietnam at that time would have been able to highlight such a teletype item and perhaps inform someone within the special operations community. Obviously, none of the mail sorters were of this type. Messages that were for information only ended up on the bottom of the stack in the reading priority of busy offices. Those in higher echelons who received them presorted in their daily reading files had to go through them perhaps with a lot of scanning. I believe that a message from a small army detachment in Bangkok did not end up very high in the reading files of the State Department, CIA, DIA, and NSA, as well as at CINCPAC. It was the type of message a reader would get to on the third cup of coffee of any one day, if even then.

So it took someone like Gene Kremin, radio operator friend of Gean Clapper who, after a long search, found reference to the crash site in 1997. He located the original 1992 teletype message from the JTF-FA printed in the Congressional Record. He contacted me and then the word went out to the retired Combat Talon community.

Missing in Action Status Change

I spoke with several staffers at the personnel center about the four different dates for the changes from missing in action to killed in action. They all assured me that the air force followed prescribed protocol for changing the status of MIAs and that the same was done in these cases. Each individual's status was evaluated separately, and several factors could have influenced the process. Cited examples were interventions by the families and congressmen who pressed for more expedient resolutions because the change of status from MIA to KIA had both desirable and undesirable consequences for beneficiaries. Changes affected the pay status as well as the desires of some wives who planned to remarry without going through with divorce proceedings. Obviously, I did not want to get involved in these details. Besides that, after meeting the families at the memorial dedication, I learned that they were satisfied with the official contacts and communications they had with the air force agencies.

Then, just when I decided to leave this matter alone, I received an invitation to review a book by Michael J. Allen: *Until the Last Man Comes Home: POWs, MIAs, and the Unending Vietnam War*. This detailed, well-researched, and well-documented book informed me about the unusual and difficult situations families of MIAs had to face. There were several legislative provisions that affected the status changes, and the families that lobbied for these legislative measures were in conflict with one another.[7] Families with MIA sons and daughters had simpler situations. Once their offspring's status changed from MIA to KIA, the promotions and pay stopped and there was only the insurance with clear-cut beneficiaries. The only complications were caused by some parents who had divorced after the date of their child's loss. Husbands and fathers were a different thing. Advantages favored retention of the MIA status because of pay and benefits for dependent children. Ages of children became a factor. Adopted children and multiple marriages also complicated claims. There were also differences between the laws of different states. Military families moved from one state to another and acquired property here and there. In states with community property laws wives could not divest themselves of joint property. Selling anything would be a problem. A wife could not legally sell a jointly owned car.

I reestablished communications with Ms. Patricia Claxton, wife of my friend Charlie, after I began writing this book. She provided me with many documents that were beneficial to my research. Letters on change in crew member status from missing in action to killed in action clarified the official process and confirmed that three crew members were evaluated apart from the rest of the crew in responses to the actions their families initiated.

The director of the Office of the Air Force Military Personnel was responsible for the annual review of missing in action airmen and for informing the families of any changes in their status. Two paragraphs of the letter from his office to the Department of the Air Force Personnel testify to this review process. The first paragraph lists their names, service numbers, and ranks at the time of their aircraft loss. The other paragraphs are as follows:

> 2. Circumstances: The above listed personnel comprised the crew of a C-130 aircraft which departed Nha Trang Air Base, Republic of Vietnam, at 0030 hours, 29 December 1967, on a classified mission over North Vietnam. The mission progressed as planned and a radio report was received at 0430 hours. This was the last known contact established. At that time the aircraft's position was approximately 13 miles northeast of Lai Chau, North Vietnam, over a mountainous and densely forested area. When the aircraft failed to return to base as scheduled, an organized search was immediately initiated. Weather conditions severely hampered the search; however, an electronic

> search was conducted over the intended flight path, to no avail. Over the next two weeks an electronic search and three photographic reconnaissance missions were performed with negative results. Organized search was terminated on 29 January 1968 when a visual search scheduled for that day was cancelled. To date no additional information has been received pertaining to the missing aircraft or any of the personnel on board.
>
> 3. Discussion: Careful evaluation of the information of record compels the conclusion that a reasonable possibility exists for the continued survival of the personnel listed in paragraph one. This conclusion is supported by the fact that there were no witnesses to this incident and that definite proof is lacking as to just what befell the crew when their aircraft was lost. In the absence of information to the contrary, it is possible that favorable circumstances prevailed whereby they were able to successfully bail out of the aircraft or survive a crash landing and were subsequently captured by the enemy. The absence of a report establishing their status as prisoners is no indication that such is not the case since the North Vietnamese and their agencies reject any obligations under the Geneva Convention to report the names of personnel in their custody. Until new evidence is produced or other events occur which overcome this possibility, it is reasonable to assume that they may still be alive and any change in their status on this date may be premature and beyond the safe calculated risk of error.[8]

This 3 December 1968 letter provided the families with more information about the flight of the aircraft than any member of the detachment was authorized to give them. We could not even say at that time (one year later), that they flew over North Vietnam. The third paragraph gave a good explanation for the periodic evaluation of the missing in action status.

Annual review of the crew's missing in action continued until 30 March 1978 when the personnel office at Randolph AFB recommended to the personnel office of the secretary of the air force that the status should be changed to killed in action. This time the first paragraph lists only eight crew members with the ranks to which they had been promoted while missing in action. Consequently, Osborne went from captain to lieutenant colonel, Claxton from major to colonel, Fisher from lieutenant colonel to colonel, Parker from captain to major, Clapper from staff sergeant to chief master sergeant, Darcy from staff sergeant to master sergeant, Eckley from staff sergeant to chief master sergeant, and McCrary from technical sergeant to chief master sergeant. The second paragraph is specific:

> 2. Discussion: The review and reconsideration of all the facts and circumstances (summarized and attached hereto) resulted in determination that it is not possible to conclusively establish the members' ultimate fate. However, the likelihood that they are still alive may no longer reasonably be considered since they have not been repatriated, sufficient time has elapsed during which it is believed some word could have been received if they had survived, and they cannot otherwise be accounted for. Accordingly, with respect to the above and in the absence of any information to support a presumption of their continued survival, it is concluded that they may now no longer reasonably be presumed to be alive.[9]

A staff summary sheet from Randolph AFB personnel office with acronym DPMC whose subject is "Proposed Change of Status of Lt. Col. Edwin N. Osborne, Jr. and Seven Crew Members" sheds some light on the three crew members who were not included in that office's 30 March letter.

> 3. The attached letter which constitutes a proposed change of status from missing in action to killed in action on Lt Col Edwin N. Osborne, Col Charles P. Claxton, Col Donald E. Fisher, Maj Frank C. Parker, III, CMSgt Gean P. Clapper, CMSgt Edward J. Darcy, CMSgt Wayne A. Eckley, and CMSgt Jack McCrary is forwarded for review by the Secretary prior to any announcement. The status of the remaining crew members is: CMSgt Williams, KIA (555), 24 Jun 77 and Lt Col VanBuren, KIA (555), 29 Aug 77. Lt Col Wenaas remains MIA and his status will be reviewed by separate action.[10]

Note that Captains Van Buren and Wenaas were promoted to lieutenant colonels and Sergeant Williams to chief master sergeant during their time in MIA status.

The secretary of the air force accepted the recommendation of the status review, and on 27 April 1978 the deputy assistant for Military Personnel changed the status of eight crew members to killed in action by these words: "the date deaths are presumed to have occurred is the date I have signed this action." This status review letter also added that: "Deaths are held to have occurred while the members, except Colonel Fisher, were in a pay, flying pay, and duty status. Colonel Fisher was in a pay and duty status."[11]

There came a time in the 1970s when colonels could no longer receive flight pay even though they were still on flying status. Colonel Fisher reached this stage when he attained that rank while he was carried on the air force rolls as missing in action. This shows how closely the personnel office followed the evolution of careers for those who were classified as MIAs. One other detail regarding pay of missing in action and prisoners of war personnel was followed. There was a Uniformed Services Savings Deposit Program (USSDP) for soldiers serving in Vietnam. Qualified soldiers could designate a percentage of their monthly pay to go into this savings account, which guaranteed a 10 percent annual interest rate. These designated amounts continued to be invested with a 10 percent interest accumulation as long as the individual was in a POW or MIA status.[12]

Communication with the Families

The families were satisfied with the way the air force communicated with them concerning the status of their loved ones. Staffs in various personnel offices that maintained contact with the families were well trained in handling grieving people who were anxiously awaiting new information on the tragedy and the efforts to locate the missing aircraft and bringing the remains of their loved ones back home. As time went by, they understood the difficult process better and appreciated all timely contacts that they had with the personnel staffers.

Initial contact with the families was quick and appropriate. All wives received surprise visits from a pair of air force officers from nearby air force facilities who notified them about the aircraft loss and offered any immediate assistance the families needed. This was followed by letters from the detachment commander, Lt. Col. Dow Rogers, and the 14th Special Operations Wing commander, Col. John M. Patton, with each expressing condolences and promises of continued search for the missing aircraft. Then came the communications from the summary court officers who processed and shipped personal possessions of the missing crew members to their wives. All wives were disappointed with the information they received from these men, who were obviously the closest to their loved ones at the time of loss. Even though they understood that those who wrote the letters were not free to divulge the secret nature of their wartime work, they wanted to know more about what they were doing that night. They wanted to appreciate the sacrifice their men made in the service of their country. Their friends and neighbors at home wanted to know what happened to their husbands. All they were told by us was that the C-130 aircraft was lost somewhere in Vietnam on the early morning of 29 December 1967. It was difficult not to learn the details until thirty-one years later, at the 1998 memorial dedication ceremony at Hurlburt Field in Florida. Many older family members had passed away during that time, and the children who had grown up not knowing how their fathers had perished had grown children of their own. I am still distraught because so many family members had died before they learned about what happened to their loved ones on the S-01 crew.

The air force was good about contacting the wives of the missing crew. Don Fisher's wife and three children joined him on his R&R (rest and recuperation) one-week visit to Hawaii. The family stayed with Don's niece's family, whose husband was based in Hawaii in the air force. Before Ann Fisher and the children left Hawaii, an air force chaplain accompanied by another officer showed up at the Fisher home in Abilene, Texas. There they met Ann's mother, who was taking care of the home during the family's visit to Hawaii. She gave them the address where the family could be reached in Hawaii. After that, three air force officers, one of them a nurse, presented themselves to Ann and her children in Hawaii with the sad news about her husband Don, who had been with them just three days before.[13]

Patricia C. Claxton received a personal visit from the base commander at the Kincheloe Air Force Base in Michigan. Because Charlie was on my S-05 crew, she assumed that our whole crew was involved in this loss.[14] She kept calling my wife in Bryan, Texas, to find out what she had learned about the tragedy, but my wife could not be reached. She and our children were spending Christmas with her family in the Rio Grande Valley. She did not return home until after New Year 1968, and that is when she learned about the aircraft loss. Believing that I flew with Charlie, she called my former boss, Col. Vernon Head, at the Texas A&M AFROTC Detachment, with what she had just learned. He called the appropriate personnel office at Randolph AFB immediately and learned that my name was not on the missing crew. He then related the good news to my distraught wife. My wife and I exchanged tape-recorded messages every day during my tour in Vietnam, and she found my last taped letter in the mail that had accumulated during the holidays. She heard me tell her about the aircraft we lost and that Charlie flew as a substitute pilot with another crew.

Thereafter, the previous offices of the Air Force Military Personnel branch at Randolph AFB assumed contact with the families and maintained it until the internment of the remains at Arlington National Cemetery. For a long time, these contacts were reduced to communications concerning the review of the status of missing in action of individuals. There was nothing to report about the crash site. All other correspondence with the air force concerning pay, promotions in rank, and benefits were properly processed through the various offices. Change from MIA to KIA status of the crew generated new correspondence contacts dealing with survival benefits and other financial matters that affected the widows and children of the families.

The location of the crash site in 1992 was promptly reported to the families. The air force personnel office contacted the wives by phone as soon as the Joint Task Force—Final Accounting released the report of the survey, which provided the location and positive identification of the crash site as being that of the C-130 missing since 29 December 1967. Ms. Pat Claxton received a follow-on letter on 3 February 1993 with an attached copy of "Detailed Report of Survey" from the 230220Z Nov 92 teletype message. The letter was short, but it assured her that they would keep her informed about future developments.

> Dear Mrs. Claxton
>
> The attached report which we received from the Joint Task Force—Full Accounting (JTF-FA), is forwarded for your information. This information which was correlated to your husband, Colonel Charles P. Claxton, was previously provided during your telephone conversation with Mr. George Atkinson.
>
> We are furnishing this material in keeping with our policy of providing everything we receive which may relate to your husband.
>
> If you have any questions concerning this report please call us on toll free telephone line (800-XXX-XXXX).[15]

All families received similar letters and remained in the prescribed communication loop. I conclude that the military members and civilians from the Air Force Personnel Center offices maintained proper and professional contact with the families of S-01 crew members. Their entire focus was directed toward the families. I found no evidence for their obligation to locate and communicate with organizations to which the crew members were assigned at the time of their loss. However, they had an obligation to respond to inquiries from organizations or persons seeking information about ongoing cases under their care.

Conclusion

In conclusion, Detachment 1, based in Bangkok, Thailand, responded to the crash site alert and submitted a detailed report of its site survey to the headquarters of Joint Task Force—Final Accounting in Hawaii on 23 November 1992. This teletype message was also sent as an information message to a host of agencies, none of which were tasked to follow up on that report. The JTF-FA then sent the same message as an attachment to a letter to the Air Force Military Personnel Center, Attention DPMCB, on 3 December 1992. The letter stated that the enclosed information was "provided for release to the next of kin." Thereafter, this office, which was responsible for air force missing persons and its acronym successors, took up the task of communicating with the wives and families of the missing crew members. They stayed with this until the men were buried at Arlington National Cemetery and the postmortem legal affairs were completed. The only shortcoming in the long-drawn-out communication with the families was the lack of information available on what the men were doing when they died. Unfortunately, many of their parents and older relatives passed away before they learned the story about their last mission.

All Americans should be proud of the way the US government persists in identifying and returning the remains of fallen soldiers. We have lost so many in so many foreign lands. Many now rest in cemeteries in countries where they died. We did not always have the means to bring them home. But today's means of transportation and technology allow us to recover and identify them better than in the past, and we are not sparing the cost. We have dedicated people conducting recoveries and identification of remains whose scale cannot be matched by any other country. My long quest taught me that and I am proud that I was associated with both the military and civilians who serve this country.

Epilogue

Memorial Air Park

Hurlburt Field is part of the vast Eglin Air Force Base complex located in the Florida Panhandle. It is the home of the AFSOC. In many neighboring towns hundreds of retired special operations veterans and their families have made their homes. Several prominent retirees who flew in a variety of special operations aircraft got together with the 16th SOW's active duty officials to secure a piece of land at the entrance to Hurlburt Field where they could display decommissioned aircraft and erect memorials to those who died in various special operations. This well-conceived idea received enthusiastic support and resulted in the establishment of the Memorial Air Park. It is now home to a growing number of decommissioned special

Hurlburt Field Memorial Air Park (1st SOW photo)

operations aircraft that were preserved and are now well cared for by the host wing and the surrounding community of loyal retirees.

The main organization involved in the maintenance of the park is the Air Commando Association (ACA). Its membership includes airmen from all special operations aircraft and campaigns dating back to 1943. The exploits back then of the 1st Air Commandos and their legendary leader, Col. Phil "Flip" Cochran, who was portrayed as heroic "Flip" Corkin, appeared in the comic strip "Terry and the Pirates." ACA has a small museum and a growing Hall of Fame for those who had died in combat or distinguished themselves while serving in various special operations units. Its members hold well-attended annual reunions in October in Fort Walton Beach. Many Air Commandos hold memberships in other smaller organizations for specific aircraft or special operations units. They hold their less frequent reunions at the same time as their umbrella Air Commando Association. Two of these are Combat Talon organizations that are also based at Fort Walton Beach. They are the Stray Goose International (SGI) and the 7th Special Operations Squadron/Air Commando Squadron Society (7th SOS/ACS).

Stray Goose International

Stray Goose International was conceived in 1993 by six early commanders of Combat Spear squadrons. They were Cols. Bob Pinard (1971–75), Ray Turczynski (1979–81), Lee Hess (1983–85), Terry Jahnke (1985–87), T. J. Doherty (1987–89), and Terry Silvester (1989–90). They succeeded in bringing together those who served in the Pacific in the unit that changed names and parent wings as it moved from CCK in Taiwan to Nha Trang in Vietnam, then to Cam Ranh Bay in Vietnam, then to Kadena, Okinawa, then to Clark AB in the Philippines, and then back again to Kadena, Okinawa. Its regular membership is restricted to those who served in that Pacific-based Combat Spear unit.

Patches for the Air Commando Association, Stray Goose International, and the 7th Air Commando Squadron / 7th Special Operations Squadron Society. (Composite photo by John Gargus)

The SGI is one of the leading groups supporting the Memorial Air Park. Its members were responsible for organizing the 1998 memorial dedication to the S-01 crew and then for ensuring a big turnout for the funeral at Arlington National Cemetery on 15 November 2000. The SGI deserves much credit for bringing together Combat Talon airmen and preserving the original Stray Goose name, which applied exclusively to the first crews that deployed to Vietnam. The Stray Goose name was retained by the follow-on Combat Spear crews even after the Combat Talon name superseded it.

The Stray Goose name did not catch on in the 7th Air Commando Squadron in Europe even though the first Combat Talon crews that deployed to Ramstein Air Base in 1968 were the Stray Goose veterans from Vietnam. Perhaps it was because that squadron was already well established and flew C-47s, C-123s, U-10s, and UH-1Ns. New Combat Arrow MC-130Es became its newest aircraft and the old-timers did not highlight project aircraft nicknames for their other birds.

7th SOS/ACS Society

The 7th Special Operations Squadron / Air Commando Squadron Society (SOS/ACS) was organized in 1997 at the first reunion of the unit's veterans from the days when they served in Germany. The organizational effort was spearheaded by Lt. Col. Max Friedauer, who kept the organization running to 2015. Its members include those who flew in OV-10s, UH-1Ns, C-47s, and C-123s before the Combat Arrow Talons came to Germany in 1967. Likewise, the organization is open to combat controller, maintenance, and intelligence personnel who have been supporting the Combat Talons. Consequently, anyone who had served with Combat Talons can qualify for membership either in the Stray Goose International or the 7th SOS/ACS Society.

Memorial Park Monuments

Visitors to the park are greeted at the entrance by three wall monuments commemorating the 1st Air Commandos of World War II. The one on the left is a memorial to the 1st Air Commando Group, listing their names. The center one is engraved with the history of the Air Commando Force. The monument on the right describes the 1st Air Commando Group's heritage. The wall monuments give the visitors insight into the early history of the air commandos. Engraved words are carefully crafted and are worth the plain book print that follows their photographs.

Three memorial walls at the entrance to the Memorial Air Park pay tribute to the 1st Air Commandos. (Photo by John Gargus)

1ST AIR COMMANDO FORCE

AT THE QUEBEC CONFERENCE IN AUGUST 1943, PRESIDENT ROOSEVELT AGREED TO PRIME MINISTER CHURCHILL'S REQUEST FOR US AIR SUPPORT OF THE BRITISH "CHINDITS," COMMANDED BY GENERAL ORDE WINGATE.

GENERAL H. H. ARNOLD SEIZED ON THIS OPPORTUNITY TO USE THE FLEXIBILITY OF AIR POWER TO FULLY SUPPORT GROUND COMBAT OPERATIONS. RECRUITING OF A 528-MAN ALL-VOLUNTEER FORCE BEGAN IN SEPTEMBER, 1943, AND BY DECEMBER 1943, MEN AND EQUIPMENT WERE IN PLACE IN INDIA AND EARLY OPERATION BEGAN.

ON MARCH 5, 1944, "OPERATION THURSDAY" WAS LAUNCHED. BRITISH "CHINDITS" WERE GLIDER-BORNE AT NIGHT TO A FIELD 150 MILES BEHIND JAPANESE LINES IN BURMA. A DIRT STRIP WAS CARVED OUT THE NEXT DAY, AND WITHIN A WEEK 12,000 ADDITIONAL TROOPS, 1300 MULES AND TONS OF EQUIPMENT AND SUPPLIES WERE AIRLIFTED INTO "BROADWAY."

L-1 AND L-5 LIGHT PLANES, GLIDERS, AND A YR-4 HELICOPTER EVACUATED THE SICK AND WOUNDED. C-47S AND UC-64'S MADE RESUPPLY FLIGHTS.

P-51'S, AND B-25'S FURNISHED AIR COVER, CLOSE AIR SUPPORT AND INTERDICTION OF TARGETS.

AFTER MAY, 1944, THE REDESIGNATED GROUPS' EFFORTS WERE THEN DIRECTED TO THE SUPPORT OF THE BRITISH 14TH ARMY IN ITS VICTORIOUS DRIVE TO RANGOON. ADDITIONAL PERSONNEL WERE ASSIGNED TO THE GROUP. P-47'S REPLACED THE P-51'S AND OPERATIONS CONTINUED WITH THE SAME ESPRIT DE CORPS.

THE FAR SIGHTED STRATEGY OF GENERAL ARNOLD, THE IMAGINATIVE LEADERSHIP OF COLONELS PHILLIP COCHRAN AND JOHN ALISON, TOGETHER WITH THE BRAVERY OF THE 1ST COMMANDOS PLAYED A SIGNIFICANT ROLE IN THE DEFEAT OF THE JAPANESE IN BURMA.

TODAY SPECIAL OPERATIONS AIR COMMANDOS CONTINUE THIS TRADITION OF DEDICATED SERVICE IN MISSIONS AROUND THE WORLD.

1ST AIR COMMANDO GROUP
HERITAGE

THE NAME AIR COMMANDO WAS CHOSEN BY GENERAL H. H. ARNOLD AS A TRIBUTE TO ADMIRAL LOUIS MOUNTBATTEN WHO FORMED AND TRAINED THE FIRST BRITISH COMMANDOS. MOUNTBATTEN WAS SUPREME ALLIED COMMANDER FOR SOUTHEAST ASIA.

AIR COMMANDO MOTTO

DURING NIGHT TRAINING A GLIDER CRASHED KILLING BRITISH CHINDITS. THERE WAS GREAT CONCERN THIS WOULD LOWER MORALE OF THE VINTAGE TROOPS ASSIGNED TO THE GLIDER OPERATIONS. A WRITTEN MESSAGE WAS RECEIVED FROM THE BRITISH COMMANDER ADVISING:

> PLEASE BE ASSURED THAT WE WILL GO WITH YOUR BOYS,
> ANY PLACE, ANY TIME, ANY WHERE.

THIS PHRASE WAS ADOPTED AS A MOTTO FOR THE 1ST AIR COMMANDO GROUP. IT IS STILL USED IN AN ABBREVIATED FORM BY SPECIAL OPERATIONS COMMAND OF THE US AIR FORCE.

THE CHINDITS

THE CHINDITS WERE HIGHLY TRAINED JUNGLE FIGHTERS WHO WERE ORGANIZED AS A REINFORCED DIVISION. THEIR MISSION WAS TO INFILTRATE BEHIND THE JAPANESE AND DISRUPT COMMUNICATIONS AND

SUPPLY LINES. CHINDITS WAS A VARIATION OF "CHINTHE" THE MYTHICAL FIGURE THAT GUARDS BURMESE TEMPLES. IT WAS THE HIGH CASUALTY RATES OF THE CHINDITS THAT PRECIPITATED THE REQUEST FOR HELP FROM THE UNITED STATES IN EVACUATION OF WOUNDED.

Combat Talon and Stray Goose Brass Plates

Equally fitting and full of historical content are the pedestal-mounted brass plates that tell the story of the Combat Talons.

> Combat Talons were first used in Southeast Asia in 1966 when four aircraft deployed from Pope AFB under Project Stray Goose. In 1967 the program suffered its only combat loss when a plane crashed in hostile territory. During the 1970 Son Tay mission to rescue American prisoners of war from a North Vietnamese camp, two Combat Talons led an assault force into heavily defended enemy territory. A decade later, MC-130Es would once again play a pivotal role by leading a rescue attempt of American citizens held hostage in Iran. On 24 April 1980, the Talons flew into the rendezvous site known as Desert One to deliver resources and personnel for the daring assault. Although the mission was aborted and eight US Airmen and Marines perished, Operation Eagle Claw became the catalyst for far reaching changes in the special operations community and the creation of

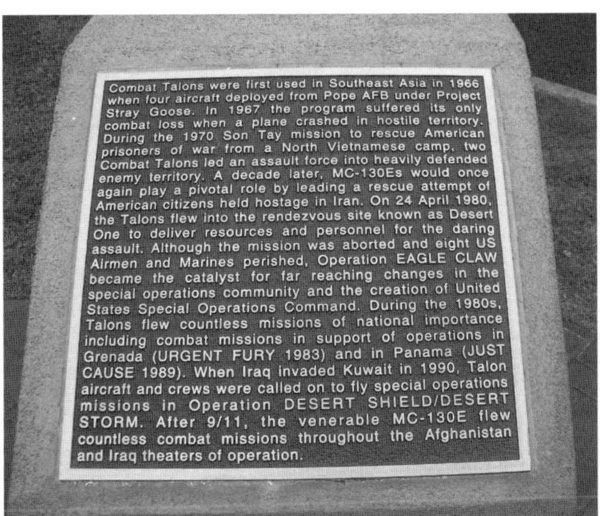

This pedestal-mounted brass plaque gives a short history of the first Combat Talons (Combat Talons Is), which included the first ones known as Stray Goose. It features the aircraft #64–0567 that is on display. (Photo by John Gargus)

the United States Special Operations Command. During the 1980s, Talons flew countless missions in support of operations in Granada (Urgent Fury 1983) and in Panama (Just Cause 1989). When Iraq invaded Kuwait in 1990, Talon aircraft and crews were called on to fly special operations missions in Operation Desert Shield/Desert Storm. After 9/11, the venerable MC-130E flew countless combat missions throughout the Afghanistan and Iraq theaters of operation.

The MC-130E Combat Talon I is a specially modified Lockheed C-130E Hercules designed to provide a unique airpower capability for United States Special Operations Forces. From its origin in 1965, The Combat Talon I performed infiltration, exfiltration, resupply, aerial and ground refueling, and Fulton surface to air recovery missions supporting our nation's most sensitive and demanding missions. A total of eighteen Talons were fielded through the Air Force Big Safari program, and at the peak of the program fourteen of these extremely capable and versatile aircraft were in service throughout the major theaters of operation. Remarkably, only 4 have been lost to hostilities or accidents despite the complex and high risk Talon mission. Early MC-130Es were camouflaged with black and green paint scheme, and were commonly referred to as "Blackbirds." During the forty five year plus life span, the configuration of the Combat Talon evolved to remain in step with emerging technology and challenges of changing enemy threats. At the heart of this unique aircraft is a terrain following radar, forward looking infrared system, and sophisticated electronic counter measure equipment. Over the years,

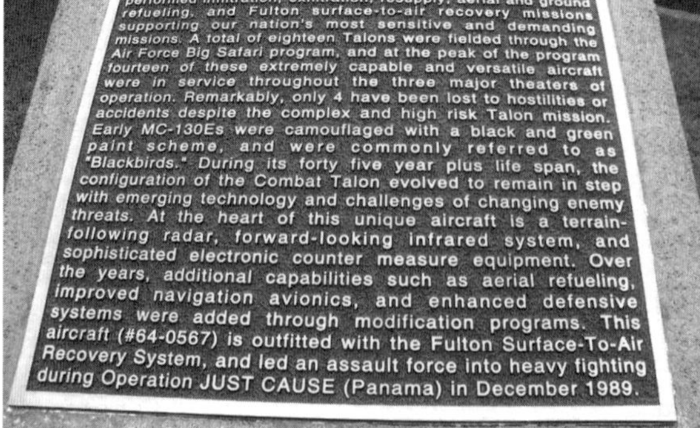

This pedestal-mounted brass plaque gives a short history of the Combat Talon fleet. (Photo by John Gargus)

Note the two pedestals on the left. They hold the brass plaques with the history of the Combat Talons. (Photo by John Gargus)

> additional capabilities such as aerial refueling, improved navigation avionics, and enhanced defensive systems were added through modification programs. This aircraft (#64–0567) is outfitted with the Fulton Surface-To-Air Recovery System, and led an assault force into heavy fighting during Operation Just Cause (Panama) in December 1989.

The Air Commandos are proud of their history and achievements. They recall their memorable missions and past camaraderie at their reunions and honor those who pass away by a somber ceremony at the Memorial Park at the conclusion of each annual reunion. Combat Talon veterans gather at the memorial pedestals dedicated to the lost crews after the memorial ceremony before they disperse and head for home. There are three individual memorials dedicated to lost crews. Two are plaque-mounted pedestals to the S-01 crew of MC-130E #64–0547 from Vietnam and to the crew of MC-130E #64–0564 from the Philippines. The third one is not a pedestal and is located at the Hurlburt chapel. It commemorates Combat Talon crew members lost on the EC-130E during the Iranian rescue operation known as Eagle Claw.

The always supporting Combat Talon community rose to the occasion once again on 24 April 2015 (on the thirty-fifth anniversary of Operation Eagle Claw) when they installed an impressive polished granite stone Combat Talon memorial. It is located in front of the displayed MC-130E - #64–0567. The memorial's front face shows four modifications of Combat Talons with colored patches of units that had flown them. The back face

New Combat Talon memorial stone installed on 24 April 2015. (Photo by Richard Hovan)

of this stone lists the aircraft and crews that were lost to date. There is empty space for any future losses that will be added should they occur.

Stray Goose Poetry

Two Air Commandos, who are no longer with us, left us poems to remember the early Stray Goose times. They are Tom Hines and Joe Sheldon. Tom was a pilot who eventually commanded the 15th SOS at Nha Trang, and Joe was an electronic technician.

Tom Hines was the operations officer at the time we lost the S-01 crew. He was greatly affected by that tragic event. He composed a Stray Goose song after the mortar attack on 25 November when we lost #64–0563 and sustained damage to the other three aircraft. He had high hopes that it would become the song we would sing at the bar, especially on those occasions when we had night combat missions and the Stray Goose painting on the wall had been flipped upside down. Tom was a banjo player with a good singing voice. I heard him practice this song in his room and then saw him perform it only once in the rooftop bar with only a few officers present. As far as I know, he never played it again after we lost the S-01 crew on 29 December 1967. It should be sung to the tune of the Blue Tail Fly.

Tom Hines was troubled by the loss of the crew for the rest of his life. He encouraged me to write the S-01 story and maintained interest

Come gather round me comrades true
A tale I must relate to you
About a bunch of fighting guys
That say: "The Goose she flies."

Give me my chute and I don't care—
Give me my chute and I don't care—
Give me my chute and I don't care
The goose she flies tonight.

The crew chief works both day and night
To keep aloft this mystic knight
The heat and mosquitos he defies
Listen—"The Goose she flies."
REFRAIN
The mortars hit! And then go off
Delta is done—her ghost aloft
Isn't this a hell of a way to die
Heaven protect the Goose that flies
REFRAIN

The night is dark the weather low
The Big Chief says: the mission goes
We launch with pride—heads held high
Listen men, "The Goose she flies."
REFRAIN
The missiles launch the flak's there too
The Goose shudders—but she's true blue
The crew they pray—their hopes still high
See! The Goose still flies
REFRAIN
The sun comes up—the sea is blue
The nest in sight—yes it's true
Let's drink a toast to those that fly!
Our blessings on—the Goose that flies

Give me my chute and I don't care—
Give me my chute and I don't care—
Give me my chute and I don't care
The goose she flies tonight

in everything I was gathering about that unfortunate accident. After he retired as a colonel and settled in College Station, Texas, he fell victim to a rare type of muscular dystrophy that kept him confined to his house and prevented him from attending military reunions. Since I lived in nearby Austin I visited him frequently, especially after attending various reunions to share the stories and well wishes from those who knew him.

We always talked about the events leading up to the loss of the crew. In so many ways, he kept expressing his responsibility for the men who were lost. He had good reasons to skip the S-01 crew and assign this mission to the next crew in line, but he opted otherwise, even though it required replacing the aircraft commander and two loadmasters. At first, he was tempted to fly on that mission as the third pilot with the copilot Ed Osborne moving up to the aircraft commander's position. After all, he had a policy to fly at least one combat mission with each one of the six crews. However, he did not feel right to be on the flight deck looking over Osborne's shoulder while he flew on his first mission as an aircraft commander. There would have been no problems getting volunteers to fill the third pilot's slot, but he decided that Charlie Claxton, third pilot from my S-05 crew, who did not fly on our combat mission in November, should make up that missed flight. Later I learned from Pat Watson, who had flown in Charlie's slot on that November night, that he was willing to go in Charlie's place again. This might have tempted Charlie, but he had already committed himself to Hines, who had picked him to fly with the S-01 crew. Because this subject came up between me and Hines so many times, I could tell that he was troubled by the decision he had made as the man in charge of our flight operations.

I provided Hines with videotape copies of the Hurlburt memorial service for the S-01 crew and of the funeral at Arlington. I don't know how many times he had viewed them, but we watched the funeral video together on my last visit to him before he passed away.

Retired MSgt. Joe Sheldon, who retired after twenty-five years of service as an electronics technician and who maintained our highly classified electronic warfare equipment, was moved by the memorial ceremony for the crew that had taken place at Hurlburt Field Memorial Park in 1998 to write a tribute poem to the eleven men we lost. It is appropriate to publish it here:

On Christmas Day of '67,
Planning had begun,
Where to go and what to do,
For Stray Goose S-01.
Mission routes were plotted,
And the weather would be fine.
For a takeoff after midnight,
On December 29.

They were warriors, they were brothers,
They were heroes of the war.
And they flew the Combat Talon,
Where no plane had gone before.
And what happened on that fateful night,
Oh so long ago.
Only they and only God,
Will ever know.

The Aircraft, 547,
On the runway at Nha Trang
Midnight skies awaited,
The arrival of the plane
Turbos came to power,
And the four props took the bite,
Then Lockheed's mighty Hercules
Leaped into the night.

They were tasked to fly a leaflet drop,
And then a re-supply,
Just Southwest of Hanoi,
What a scary place to fly.
The first half of the mission,
Was successful so 'tis said,
It's the second half,
That we've come to dread.

The Talon made their TOT,
And everything was fine.
RO called "OPS NORMAL,"
0430 was the time.
Before they made their second drop,
Their "bogus" re-supply,
The Ops Normal the RO called,
Would be their last reply.

When morning's sun came to Nha Trang,
No S-01 was there.
It wasn't long before our Photo Recon,
Took to air.
They searched the route for days on end,
It's sad but it is true.
The Talon's final resting place,
Stayed hid till '92.

When '97 rolled around,
The truth was brought to light.
The mission was declassified,
And what took place that night.
By eleven unsung heroes,
In a Talon far away,
Who gave their lives for freedom,
Such a heavy price to pay.

Now 30 years had come and gone,
Since S-01 went down.
We did not forget our friends,
We're glad that they were found.
We've lost 11 warriors,
But their memories guide us through.
The special ways of Special Ops,
And special things we do.

Appendix A

The Last Mission of Combat Talon's S-01 Crew

Colonel John Gargus, USAF (Ret.)

This is the story of one Combat Talon MC-130E that was lost with its eleven crew members on December 29, 1967, while conducting a TOP SECRET mission over North Vietnam. After many years of silence, Maj. John Plaster authored a book, *SOG: The Secret Wars of America's Commandos in Vietnam*, in which he described the exploits of commandos who lost their lives on missions that had not been brought to public attention for numerous security reasons. The loss of this aircraft fits into that mold. It was, according to Major Plaster, our largest single aircraft loss over North Vietnam. I hope this story honors the eleven lost crew members and acknowledges the role of all men who served in the Combat Talon unit, which was first named Detachment 1 of the 314th Tactical Airlift Wing, then the 15th Air Commando Squadron and finally the 90th Special Operations Squadron.[1]

At the time of this incident, Det. 1, 314 TAW was based at Nha Trang Air Base, Republic of Vietnam (RVN), with six eleven-member crews and four MC-130E Combat Talon I aircraft. I was a member on one of these crews. These aircraft were equipped with terrain following radar, Fulton Recovery System, and an array of passive electronic countermeasures. The planes were painted with special dark green paint that significantly reduced their reflected radar energy, and, because of their overall appearance, they were affectionately called the "Blackbirds." They provided Military Assistance Command, Vietnam–Studies and Observations Group (MACV-SOG) with dedicated airlift during daytime and conducted highly classified, clandestine missions at night. These night missions were called "combat missions" even though it was never the intent to engage in what would certainly be a one-sided battle with the enemy. The only arms we carried were the survival .38 caliber pistols. We relied on our low level terrain following capability, the element of surprise, and experienced airmanship to fly wherever tasked over North Vietnam.

The "combat missions" were generated at MACV-SOG headquarters in Saigon. They ranged from quite ordinary to some bizarre airdrop operations. We would drop teams of infiltrators behind enemy lines and then resupply them periodically. At times we would drop specially rigged personnel parachutes without infiltrators and imaginatively assembled resupply loads to convince the enemy that we had teams operating in this or that area. Sometimes the air-dropped loads were rigged to fall apart in the air or were booby trapped for the North Vietnamese Army (NVA) soldiers on the ground. And, of course, there were psychological operations consisting of high altitude leaflet drops and low altitude drops of pretuned radios or gift packages to fishermen in the Gulf of Tonkin. This was interesting and rewarding work. It made us feel that we were making a significant contribution to the overall war effort by creating considerable confusion inside the enemy's own territory.

To be effective in these clandestine air operations, we had to maintain a low profile and avoid shoptalk with airmen of other units. The geographical separation from SOG headquarters in Saigon helped us in not being visibly tied to their operations. Only a few of us, key command officials and mission planners, were able to visit SOG headquarters. There, our points of contact told us only that operational data which we needed to know. We understood the need for this arrangement and loyally carried out our role as dedicated airlifters.

As we acquired more experience in performing our assigned tasks, we became aware that there were problems with some of the teams we supported in the North. We had to make some peculiar drops with very specific instructions and, at times, execute them under the supervision of tight-lipped SOG jumpmasters who were assigned to fly with us on some missions. This led us to believe that we were dealing with probable double agents and some questionable characters. As mission planners, we did not share these concerns with our crews, but some details had to be disclosed when astonished loadmasters reported to the cockpit that our SOG jumpmasters halted the paradrop after the first man went out and that they made the rest of the team sit down without offering any explanations. Then after landing, just as the aircraft came to a halt in its parking area, a van would appear and the remaining jumpers would smartly pile into it without any comments to the crew. Events like that and cargo loads that were purposely rigged to foul up or break up upon hitting the air stream had to be explained to the crew involved.

Because the success of the missions depended on secrecy, we were naturally apprehensive about dealing with complete strangers who would not speak to us. In time, we learned that some of the teams were compromised and feared that our aircraft may become an easy target to be brought down over a drop zone. In mission planning, we dreaded the possibility that one day we could be directed to recover a questionable agent or a package from North Vietnam using the Fulton Recovery System. We were known to the enemy for delivering booby-trapped resupply bundles. A recovery of an agent, or a package, would be an opportune time for them to return the favor and bring down a Blackbird.

There was also considerable internal secrecy in our work. Crews were not allowed to discuss their combat missions with other crews. Locations of drop zones and types of delivery payloads could not be shared with others. One could not be exposed to too many details of the clandestine operations. There was always a possibility of being forced down and captured behind enemy lines. For this reason, Major Thompson, a C-130 navigator, who was not a Combat Talon qualified crew member, was assigned to our unit as a mission planner. As such, he knew about the locations of infiltrated teams and about the type of airdrops we were conducting. He did not have a crew position and was not allowed to fly "combat missions." This arrangement lasted only for the duration of his one-year tour. It also gave me, Maj. John Gargus, navigator, and 1st Lt. John Lewis, electronic warfare officer (EWO), both from the S-05 crew, the opportunity to succeed him when he rotated to his next duty station. By that time, it no longer mattered that two crew members from the same crew would become his replacements and that they continued to fly combat missions. We began our on-the-job training by helping Thompson to plan this fateful mission. Roy Thompson, who retired as a colonel, agreed to collaborate on putting this story together. Unfortunately, his contribution was lost forever. He passed away on July 25, 1997, before he could join me and John Lewis in sharing his memories of almost thirty years ago.

The fragmentary order for this fateful mission came from SOG on Christmas Day. Our whole detachment celebrated Christmas in the courtyard of Nha Trang's Roman Catholic Cathedral with Christian Boy and Girl Scouts and their parents. When we returned to the hotel after the festivities, Roy Thompson came by to tell me that First Flight Operations had a classified message tasking us with our next combat mission. He wanted to know if I was interested in going with him to review it. I was eager to see what it was all about, so we hopped into our jeep and drove to the Vietnamese side of the base where we shared secure mission planning and communications facilities with our sister unit, which was designated First Flight. The First Flight was another SOG air asset flying C-123s with some very interesting crew members. First Flight cargo specialists assembled all our airdrop packages, rigged all our parachutes, and even loaded the cargo for our combat missions. We were to trust their methods and procedures no matter how weird or foreign the resulting drop configurations looked to our loadmasters.

The frag order called for an unusual combat mission. It directed us to execute two airdrops deep inside North Vietnam. The first one was to be a high altitude leaflet drop on a north-northeast heading just west of the Red River and the second one a low level resupply drop on a southerly heading just west of the Black River. We positioned ourselves in front of a large-scale classified wall chart with numerous circles of various diameters and colors that depicted locations of known enemy defenses. We traced a probable inbound and outbound route with our fingers and concluded that the mission was a feasible one. The only possible threat to our aircraft would come during the "short look," the leaflet drop, when the Blackbird would be in close proximity to the Yen Bai Air Base and its MIG interceptors, or from any other Hanoi area base that had MIGs on night alert. Otherwise, everything else looked good. We would be able to lay out a flight path that would be clear of lethal ranges of all known surface to air missiles (SAMs) and anti-aircraft artillery (AAA).

With this accomplished, we returned to the Ahn Hoa Hotel to brief the detachment commander, Lt. Col. Dow Rogers, and the operations officer, Lt. Col. Tom Hines, on the forthcoming combat mission. The mission was scheduled for the night of 28 and early morning of 29 December 1967.

At Ahn Hoa, things were in a festive mood. Maj. Charlie Claxton, who had performed the role of Santa Claus, was now busy in the kitchen making sure that everything was on schedule for the big evening meal. We were hosting the American officers of First Flight and borrowed their gourmet cook to assist our own very capable Chinese kitchen staff. Capt. Gerald Van Buren, the officers open mess steward, had already done his job. He made sure that all needed kitchen supplies were either procured in the Saigon commissary, or that they were obtained from his various contacts at Special Forces operating locations. We would trade with the Special Forces outposts on almost every visit to their remote sites. We would trade San Miguel beer, obtained on our visits to Taiwan or to the Philippines, for crates of fresh vegetables grown in their neighboring Montagnard villages. Charlie Claxton was aspiring to replace Gerald Van Buren as the mess steward when Jerry completed his one-year tour in Vietnam.

That evening we had what must have been the best feast of our Vietnam tour. We all complimented our kitchen staff as well as Charlie Claxton and Gerald Van Buren for their superb performance. The rooftop bar activity that night was somewhat subdued; most of us retreated to our rooms early to make audiotapes for our families. We all owed special thanks to our wives for making the Vietnamese Christmas as good as it could have been. All the sweets, toys, and clothing for the cathedral party and gift dispensing visits to several local orphanages were sent to us by our well-organized wives. They enlisted support of their local chambers of commerce for donations of clothing, candy, and gifts and arranged with the USAF for shipment of assembled goods by opportune C-130 airlift. We were proud of them for their contribution to this civil action effort. Sorting of donated clothing became a major undertaking that took us several days to complete. We sized and sorted the clothing in the hot unventilated upstairs storage rooms of the operations building. Sgt. Jim Williams spent countless hours helping me in my capacity as the unit's civil action officer. He took charge of keeping the effort going when some other volunteers gave up because of uncomfortable heat and troublesome clothing lint and dust in the improvised Santa's workshop. It was he who recruited SSgt. Ed Darcy to help us until the clothing was finally sorted, boxed, and labeled for distribution. During the festivities in the cathedral courtyard, both of these young men displayed great enthusiasm in playing games with the scouts. We all had a great time. Christmas spirit and joy overcame all language and age barriers.

Early next morning, Roy Thompson, John Lewis, and I settled down in the secure planning room where we drew out the route and prepared master charts for the crew that was going to fly the mission. Our master charts would be used the next day by the mission crew members who would study them and customize them for their own personal use.

The entire flight would take about eight hours. It would follow the often-repeated high-level route from Nha Trang to the Skyline TACAN in Laos. There the Blackbird would descend to a terrain following altitude and fly a short zigzagging route toward the first leaflet drop area. Then, after a "short look" (rapid climb to high altitude, quick drop, and rapid descent), the aircraft would resume terrain following through the low level resupply drop and return to the Skyline TACAN. From that point the aircraft would continue back home at normal cruising altitude.

In planning the terrain following routes, we always tried to stay away from populated areas and selected prominent geographical features as radar return targets for turning points and navigational instrument updates. A unique feature of the terrain following flights was that we flew at controlled ground speeds rather than constant airspeeds. Our aircraft was equipped with the APQ-115 terrain following radar that used the aircraft's speed over the ground in its computations for maintaining desired altitude above the ground. Typically, we flew at 500 feet above the ground during daytime and at 1,000 feet at night. Flights over uneven terrain required continuous throttle adjustments to maintain the standard 230-knot ground speed (265 miles per hour). The pilots had a Doppler ground speed indicator that they monitored continuously. The pilot (left seat) had an APQ-115 screen, which in one display mode traced the terrain directly ahead of the aircraft and in another, cross scan mode, painted the terrain 20 degrees left and right of the projected ground track. The radar navigator had a third mode option for terrain mapping. This one gave him a 45-degree left and right view of the aircraft's projected track, but when the radar was in this mode, the terrain following input used by the pilot was disabled. Flying in the left seat was very strenuous. For all practical purposes it was like flying the sustained instrument landing systems (ILS). Blackbird pilots had to fly the attitude direction indicator's (ADI's) pitch bar, which received commands based on radar terrain returns and Doppler ground speed. They had to monitor their radar scope for visual terrain signals and manipulate engine throttles to maintain the desired ground speed. During daytime, well-placed cockpit windows allowed the pilot to verify approaching terrain, but on a dark night, this was impossible. One could not fix his eyes to the outside through the ever-present glare of the cockpit's amber lights and not lose focus on the instruments by which he had to fly. For that reason, it became standard practice to have the first pilot fly in the left seat and have the aircraft commander sit on the right. This was the only way he could command his eleven-member crew. He could not take time away from the instruments to focus on even a routine in-flight problem.

Terrain following combined with special navigational and flying techniques would get us to where we needed to go, but our ultimate survivability over North Vietnam depended on the skills of the electronic warfare officers (EWOs). At that time, North Vietnam had the most formidable air defense system in the history of air warfare. It is true that their radars were not state of the art, but they were effectively used by operators who had gained considerable skills with them. The same could be said about the AAA and SAM crews. Their tours of duty were not limited to one year like ours. They were at home defending their families against the most advanced American war machines for as long as the war lasted. So these Soviet-made radars, which were first introduced in Eastern Europe, were now being combat tested. The US intelligence had appropriate nicknames for all of them. Thus we confronted Bar Locks and Spoon Rests for long-range early warning, Fan Song for SA2 surface to air missiles (SAMs) and Fire Cans for a variety of anti-aircraft artillery (AAA).

Our knowledge of the locations of these radars, combined with our low-level tactics, would get us into most target areas without detection. Once detected, however, it became the EWO's job to analyze the threats these radars posed. If all radars were in the locations we had plotted on our charts, we would be able to fly through their scanning ranges and stay away from the effective ranges of missiles or artillery they controlled. During mission planning, the EWO would prepare a scenario that would tell him at which point of flight and from which direction each radar's scan would illuminate our aircraft. If he detected radars not plotted on his chart and the received signal strength was stronger, indicating a closer proximity to our flight track, he would have to direct the pilots to get us out of there. By monitoring his state-of-the-art instruments, he could tell whether the enemy radars were in routine mode or were focused on our aircraft in sector scans with added height finders that would help them to acquire the aircraft's track, speed, and altitude. The missile and AAA crews needed all this information before they could zero in on our aircraft's position and fire. In addition, with SAM's Fan Song radar, he could tell when the radar pulse recurrence frequency changed to forecast an imminent missile launch. All that required good eyes to monitor several visual displays and good hearing to discern distinct chirping audio signals each radar propagated. In a concentrated radar signal area, such as our aircraft would enter upon its climb to drop altitude, the EWO would receive welcomed assistance from the crew radio operator who shared his instrument console and sat on his left. All the radio operators became adept EWO assistants.

Blackbird's EWOs also had the capability to detect and disrupt an attack by a MIG interceptor. Using passive electronic techniques, they could confuse a MIG long enough to enable their aircraft to escape into hilly terrain where the interceptor's radar became ineffective and the pursuing pilot risked flying into the ground. First, by monitoring aural and visual signals, they could tell that ground control intercept (GCI) radar was tracking their Blackbird and most likely vectoring a MIG for an attack from the rear. Once the EWO picked up the interceptor's radar, he could play with the target a pursuing pilot would see on his radarscope. By manipulating the radar echoes reflected from the Blackbird to the interceptor's radar they could offset the pursuing pilot's target to the left or right. Then just as the MIG was ready to fire, they would call for a sharp break away from the established aircraft heading, causing the interceptor to miss his radar target. After the first missed pass the GCI site and the interceptor pilot would get smarter and come around for another pass. In the meantime, the Blackbird would make a rapid descent to the treetop level and get lost in the ground clutter where the airborne radar could not find it. The interceptor would have to abort the chase or risk flying into the ground.

In addition, Blackbird's EWOs could dispense highly reflective chaff, which would instantly paint a brighter and larger target than the aircraft. With all that equipment and our special training, we had what we needed to conduct gutsy, but safe operations in the hostile skies of North Vietnam. No one expected a large, slow, and unarmed transport aircraft to operate in the same North Vietnamese air space that proved to be so challenging to the most advanced high performance aircraft in the US inventory.

Our success rate over the enemy territory was commendable. Many of our low-level missions through the North Vietnamese air space went undetected. Some were tracked during portions of the flight, but always succeeded in avoiding AAA fire. A few had to abort high altitude leaflet drops when a missile control radar locked on to them and the EWO detected a frequency shift, which signaled an imminent SA2 missile launch. They always managed to break the radar lock on during a rapid roller coaster dive down to the minimum safe altitude. Fewer still experienced a MIG chase with an airborne radar lock on. The EWOs always saved the night for us. Consequently, it didn't take long for the Blackbird crews to develop a due respect for their skills.

Two months before, in mid-October, the S-05 crew's EWO, John Lewis, defeated three passes of an interceptor that jumped upon us just off the coast near Haiphong Harbor. We were dropping pretuned radios to the local fishermen. Pursued, we flew as low and as fast as we could, shaking and bouncing on the air currents that our aircraft stirred off the otherwise calm seawater. When John called "Break Left," we had to pop up a few feet in order to avoid dipping the left wing into the water. The operations officer, Tom Hines, flew with us that night. It was daylight when we landed at Nha Trang. The wings and the fuselage of the Blackbird were white with salt. John Lewis may still hold the Combat Talon record for besting a pursuing fighter pilot three times on a single "combat mission."

Our first problem on the 29 December mission would be the early warning radar at Na San. We had to stay as low and as far south of its range as possible in order to avoid detection while crossing into North Vietnam. Once inside of North Vietnam, we had to get to the east side of the central mountains and stay out of range of well-placed AAA and SAM sites along the Red River valley. We tried to avoid getting picked up and tracked by the multitude of radars associated with those anti-aircraft weapons. These radars by themselves could not hurt us, but they would alert AAA and SAM crews for possible action if we came within range of their weapons. Our best scenario was to have no radar track us until we began our rapid climb to 30,000+ feet for the leaflet drop. We knew that once the aircraft reached 9,000–10,000 feet, all available radars would come up and keep the EWO extremely busy. If the enemy did not respond with a launch of interceptors, the leaflet drop would be completed and the aircraft would resume low-level terrain following proceeding westward just south of the China border along the 22nd parallel until reaching the Black River valley. At that point they would turn southbound and staying in the mountains along the western side of the river to execute the second airdrop northwest of the Na San early warning radar.

Detection by the Na San radar was not our concern at this point in the mission. By this time a warning would have been issued from the Hanoi side of the mountains that a leaflet dropping intruder was moving westward toward Dien Bien Phu. Consequently, this early warning radar would be scanning in a northwest direction, expecting the emergence of the Blackbird. Na San's detection of our flight at this time could actually assist in the accomplishment of the second portion of the mission. Our resupply drop was what we called a "notional" drop, or a diversionary drop. There was no friendly team to receive the two resupply bundles. These bundles were carefully planned by imaginative minds at SOG to confuse the North Vietnamese and to have them expend considerable resources searching for infiltrators that did not exist. So the resupply bundles were meant to be captured by the enemy. Na San's detection of our aircraft's slow-down could assist them in locating this bogus cargo.

By the time we finished with the planning, we learned that augmented S-01 crew would fly the mission. It was S-01's turn to take the next mission, but there were some questions about the possibility of having them skip their turn. Aircraft commander Maj. Dick Day and one of the crew's loadmasters were on duty not involving flying (DNIF). Their senior navigator, Lt. Col. Don Fisher, was not yet back from his R&R (rest and recuperation) in Hawaii. His earliest expected return was on that day, 26 December. Earlier on this day, the other crew loadmaster departed with the S-03 crew to the parent 314th Wing in Taiwan. He had made arrangements with Staff Sergeant Darcy from the S-03 crew to switch places. Ed Darcy, a quiet, conscientious young man, planned to save some money by staying in Nha Trang. He did not want to spend it on a three- to five-day stay in Taiwan while the ferried Blackbird went through its scheduled inspection and repair as necessary (IRAN) in a maintenance facility that was equipped to handle C130s. All crews looked forward to their turn to ferry a Blackbird for an IRAN in Taiwan. It was the most welcomed vacation break from the wartime conditions in Vietnam. So, Ed Darcy became a volunteer replacement for one S-01 loadmaster. Sgt. James Williams agreed to take the place of the loadmaster who was DNIF.

This mission provided an opportunity for Capt. Edwin Osborne to take command of the S-01 crew and for Capt. Gerald Van Buren to move up to the first pilot's position. The second pilot's slot was filled by Maj. Charlie Claxton from my S-05 crew. He had missed an earlier combat mission when he was DNIF, so this would become a make-up mission for him. I made up my mind that I would take Don Fisher's place if he did not return in time from Hawaii. I would have been the logical replacement in any case because I already knew the route and mission details and could be used to step in to replace him up to the last minute.

Later on that evening I heard that Don Fisher was back. I went to see him and found him in a most jovial mood. He had just returned from a memorable R&R in Hawaii with his whole family. He had just had the greatest of Christmases and repeated to me and to others that he was "in love with the whole world." He was ready to fly his own combat mission.

Edwin Osborne was also ready to fly as an aircraft commander of a combat mission. All our first pilots were highly experienced as C-130 airlift aircraft commanders before becoming qualified in the Combat Talon Blackbirds. Many felt that to become a highly qualified copilot in the Combat Talon program was somewhat of a career regression even though they understood the need for such demanding pilot qualifications. As experienced pilots, they were simply outranked by others with more impressive pilot credentials who became Combat Talon aircraft commanders. Edwin Osborne was clearly a pilot who should not be taking a back seat to anyone. He was an excellent pilot qualified as an instructor pilot in the Blackbirds.

The next day John Lewis and I rode with the S-01 officer crew to the mission planning room. Van Buren drove the crew van. He normally drove whenever his crew went places. I was told that as our commissary officer he even drove through Saigon on his crew's periodic commissary runs. His crew always got some extra ground time at Tan Son Nhut to accommodate his grocery shopping. Since Charlie Claxton was destined to inherit that duty from him, it meant that my S-05 crew would get the long ground time on some future transits through Saigon.

On the way to our secure mission planning room, I sat across from Capt. Frank Parker, a tall, blond young man who was the crew's EWO. He was telling several of us how fortunate we were in having missions where we could sneak in and sneak out without stirring up a hornet's nest. He had recently returned from Thailand where he ran into several of his EWO classmates who were flying in RB-66s. Their mission was to deliberately challenge the enemy's electronic detection systems and face deadly retaliation in their efforts to pinpoint locations of enemy radars. He used the term we sometimes applied to those situations when one would prefer to be on the ground rather than in the air. He said that his friends were "eating their livers" on their RB-66 missions.

Roy Thompson had everything ready for us when we arrived. All the charts we prepared the day before were either posted on easels or laid out on worktables. Fresh, unmarked charts, flight plan logs, and other necessary mission forms were placed on tables where the crew members would use them. Roy gave a brief overview of what the mission entailed. About the only unusual thing that he noted was that times on targets (TOTs) were not prescribed because neither drop zone had a reception team. The psyops (leaflet) drop had a fixed drop leg at an altitude of 30,000 or more feet, depending on the wind velocity and direction. Weaker winds would require a higher altitude. The heart of Hanoi would be from 65 to 70 miles away, and it was hoped that some of the leaflets would make it that far before the sunrise. Lack of TOTs also explained why their flight plan was not completed with time of arrival at turning points. They were to calculate these by themselves, planning on a 260–265 true air speed at high altitudes and a standard 230 ground speed at terrain following levels.

Once Roy Thompson was finished with his mission introduction, I joined Don Fisher and Gordie Wenaas, the two crew navigators, to work on the flight planned route. John Lewis and Frank Parker got together to work on the enemy's defenses. Roy joined the three pilots. Our enlisted crew members: two flight engineers, two loadmasters, and one radio operator, normally did not participate in mission planning.

Gordie Wenaas thought the mission would be a "piece of cake." He quickly noted that there were practically no threat circles anywhere near our track. Then he started crunching out flight plan times between turning points. Don and I went over each low-level turning point, examining the terrain in its vicinity. Practically all were river bends or rivers that would show up well on radar. Some turning points had been used on previous missions and were reported to be good ones. The selected drop zone for the second drop was a location with good radar targets everywhere. He was satisfied with everything and began to prepare his own navigational chart. In this task, Gordie was way ahead of him.

Gordie was a man who undertook every single task seriously. I remember him going around our hotel taking care of chores whenever his S-01 crew was scheduled to be the hotel's duty crew. Each crew was regularly scheduled for hotel crew duty by the operations scheduling as if it were a flight assignment. These duties consisted of servicing the two electrical generators, bringing in fresh potable water from the air base, taking care of mail, stocking the rooftop bar, and performing whatever maintenance chores were needed at the hotel. Gordie Wenaas was conspicuous in keeping himself occupied with these chores. He showed me how to start up and switch on the two noisy generators.

I was then drawn into a conversation with the pilots. Osborne liked the route and had only one concern. It was the time interval between the end of the first drop and the start of the second one. Would his two loadmasters have enough time to move the cargo to the ramp for this drop? How many bundles would there be? How much would they weigh? And, of course, "What is this notional stuff?" The answer to the last question could only be provided by the cargo rigger, a warrant officer from the First Flight. Van Buren was dispatched to go next door to get him. He returned alone, but he brought the information we needed. He also succeeded in making arrangements for the loadmasters and the flight engineers to be at the aircraft next morning to witness the cargo loading. He commented that the warrant officer told him that no one was to mess with the cargo and question its rigging. Everything would be set up by the First Flight crew just the way it should be dropped. Anything nonstandard or out of place should be ignored. Our job was to fly it there and drop it just as it was configured.

Ed Osborne showed much interest in the terrain following portion of the flight. So the pilots gathered around Don Fisher, who had already drawn his chart. He walked through every leg of the flight and explained each turning point. Charlie Claxton had the weight of the aircraft calculated at the point of acceleration and climb to high altitude. There were questions about how much of the area west of Hanoi the crew would be able to see. The aircraft's track was over the eastern slopes of the central highlands. Numerous peaks with elevations of up to 9,000 feet were immediately to the left and the sprawling Red River valley with level terrain west of Hanoi was to the right. It was to be a dark night with a new moon beginning on 30 December. There would be total darkness. Some lights from Hanoi would no doubt be on. Our prior flights noted that North Vietnam did not have a complete nighttime blackout. The night would be perfect for Gordie Wenaas and Charlie Claxton, the two designated map readers, to use the somewhat cumbersome starlight scope to monitor the terrain below. The scope was of little use at terrain following levels because it had excessive tunnel vision. This made the terrain whiz by so fast that it caused the images to blur. But at the high drop altitude, where the Blackbird would seem to be at a standstill in relation to the ground below, the scope would give its user a fascinating view of terrain otherwise hidden in total darkness. Very little cloud coverage was predicted for that night.

We pointed out the location of Yen Bai Air Base that would be at the aircraft's one to two o'clock position during the drop. If there were any MIGs on night alert, that base would pose their greatest threat. This would also be Frank Parker's greatest challenge that night. He would have to defend against a possible interceptor activity.

Ed Osborne examined the terrain into which the aircraft would descend after the leaflet drop. He was concerned about the rapidly approaching ground during their maximum rate of descent when the radar stabilization was habitually, but only temporarily, lost and the Doppler limits were also exceeded. Here I pointed out that a rapid descent should not be executed unless the aircraft was in jeopardy due to SAM or interceptor attack. All crews seemed to have the same Pope Air Force Base training mind-set. During our training there, each short look was followed by a maximum rate descent, a maneuver that put a lot of stress on the aircraft. This needed to be practiced at every opportunity at Pope. Now in real life, if a threat to our aircraft did not materialize, there was no need to put it through such a stressful maneuver where the crew experienced weightlessness and everything not tied down started floating about. Then at the point of level off, the tremendous g load would force the standing crew members down to their knees. On this mission there would be additional cargo just behind the EWO and the radio operator compartment. We did not want any of it to break loose during such a stressful maneuver.

Ed was concerned with the time remaining before the second drop. His loadmasters and the second flight engineer would have to move the cargo to the back of the aircraft and get it set for the drop. Normally, the cargo would be all set from the point of takeoff. But not this time. The back of the aircraft would have to be cleared of any remaining restraining straps from the leaflet drop. Then the resupply bundles would have to be moved into place toward the ramp. Normally this would not be that difficult because the palletized bundles were on rollers. But being on rollers in a straight and level flight is one thing, being on rollers in an up and down terrain following flight is another. Great care was needed to avoid an injury or have the cargo slip off the rollers at an angle where its pallet would jam. This would no doubt be a new experience for these loadmasters. Ed noted with some satisfaction that the terrain following leg going westbound along the 22nd parallel was relatively level because we were taking advantage of the break between 10,000-foot-high peaks on the right and 9,000-foot peaks on the left.

At a prominent turning point over the Black River the mission would turn south. The Blackbird would fly almost due south hiding behind the high terrain west of the river. This would keep it west of the valley's populated areas. Ahead at the aircraft's ten to eleven o'clock position would be the Na San early warning radar. This radar would be looking for the reappearance of the intruder that was sure to excite the radars on the Hanoi side of the mountains in the Red River valley. This radar was not capable of directing MIG interceptors, and none were expected to come west out of the Red River valley.

The second drop zone was in an isolated area in the vicinity of Highway 6. It was a logical place for a drop zone. Its location would no doubt add credibility to the nonexistent team's presence. Roy Thompson explained the deceptive nature of this drop. There would be no ground markings or signals. The drop would occur on Don Fisher's green light command when his Doppler distance to go ran out. After this drop the crew would continue terrain following into Laos where the high altitude route home would resume at the Skyline TACAN.

At some point during this low-level route review we were joined by Frank Parker and John Lewis, who had concluded their study of the enemy's electronic air order of battle. They pointed out correctly that once the aircraft crossed into the Black River region the enemy defenses were such that a return home at any altitude would be safe. That was a good thought in case of any in-flight problems, such as navigational, mechanical, or outside visibility degradation due to weather.

Then the group gathered around Frank Parker's chart. His chart differed from those of Don Fisher and the map readers Charlie Claxton and Gordie Wenaas. They had smaller threat circles along the flight-planned track that represented lethal ranges of SAMs and AAA. Frank's chart had the mission flying through much larger circles that outlined scan ranges of various radars. His chart showed that the aircraft would be exposed to many types of radar throughout its northbound portion of flight along the Red River. He estimated that even before the aircraft would reach its drop altitude of 30,000+ feet, all available radars would be alerted to their presence and that he would be saturated with a tremendous amount of visual and aural signals. He acknowledged that he would have to rely on able assistance from Gean Clapper, the crew radio operator, who would be sharing his console behind the cargo compartment curtain.

Gean Clapper was a true professional in his field. He had many years of experience as a HAM radio operator. As such he had contacts with colleagues throughout the world. On flights over international waters, where it was permissible, he would raise his contacts and relay personal greetings and messages to families back home. He was also very good at electronic warfare. He could positively recognize the chirping sounds of various radars. This should be a great asset on a flight such as this one where, sound-wise, things would get extremely noisy for Frank.

Frank concluded that with Gean's help he should be able to detect anything out of the ordinary and call for evasive action before any harm could come to the Blackbird. It would be Don Fisher's task to find a safe evasive flight path through the mountains on the left.

After that each crew member went on his own, putting finishing touches on all paperwork. We three mission planners assisted them with anything they needed and ensured that all mission documents they produced were properly stamped TOP SECRET. None of the documents could leave with the crew. We collected everything and locked it in the First Flight's safe. Documents would not be released to the crew until the next night before the predeparture mission briefing.

The next day's mission briefing was a whole crew affair attended by the commander and operations officer. This would be the first time the enlisted crew members learned about the target area. All five—the two engineers, two loadmasters, and the radio operator—were present when the First Flight's cargo handlers loaded the aircraft. Flight engineer TSgt. Jack McCrary gave us thumbs up on the condition of the aircraft. He was a meticulous crew member, well regarded, not just by Ed Osborne, but also by his flight engineer peers. I wondered how much sleep he had gotten during the day. His eyes looked red as if he had not slept at all. But we all knew that his nickname was "Red Eye." He had an eye condition that made them look red and bloodshot all the time. His second, SSgt. Wayne Eckley, was an engineer of lesser experience, but not short on enthusiasm. His nickname was "Bones." The jungle fatigue uniforms (designed as one size fits all) exaggerated his lean, bony body. There was so much more space left for him inside his fatigues.

The mission briefing started with Roy Thompson, who stood in front of several chart-filled easels placed in the front of the briefing room. He briefed the weather. It was going to be favorable for this flight with very few clouds on the east side of the mountains in North Vietnam and strong favorable WNW winds at drop altitude. A low-level pressure was moving southeast from China, bringing some cloudiness into the target area in the Black River valley late in the morning.

Then the mission briefing was turned over to Don Fisher, who briefed the route and the drop sequences. He was followed by Frank Parker, who covered the enemy order of battle. He presented the latest SOG intelligence that included known numbers of different MIG interceptors available to North Vietnamese defenses. As always, he mentioned the standard radio silence precautions. Minimum chatter on the intercom! He was going to run every one of his sophisticated tape recorders that registered all electronic signals generated by enemy radars and also captured crew's intercom transmissions. This was going to be a special night for him to gather electronic intelligence signals for future use. We should end up with a sizable amount of signals from all types of radars. These tapes would then be used by other crew EWOs interested in sharpening their listening and signal interpretation skills.

Frank's briefing was followed by the aircraft commander, Osborne. He briefed the crew assignments that had been previously reviewed with the operations officer, Tom Hines. He would fly the entire mission in the right seat. Van Buren would be in the left seat from the takeoff through the low-level terrain following part of the flight. Charlie Claxton would map read from behind Van Buren during terrain following and then take the left seat at high altitude on the way home. Don Fisher would ride the radar navigator's seat with the curtain drawn during terrain following and the leaflet drop. Gordie Wenaas would stand behind Osborne's right seat and map read from there. Jack McCrary would fly in the engineer's seat during terrain following. Wayne Eckley would spend his time in the back playing the safety observer role and provide assistance to the loadmasters. Frank Parker and Gean Clapper were to man their console behind the bulkhead curtain, and the two substitute loadmasters, Jim Williams and Ed Darcy, were to make sure they kept their restraining harnesses on during the drops. All crew members were to go on demand regulator oxygen upon entering North Vietnam and then on 100 percent oxygen during the leaflet drop.

There were a few standard questions from Lieutenant Colonels Rogers and Hines about everyone's fitness and emphasis on safety. Finally, they wished the crew good luck.

After this we sanitized the crew. We collected all personal effects: identification cards, family photographs, and even jewelry. We placed everything into individual plastic bags and saved them for their return. Each crew member was left only with his dog tags and Geneva Convention card as identifying documents. That was the standard procedure for all combat missions.

Because we had to secure all the classified mission documents and personal effects, the crew members were already in their assigned positions running their predeparture checklists when we rejoined them at the aircraft. We witnessed an orderly engine start and watched the Blackbird taxi out to the end of the runway. From our vantage point we saw them take off and disappear into the darkness over the South China Sea.

About three hours later, I returned with Roy Thompson to the operations office to monitor the North Vietnamese portion of the mission. One of the radio operators monitored a special HF radio frequency over which Gean Clapper transmitted coded mission progress reports every thirty to forty minutes when the aircraft reached a significant flight planned turning point. A radio station in an unknown location would broadcast continuous one-letter Morse code at regular intervals. The airborne operator would monitor the same frequency and at proper moments would insert a two-letter Morse code signal, which would let us know which point of the route was reached and gave us the status of the mission's progress. This was such a short burst of transmitted energy that our enemy, who was sure to monitor the same frequency, would not have enough time to zero in his direction finders to locate the position of the aircraft. These transmissions were the only breaks in radio silence allowed during combat missions.

Upon checking with the radio operator, we learned that the flight was already over North Vietnam and right on time. We did not have any mission documents with us other than the radio operator's log with numbered points and corresponding estimated times of arrival over them, but we had a good mental picture of what must have been happening in the cockpit. So as we sat there, sipping strong coffee that the radio operator prepared, we made occasional comments on what the crew must have been going through.

For the leaflet drop, all the lights were at their dimmest and the radar navigator and EWO/radio operator compartment curtains were drawn to prevent any outside light to affect the night vision of the rest of the crew. All were on oxygen and their intercom voices were muffled by the oxygen mask microphones that registered and exaggerated the sound of every breath they took. The aircraft began its acceleration prior to the rapid climb. Maximum aircraft acceleration to 932-degree turbine inlet temperature was attained in relatively short level flight with aircraft shaking as if its four turbojets were ready to tear loose and leave the bulky aircraft carcass behind.

Then, as the aircraft began its rapid climb, Frank Parker's console surely began to light up. At first he would pick up a number of AAA and SAM radars, which would routinely scan their assigned areas. As they detected the Blackbird, they would focus their scans on the just-discovered target and activate their height finders to establish the aircraft's altitude. They would pass this acquired target data through their established notification channels. Then even more radars would come up and focus on this rapidly rising, but now slow-moving target. The crew would hear Frank reporting the inevitable. Two or three AAA radars were tracking them, but from a safe distance. Of greater concern would be the SAM radars. These had longer reach, but were expected to be out of range. He would certainly be calling these to Osborne's attention. Then would come the level off and the start of drop. Each man could tell when each cardboard box exited the aircraft. There was a whoosh sound to each exit as the departing load created an added vacuum in the rare atmosphere of the cargo compartment. The aircraft would seem to stand still, just hanging on in the thin air, being as high as it could climb on the thin cushion of available air. And as Frank watched for the emergence of a GCI radar and its tracking pattern in order to determine if there was an intent to launch a MIG, Gordie Wenaas must have struggled with the night vision scope looking for Yen Bai Air Base some 30 miles away. This was the place from which the nearest MIGs could come. His night vision scope would certainly pick up the heat of an interceptor at takeoff. He would have to be pointed in the right direction. Others in the cockpit were getting the answer to whether they could see the lights of distant Hanoi now at their three o'clock position. Don Fisher must have had his face buried in the hood of his radar as he carefully traced every mile of ground covered by the aircraft. He had to know exactly where he was in case Frank reported radar or interceptor lock on, which would demand an immediate descent to a safe terrain between the mountain peaks on the left.

We did not hear any interruptions to the monotonous "V" sound on the radio, so we assumed that all was okay. All the leaflets were delivered. The aircraft was on its way down and proceeding westward to its turning point over the Black River. The next report came just as expected. All was still okay. The aircraft was now southbound running its checklist for the bundle drop by Highway 6.

Roy and I planned to return to the hotel right after the next report and get a couple of hours of sleep before coming back to greet the returning crew. But as we waited, nothing happened. There were no further reports from the aircraft. Our first assumption was that something went wrong with Clapper's radio. We would surely hear something once the aircraft emerged from its radio silence over the Skyline TACAN. That is where the aircraft would report a small problem like that to our radar sites in Thailand. Once again, there was nothing. With that we returned to the hotel and reported our concerns to Dow Rogers and Tom Hines.

There were anxious moments as the aircraft's return time approached. Calls were made to find out if any landings were made in Thailand or at Da Nang. Then we notified the command at SOG. They took over all search and rescue efforts. Several F-4 Phantoms were launched to survey the area south of the last known reported position. The weather turned bad. The front moved in as expected and the F-4s could not see a thing on the ground. They monitored radios for signals from the aircraft's crash position indicator and from crew member survival radios. They heard nothing. After several attempts, the search was given up. The crew of eleven was declared as missing in action (MIA).

There were many guesses and opinions as to what might have happened. A loss to enemy action was discounted. The aircraft was proceeding normally on its assigned mission after the leaflet drop, which was the most hazardous part of the flight. Enemy attack on the aircraft would have been reported. The enemy had a chance to detect our aircraft by Na San radar, which must have been alerted about our aircraft's escape toward Dien Bien Phu. Had this happened, there might have been some forces in the vicinity of the drop zone capable of bringing down a low-flying aircraft with small arms fire. But such an act would have been heralded as a great victory by North Vietnam. The enemy would have learned of our aircraft's fate almost immediately. Even with a low profile, the failure of the aircraft to return to Nha Trang could not be concealed for very long. The enemy should have concluded that it was the aircraft that had dropped several million leaflets west of Hanoi. They did not take credit for its disappearance during this mission. But some thought of a more sinister scenario. The enemy had the aircraft and perhaps some members of the crew and they would use them for propaganda purposes. However, as time went on this probability dissipated. It became clearer and clearer that the aircraft must have impacted a mountain in an isolated area sometime after making its last position report. The return of our POWs in 1973 confirmed that. The names of the S-01 crew members were not known to any of the returning POWs.

The location of Blackbird 64–0547 continued to be a mystery for twenty-five years. In 1991, when the villagers of Phu Nhung heard that the United States was searching for remains of American airmen, various individuals reported that they knew of a crash site in their vicinity. In November 1992 a joint US-Vietnam team was led to an isolated location at coordinates 21–39.80N 103–31.20E (Grid 48QUJ 4744596161) where they found a few remaining parts of an aircraft that turned out to be the Blackbird.

The crash site is located in a rugged mountainous terrain of Lai Chau province some 32 miles northeast of Dien Bien Phu. It lies just a few miles east of the route that many of our crews flew in the opposite direction toward the same prominent bend in the river over which the last aircraft position report was made. This river bend was a distinct radar return, and we used it on those missions that required our undetected entry into areas between Hanoi and the China border. Since we are unable to retrieve the flight plan for this mission, we do not have the exact location of the initial point for the drop or for the drop zone. I must rely only on my memory and conclude that the aircraft was either on its planned route to the initial point or making a course correction to it. Distance wise, the crash occurred seven and a half minutes from the reporting point at the river bend. Description of the aircraft's impact point reveals that it was heading directly toward the Na San radar site that was about 45 nautical miles away.

The US recovery team pinpointed the crash location on the best available 1 to 50,000-scale chart. This chart shows it to be at 4,780 feet on a steep 60-degree slope of a north-northwest-facing crescent-shaped mountain. The crest of this mountain goes only up to 4,870 feet. The main peak of this karst-studded mountain, known as Nam Bo, rises to 5,174 feet and is 1 mile due west of the crash site. The crash site is very small. Its measurements established by the recovery team are given as 105 by 72 feet. This is a very small area for an aircraft as large as a C-130. Since all the crew remains were recovered from this small location, it can be safely concluded that the aircraft did not bounce and break up along its track before coming to a stop. Its crash heading must have been perpendicular to the face of the mountain. With that, the destruction of the aircraft must have been instantaneous.

At the time of the crash the crew was getting ready for the second drop. Eckley, Darcy, and Williams were in the cargo compartment making sure that the load was properly positioned for the drop. They were moving about and did not yet have their restraining harnesses hooked on. Claxton and Wenaas were the other two crew members who were not fastened to any seats. Their map-reading duties called for them to stand behind the pilots and peer outside through the side windows.

The first person on the scene of the crash was a twelve-year-old boy. He reported that the aircraft was in many pieces and that it was still burning. He saw several bodies, many of them burned. He did not find any survivors.

The team found very little at the crash scene. The villagers had pilfered the site within days after the crash and over the years carted away all aircraft parts they could use. In 1991 when they learned about the US search for the remains of airmen, they returned to the site and dug up all the human remains they could find. They turned them over to the proper authorities who concluded that they accounted for eight crew members. When the team returned to the site one year later, they found only a few fragments of human remains, and the team leader recommended that any further attempts at recovery should be abandoned. All recovered remains were sent to Hawaii for proper identification.

There is a question why the site went so long without being reported. The team's investigation revealed that the crash site was reported to the village authorities immediately. It may be that the village leaders were so isolated from the governmental authorities that they didn't know what to do. Or, on the other hand, they were astute enough to realize what kind of fate would descend upon them for pilfering the crash site and keeping the crew weapons as well as those that must have been packaged in the airdrop cargo. Consequently, keeping the news of the crash a village secret had some benefits for the isolated indigenous population. Then, once the American rewards for locating aircraft crash sites became known and profitable, the villagers revealed their secret.

Our own information channels were also flawed. Personnel associated with Combat Talon were never officially informed about the crash site discovery. In mid-1997, plans were put in motion at Hurlburt to erect a memorial for the eleven lost crew members whose status had been changed from MIA to KIA in 1978. As an individual who was closely tied to this unfortunate mission, I agreed to write this story so that the families of the lost airmen would learn about the work their loved ones did in Vietnam and so that those who flew the Blackbirds in that war would recall and share their mission recollections with others. I finished the first draft of this story in July, hoping that John Lewis's and my recollections of the route and events of thirty years ago would help someone to locate the missing aircraft. The title of this first draft was "Missing Combat Talon C-130E." The word of my writing went out and in August I received a surprise phone call from a man who had been looking for information about his friend who flew on that mission. It was Gene Kremin, a radio operator buddy of Gean Clapper. He informed me that the aircraft had been located almost five years before and that his information about the crash site came from the Library of Congress in Washington, DC.

Appendix B

Transcribed Teletype Messages

Teletype messages used by the US military services in the 1990s had a specific format. They were typed in uppercase letters with text printed in two columns. Each page began with identical date, time, sender, and addressee information before the dual column text continued from one page to the next. This was done to ensure that the incoming pages, which rolled off the printer and got separated when the perforated sheets were torn from the accumulated stacks, could be properly collated in appropriate order.

Transcribed teletype messages of this annex are printed in regular single column text format. Date, time, sender, and addressee information is given only at the beginning of each document. The flow of the transcribed text is interrupted by references to the page number of the original document for proper source documentation in the book.

This appendix contains the following messages from the Joint Task Force–Final Accounting to various Department of Defense agencies about the lost Combat Talon aircraft in North Vietnam on December 29, 1967:

1. November 23, 1992—Detailed Report of Survey of Case 0954. Initial visit to the crash site and interview of witnesses.

2. March 31, 1993—Second Survey Report. (Internal JTF-FA fax message). Follow on visit with recommendation for another crash site recovery.

3. November 22, 1993—Detailed Search and Recovery Report for Case 0954. Extensive final excavation and interview of native visitors to the crash site.

4. June 17, 1994—Report of Investigation of Leads Pertaining to Possible Remains of U.S. Servicemen Reported by a Vietnamese Citizen.

#1. 23 Nov 1992 Teletype

Transcribed Teletype message from CJTFFA Det. 1, Bangkok, Thailand.

ROUTINE

R 230220Z NOV 92 PSN 893971P33

FM CJTFFA DET ONE BANGKOK TH

TO CDR JTF-FA HONOLULU HI

INFO SECDEF WASHDC//OCJCS-PW-MIA/J5//

SECDEF WASHDC//OASD-ISA/PW-MIA USCINCPAC HONOLULU HI//J3//

USCINCPAC IO WASHDC// DIA WASHDC//POW-MIA//

CORUSACILHI HICKAM AFB HI// NSC WASHDC

SECSTATE WASHDC//CA/OCS/CCS/EAP//

CIA WASHDC//OEA/SEA/IB/DDO/EA/ICOG//

UNCLAS SECTION 01 OF 08 BANGKOK TH 52313

UNCLASSIFIED 0371 NOV 92

DIA pass to DOD POW-MIA Central Documentation Office

Subj: Detailed report of survey of case 0954.

1. Summary:

A. On 29 Oct 92 a joint U.S.-Vietnam team attempted to survey a crash site at grid coordinates UJ4744596161, near Phu Nhung Village, Tuan Giao District, Lai Chau Province. Because of logistical constraints, the survey was not conducted at this time. On 30 Oct 92 the team interviewed two witnesses who provided information concerning the crash site. On 30 and 31 Oct 92. The team examined a total of eight sets of human remains, and one set of identification data. On 7 Nov 92, one of the witnesses was reinterviewed. On the morning of 8 Nov 92 the team began an arduous trek to the alleged crash site of REFNO 0954. On 8 Nov 92, the investigative element completed a site survey of REFNO 0954. A total of three witnesses provided more information on the site and one witness was able to point out the location of more human remains. This site is not recommended for recovery effort.

B. US team members were:

CPT Sanders (Team Leader)
SFC Thornhill (Medic)
MSGT Maynard (Life Support Technician)

DR. Davis (Archaeologist)
TSGT Cheek (Linguist/Analyst)
CT12 Foster (Linguist)
SSG Arnold (Mortuary Affairs Specialist)
SGT Hudson (Mortuary Affairs Specialist)
Vietnamese:
MR. Khuynh—VNOSMP
MR. Hung

2. Details of investigation:

A. On 29 Oct 92, CPT Sanders was scheduled to meet with VNOSMP and district officials in Tuan Giao District, Lai Chau Province to discuss REFNO 0954. While en route to Lai Chau Province the MI-8 helicopter pilot was instructed to overfly the site allegedly associated with REFNO 0954. Throughout the time over the alleged site, no US team member observed any possible aircraft wreckage. The pilot attempted to land at an apparent landing zone that was still in the process of being cut. He was unable to land because of concerns of the tail rotor blade striking the ground due to the slope on which the landing zone was being cut. Upon returning to Tuan Giao, CPT Sanders discussed with VNOSMP representative alternate means of getting to the crash site. At this time, CPT Sanders was informed that it would take six hours by truck and then a possible four or five hour walk. The US team leader decided to make an attempt by truck. The investigation team rode about forty five minutes to Phu Nhung village and stopped. At this time CPT Sanders was informed that the trucks could not proceed any further and it would take seven to eight hours on foot from the village to reach the site. Because this information was not consistent with what was told to CPT Sanders earlier, the investigation team was logistically unprepared to continue the mission. At this point the US team leader made the decision to return to Tuan Giao district headquarters to consult via landline with IRT commander in Hanoi. At 1600 hours, CPT Sanders notified Det 2 commander of situation and informed him of the concerns that would be presented to VNOSMP representative on the following morning. The concerns were as follows:

(1) That the investigative element be allowed to see the alleged remains.

(2) That investigative element be allowed to interview witnesses.

(3) The investigative element would return to Tuan Giao/Lai Chau on 6 Nov 92 after making necessary preparations.

End of page 1 of 8

(4) That local villagers were to cut out a usable landing zone closer to the crash site.

B. On 30 Oct 92, at approximately 1100, while waiting for the weather to clear for return flight to Son La Province, VNOSMP representative informed CPT Sanders that the witnesses and remains would be made available to us later in the day. At 1400 hours, in Tuan Giao district headquarters, both witnesses and alleged remains believed to be associated with REFNO 0954 were provided (see enclosure) a total of four sets of possible human remains were examined by the on-site archeologist and photographed. After completing the examination and photographing of the alleged remains and identification data, we were allowed to identify the two alleged witnesses.

US team members present at the interview:
CPT Sanders (Team Leader)
DR. Davis (Archaeologist)
MSGT Maynard Life Support Technician)
TSGT Cheek (Linguist/Analyst)
SSG Arnold (Photographer)
Present from the Vietnamese delegation:
MR. Khuynh—VNOSMP Representative
MR. Nguyen Quoc Dat (Nguyeenx Quoocs Dat)—Asst District Chief-Tuan Giao District
MR. Than Du (Traanf Zu)—District MIA Team Member
MR. Nguyen Sang (Nguyeenx Sangs)—District MIA Team Member
MR. Io Van On (IooVawn Ons)—District MIA Team Member
MR. Ngo Van Cu (NgooVawn Cws)—District MIA Team Member
MR. Sung Giong (Sungs Gioong Ly)—Witness 0954
MR. Vu Xuan Hung (Vws Xuaan Hungf)—Witness 0954

C. The first witness interviewed was Mr. Vu Xuan Hung (Vws Xuaan Hungf). Mr. Hung, 36 YOA, is a resident of Phu Nhung village, Tuan Giao district, Lai Chau province. Mr. Hung stated that as far as he could remember, the incident happened at the end of 1967 or beginning of 1978. Mr. Hung stated that he couldn't remember the date, month, nor the time of day that the crash took place. He said that when the aircraft crashed, he was in his village (Phu Nhung). The witness said that he "saw" the aircraft crash. When questioned further on this point, Mr. Hung stated that he did not remember seeing which direction the aircraft was coming from, or which direction it was headed. Mr. Hung also said that he did not hear any explosions, nor did he see any parachutes. Mr. Hung said that after the aircraft crashed, no one went to the crash site because there were "too many American aircraft flying around." He was unable to tell what type of aircraft were flying around. Mr. Hung stated that he didn't remember what time he set out to go to the site but he didn't get there until late afternoon. He said that at first he was unable to get too close to the site because the area was ablaze. After an unspecified time, Mr. Hung stated that he was able to get close to the aircraft wreckage. When asked about bodies, Mr. Hung stated that he doesn't remember anyone still alive, but the bodies he saw were probably all dead due to the fire. Mr. Hung stated that because the fire was so bad, he could not tell how many bodies were at the site. He also stated that because everything was so badly burned, he could not tell what kind of aircraft, how many engines, nor could he distinguish any markings on the aircraft. Mr. Hung said that he left the site and returned to his village without taking anything from the site. He didn't remember telling anyone of what he had seen (see comments). Mr. Hung stated that he went to the crash site a total of two times. He stated that though he didn't know when they began, people (local ethnic villagers) soon began going to the site to take away pieces of metal from the aircraft wreckage for use in their villages. Mr. Hung stated that after learning of

End of page 2 of 8

government (VN) efforts to locate missing Americans in November of 1991, he told local authorities of what he had seen. At that time district and province authorities were informed of the crash site.

D. The second witness interviewed was Mr. Sung Giong Ly (Sungs Gio-ong Ly), a 65 YOA resident of Phu Nhung village, Tuan Giao district, Lai Chau province. Mr. Ly could not remember any details as to when the incident occurred. He couldn't remember the date, day, month, year, nor time of day. He also couldn't remember if the incident happened during the day or night. Mr. Ly stated that he did not see the aircraft crash. He did not remember hearing or seeing the aircraft overfly his village. Mr. Ly said that he saw an area burning and thought it might have been an aircraft and decided to go see. Mr. Ly didn't know the distance from his village to the area that was burning, but he stated that he started at sunrise and didn't get there until noon (approx. 6 hours on foot). Mr. Ly remembered that he didn't go alone, but he couldn't remember who went along with him to the site. Mr. Ly said that upon reaching the site, he didn't know what type of aircraft it was, but that it was a "large" aircraft. Mr. Ly said that he couldn't distinguish any markings, or even how many engines, because everything was so badly burned. Mr. Ly, however, said that he saw bodies with what he thought was "American clothing." He was unable to remember what type of clothing it was to make him think American. Because of the wreckage and burning, he could not tell how many bodies there were. Mr. Ly was certain that he saw no one still alive. He stated that this was because everything was so badly burned. Mr. Ly didn't remember how long it took for him to report what he saw, but he remembered that he did report what he had seen to village authorities. Mr. Ly stated that he went to the site a total of three times. Mr. Ly stated that he had no knowledge/recollection of anyone else going to the site, or of anyone taking anything away from the site. Mr. Ly couldn't remember nor relate any other information concerning the incident of REFNO 0954. After thanking the witnesses for their help and cooperation, the interview session was terminated and the witnesses dismissed.

E. After the witnesses were dismissed, Mr. Dai, Tuan Giao district assistant chief explained why it took so long for district, province and national level officials to learn of this incident. Mr. Dai stated that the crash happened in an area inhabited by many ethnic minorities who are not always in touch with local and district authorities because of terrain and distance. He stated that when local village authorities were informed, no one knew exactly what to do not only with the information, but also with any remains or identification data that had been removed from the site. When the American and Vietnamese governments increased their efforts to account for Americans missing during the war, government news of the effort began to reach down to the ethnic village local authorities. They then knew that the incident that they had been aware of for so long needed to be reported to district and province authorities. That is why reports of this incident didn't begin to flow until after Nov 1991.

F. Linguist/analyst comments: the first witness, Mr. Hung, was noticeably nervous throughout the entire interview. Other than remembering that it happened at the end of 1967 or beginning of 1968 (which corroborates the time frame), he didn't have a lot of specifics to relate. It is very probable that he didn't know what it was he was seeing because at the time of the incident he would have been only 11 or 12 years of age. The second witness, Mr. Ly was also unable to relate very much specific information concerning the circumstances around the crash itself. The apparent highlight of his testimony was seeing what he thought to be American clothes. The authority's explanation for the time lapse between the time of the crash and the time the province/national authorities became aware, is

End of page 3 of 8

definitely plausible due to the physical isolation, lack of established lines of communication, and ethnic differences.

G. On 31 Oct 92, an additional four sets of human remains (see enclosure) were made available to the investigative element. Materials made available included a Geneva Convention card, an identification tag, and an aircraft data plate.

H. On 7 Nov 92, at Lai Chau district headquarters, all eight sets of remains, identification data, aircraft data plate, and a screwdriver, were measured and photographed. After this was completed, Mr. Vu Xuang Hung (Vws Xuaan Hungf) was reinterviewed to see if he could provide further information concerning REFNO 0954. Mr. Hung stated that in November of 1991 he heard that the government (VN) was looking for MIAs and remains. He said that after hearing that information he went to search for bones. He stated that at the time of the incident, the nearest house was seven to eight kilometers from the crash site. He said that presently the nearest to the crash site is about one kilometer from the site. Mr. Hung stated that there are no roads or trails to, around, or thru the site. He said that the crash site covered about 200 square meters. Mr. Hung stated that when he decided to go to the site to search for bones, he went alone. He stated that when he reached the site he saw no apparent grave sites to indicate that villagers might have buried the bodies. Mr. Hung stated that the aircraft wreckage had been carted away by local villagers, but that there were still some heavy pieces remaining in the area. He said that he was not able to tell what type of aircraft it was because everything was so badly burned. Mr. Hung stated that he does not personally know anyone who might have taken wreckage from the site, or anyone that might be presently holding remains. Mr. Hung said that upon reaching the site, he dug several holes approximately 40 to 70 centimeters deep and that bones were spread out throughout the holes. Mr. Hung stated that he has been to the crash site three times. The first time to see the crash. The second time was when he went to search for bones, and the third time was to guide Mr. Pham Teo (VNOSMP team leader) to the site. Mr. Hung then stated that "the first time he had been to the site was approximately 10 years ago." He said that he couldn't remember the month or year of tat visit.

I. Upon arrival at the crash site, on 8 Nov 1992, two witnesses were interviewed. Both of them had been to the site, had recovered remains and turned them over to district and province authorities. The first witness interviewed was Mr. Ly A Vang (Lys A Vawng) a 36 YOA resident of Phu Nhung village, Tuan Giao district, Lai Chau province. Mr Vang provided the following information that he remembered concerning REFNO 0954. He said that he found some remains in Oct 91, finding all he had in one hole. He said that at the time that he was looking for the remains there were two other people with him who also found remains. He said that they happened on to the site while they were out hunting, and having heard the news of the government looking for MIA remains, he and the people with him began to search for bones. He said that one of the people who was with him a Mr. Va A Vang (Vaj A Vawngh) found a pair of "army boots." He was unable to supply the name of the other person and he did not know if they still were/are in possession of the remains or if they have turned them over to any officials yet. Mr. Vang stated that he had to dig for about 10 minutes before he found the remains that he turned in. He said that there were no remains lying on the surface of the ground. Mr. Vang said that he heard from others (not further identified) that the site had been there for a long time, probably since 1967 or 1968. Also interviewed at the site was Mr. Lau Gia Nu (Laau Giar Nu), 38 YOA. Mr. Nu stated that he found the remains that he had turned over in Aug 1992. He said that he found them all in one hole. He said that at the time he was at the site searching for remains, there was a total of seven people

End of page 4 of 8

searching for remains. He could not supply the names of all the people, but he said that a Mr. Lau A Co (Laau A Cowj), 17 YOA found one bone. Mr. Nu said that he found two "finger" bones in one hole. Mr. Nu said that the reason he was there searching for bones was that he had heard the news about the search for MIAs from some (not further identified) people who were from La province. He said that he looked for the bones for about one day and had not been back to the site after that time. Mr. Nu said that he knew of people (not further identified) who had remains, but had already turned them in to authorities (not further identified).

J. Also while at the site, Mr. Hung, who had been interviewed twice before, was able to go directly to a spot and indicate that remains were buried at that spot (TE-1) (see analyst's comments).

K. Linguist/analyst comments: again the witnesses were all very cooperative when questioned about this incident. However, there appears to be some contradiction in the nature and content of Mr. Hung's interviews. In the first interview there was extreme nervousness and a general inability to remember much specific information. But he was able to remember that he went to the site while the area was still burning. However on subsequent interviews, he supplied answers that were in complete contrast to what he had supplied on the first interview. An example is that in the second interview he said that the first time he had been to the site was 10 years ago and upon arrival at the site itself, he was able to go right to a spot and show where remains would be found. Inconsistencies were numerous in his interviews. In discussions with district and provincial officials it is apparent that all remains turned in have been held by local and province authorities until they were turned over during this joint field activity.

4. Material Evidence: (*Editorial note*: *There was no paragraph 3*)

A. The following material evidence was found in the immediate area believed to be the crash site of 0945:

Struts plus brake plates from main landing gear
Shaft plus portion of the compressor
Blades from turbojet engine
Numerous small pieces of unidentifiable wreckage
Cockpit plus fuselage insulation

B. Analyst comments: the items listed above are the only identifiable portions of aircraft wreckage observed at this site. The remaining portions of the aircraft were removed by local villagers. No useful part numbers were found. Life support equipment items were observed at the site and may or may not be useful to determine the best areas for the remains recovery since it is now known whether or not the crew members were wearing their equipment at the time of this incident.

5. Survey Results:

A. The reported crash site is located at coordinates UJ4744596161 in Tuan Ciao District, Lai Chau Province, Socialist Republic of Vietnam. The site is extremely isolated and is accessible only by an arduous six hour trek overland. It lies high in the mountains at roughly 4300 feet elevation, nearly 3000 feet above the end of the road where the trail begins some 45 minutes north of the Tuan Giao district headquarters.

B. This is an aircraft crash site in extremely rugged and dangerous terrain. The immediate site area is a rocky mountain slope of 30 to 40 degree grade. For some 500 feet below this point and perhaps another 200 feet above, the rocky face angles 60 degrees and more. This a karst, limestone landscape generally covered by a mixed forest of tropical deciduous and evergreen broadleafs with dense understory of bamboo, bushy shrubs, ferns, vining lianas, and various grasses. The site itself, however, is nearly devoid of vegetation.

End of page 5 of 8

There is a noticeable, roughly circular break in the trees where the aircraft plunged through the forest canopy. The surface of the site is largely covered by limestone outcrops and highly unstable areas of scattered rocks. The latter presumably resulting from the impact of the aircraft against the mountain side. Few pockets of humic soil can be found scattered about the crash area, but for the most part this surface horizon has long been eroded downhill once whatever protective ground cover may have existed was destroyed by the crash.

C. Overall, the crash area measures some 16 meters uphill/downhill and 22 meters across the slope. From top to bottom the site falls roughly 10–15 meters and faces a generally north-northwesterly direction. While considerable amount of aircraft wreckage litters the main site area and portions of the steep slope immediately below, no large pieces of wreckage were observed with the exception of what appeared to be two struts from the main landing gear and a section of drive shaft from one of the engines. The rest of the larger wreckage appears to have been gradually carted away over the years by local villagers "mining" the site for scrap metal. Presumably these were the same people who more recently recovered the human remains presented to the survey team. There was abundant evidence of fairly recent digging at this site and at least two witnesses were able to confirm locations where they had recovered human remains.

D. The survey team tested three localities to determine the nature of the few accessible soil deposits and their potential to yield further human remains. Two test areas (TE-1 and TE-2) were previously worked by the interviewed witnesses. The third area was tested on the basis of a tooth fragment found on the surface. TE-1 at the downhill end of the crash area measured 0.1 meter and bottomed on bedrock at about 0.5 meters below surface. The matrix consisted of a very dark brown highly organic, silthy loam. This material was carefully deposited as a result of colluvial downwash trapped in pockets among the rock outcrops and as such presents little excavation potential beyond the limited occurrence of these pockets. As for material recovery TE-1 yielded one vertebral fragment and one metacarpal, or metatarsal fragment. TE-2 near the top of the site measured roughly 0.4×0.5 meters and bottomed on bedrock at 0.2 to 0.3 meters below surface. The matrix here was the same as in TE-1 but yielded no further remains beyond those already pointed out by the witnesses. TE-3 at the top of the crash area where human tooth fragment was found on the surface measured 1×1 meter and bottomed on bedrock at 0.2 to 0.3 meters below surface. Again, the matrix here was the same as in TE-1. Material remains recovered from the TE-3 included small cranial vertebral, rib long bone and tooth fragments, all of human origin. In all small bits of human bone ranging from 9 to 32 millimeters in length appear to be widely scattered across the site trapped in small discontinuous pockets of soil surrounded by bedrock outcrops and/or highly unstable scree of shattered limestone.

E. Material Evidence:

(1) Preliminary analysis of the on-site archeologist is that the eight sets of bones turned in by eight persons from Tuan Giao District are, within a few minor exceptions, human remains.

(2) Preliminary analysis of the on-site archeologist is that the bone and tooth fragments recovered by the survey team from TE-3 are human remains.

6. Recommended Future Actions

A. Although this crash site has yielded human remains, recovered by both local villagers and the present survey team, further archeological excavations

End of page 6 of 8

are not recommended. A number of very serious logistical, operational and recovery problems militate against fielding a recovery team at this site. These are:

(1) The terrain both to and at the site is extremely rugged and is considered exceedingly dangerous to even lightly equipped men. Supplying a full-scale recovery team overland would be hazardous even under the best of conditions. Rapidly changing weather conditions typical of

these high mountain localities could leave the recovery team isolated for prolonged periods of time.

(2) There is no alternative access to the site other tan overland. The closest acceptable safe landing zone is presently a three to four hour trek from the site. The possibility of finding a closer landing zone appears unlikely at this time.

(3) The availability of a safe base camp area on site is too limited for a full-scale recovery team. To alternatively place camp below the site, on the other hand, would only increase the opportunity for severe mishap in traveling between the camp and the site twice a day—not to mention a minimum of two to three hours lost in transit each day.

(4) The ruggedness and isolation combine to severely hamper the logistical support of this site, especially in terms of the heavy and cumbersome equipment needed to mount a full-scale field recovery.

(5) As already noted, the terrain of the site itself is extremely rugged. However, it is more the large areas of loose, highly unstable scree that make for hazardous working conditions once on the site.

(6) Excavatable matrix from which material remains can be reasonably recovered is limited to small pockets of colluvial soil trapped among the rocky outcrops. These soil areas represent perhaps less than 20 percent of the site as defined by the observable crash area.

(7) Few of these soil pockets have gone unworked by the local villagers, thus further reducing the recovery potential of further archeologically controlled excavation.

(8) The only other, and very problematic, possibility of archeological recovery of significant human remains is to extend into the downhill wash: however, this area is even more precipitous than the immediate crash area and there is the added factor of requiring the recovery team to work below tons of unstable scree.

B. In summary, this site offers only a marginal potential for the recovery of significant human remains beyond what has already been recovered while, at the same time, presents an unacceptably high risk factor. Further archeological recovery is therefore believed to be unwarranted at this time.

C. Recognizing the limiting conditions imposed by this site, if the decision were made to pursue further archeological recovery, the following provisional recommendations are offered:

(1) The recovery team be limited to no more than five or six American members plus an approximately reduced number of our VNOSMP counterparts and local hire. These would all be volunteers only.

(2) Isolation is the key limiting factor, so the recovery team must be totally self-contained for the duration that they are on site.

(3) The site should be mapped using a modified base line/grid system appropriate to the conditions of the site, primarily focusing on plotting the location of

End of page 7 of 8

the excavated soil pockets.

(4) Excavation should be limited to completely removing all accessible soil pockets within the immediate crash area only and avoiding the lower downwash below the crash area.

7. Pertinent data or location changes: None.

8. Analyst comments: None

9. Search and recovery specialist comments: concur with comments made in paragraph six.

10. Team chief comments: the information from the witnesses and the wreckage found at the crash site correlate with REFNO 0954. Do not recommend a recovery of this site base on all facts stated in paragraph six.

End of page 8 of 8

#2. 31 Mar 1993 Transcribed FAXed Message

DETACHMENT TWO

JOINT TASK FORCE—FULL ACCOUNTING

HANOI & VIETNAM

DATE: 31 MAR 93

TOTAL PAGES (INCLUDING COVER SHEET): 3

FROM: CDR, DET 2, JTF-FA, HANOI, SRV

OFFICE PHONE: 84–42–33709

FAX NUMBER: 84–42–33628

TO: CJTF-FA, CAMP SMITH, HI 96861

OFFICE PHONE: (808) 477–5521

FAX NUMBER: (808) 477–3001

CDR, USACILHI, HICKAM AFB, HI 96853

OFFICE PHONE: (808) 448–8903

FAX NUMBER: (808) 448–7813

EOC DUTY NCO: Please ensure a copy of this FAX gets delivered to LTC bbbb at CILHI; also provide a copy to JTF J-2 and J-3.

SUBJECT: (FAX102–93) CASE *0954

1. On 29–30 Mar 93 LTC bbbbb SSGT bbbb bbbb , two members of VNOSMP and two members of Tuan Giao District (Lai Chau Province) visited the site for case #0954. After repeated attempts to visit the site we were finally successful on this occasion. We departed Tuan Giao town and travelled by an old jeep for approx. 30 minutes to a dismount point QUJ 407981. We then hiked for 5 hours to a "village" (two residents) QUJ 455959 for an overnight stay, followed by a 1 ½ hr. hike to the crash site QUJ 474962.

2. The 6 1/2 hike/climb is tough and there is some hand-over-hand climbing up rock, particularly the last 45 min. As far as potential LZ's are concerned there are few opportunities; none

End of page 1 of 3

anywhere near the site. The top of the ridge, above the crash site, was explored but it would require extensive work (to include some demolitions of boulders, which would most likely have an adverse effect on the crash site) to construct any type of LZ and this is not recommended. The next possibility is via UJ466963 but this would require some demolition work to reduce/remove boulders. This area would knock off about 6 hrs. of hiking but the climb would still be required. The last possibility is QUJ 439974 and this is relatively easy LZ for the locals to clear/prepare. It will knock 4 hrs. off of the hike; the remaining 2 ½ hrs. would consist of 2 hrs. of using pack horses for equipment, followed by 30–45 min. of climbing to the actual site. During the last portion, there will be a requirement for construction of vertical hauling lines for equipment; I believe there is an NCO at CILHI who has served in the rangers and he could very well conduct the proper train-up for rope work. Once on site, there is sufficient space for sleeping, albeit the U.S. team (and its Vietnamese contingent) would have to be a reduced size team. A suggested team would be: team leader, anthropologist, medic, linguist and two graves registration specialists; all must be fully capable of hard climbing and harsh living conditions.

3. At the crash site there is an ample amount of wreckage still visible and immediately sub-surface although the preponderance of aircraft wreckage has been scavenged. The surface conditions are:

A. The site is located in rock formations on a steep mountain slope, approx.150 meters down from the ridgeline.

B. There are areas that should be excavated and the surface is composed of small boulders (that can be manhandled) underneath which is soft, fine granular soil, mixed with rock. It is recommended the small boulders be removed and placed in a "staging area" approx. 75 meters west of the crash site. Excavation and sifting can then be accomplished more effectively.

C. The remaining area of the crash site, where remains could expect to be discovered measures 100 × 100 yards, approximately.

4. Material evidence found: although numerous pieces of wreckage were observed on the surface, a greater amount was uncovered with minimal effort. One piece of evidence discovered on the surface was some sort of coupling arm that had two pieces of rubber as some sort of absorber on both ends; one piece of the rubber remained whereas thee other piece had been "replaced" by solid rock, a portion of the mountainside. This would indicate to me the extent of the velocity at which the aircraft impacted into the mountain. A reasonable conclusion would be that no crewmembers could have been expected to survive such an impact. A photograph of this piece of wreckage, and others, will be forwarded to HQJTF soonest. Additionally found and removed from the site by the undersigned were: a portion of hose from an oxygen mask system; a portion of nylon webbing (—in. width) with a loop (hand sized) tied at the end of it; a snap connector

End of page 2 of 3

from a parachute; and a portion of a map. The map was discovered under less than 10 cm of loose granular soil and was still readable and in excellent condition (the portion recovered was of the a Luoi area (Thua Thien-Hue Province).

5. Vietnamese counterparts' comments, after several trips to this region, and more specifically during this past one, it is clear that the Vietnamese aren't too excited about trekking to this site. They made repeated statements to try and dissuade us from making the hike; our determination may have provided them with an indication that we are very serious about excavating this site. Local officials recommended that, if we decide to excavate, then we do so in may before the bad weather sets in. Vietnamese cooperation was good, once the hike started. Initially there was a problem because (we were told) VNOSMP had not contacted the local officials and told them of our intentions. After waiting for over 2 1/2 hrs. at the helicopter in Tuan Giao, we finally started on our journey.

6. Recommendation. Although this site could be considered for group burial status, I recommend a recovery of this site during a future JFA when we have excavation teams operating in the northern portion of Vietnam. Team composition should be as stated in Para 2, and there should be a train-up for team members of the use of ropes prior to deploying to SRV. The team should be equipped with sleeping pads/mats, much insect repellant, plenty of water, ropes w/snaplinks, for climbing/vertical hauling lines, safety lines, etc., and MREs. It is further recommended that, for the sake of SRVG "approval" at future tech talks, this "team" be part of an 18 man recovery element which would give CJTF the negotiating leverage with his counterpart to say that we want to bring in only three REs, however, one of them will be a bit larger than the other two.

BBBB BB BBBBBB

USA

COMMANDER

End of page 3 of 3

#3. 22 Nov 1993 Teletype

Transcribed Teletype message from CJTFFA Det. 1, Bangkok, Thailand.

ROUTINE

R 221030Z NOV 93 PSN 937404P27

FM CJTFFA DET ONE BANGKOK TH

TO CDR FTF-FA HONOLULU HI

INFO JCS WASHDC//OCJCS-PW-MIA/J5//

USCINCPAC HONOLULU HI//J2/J3/J30M//

USCINCPAC LO WASHDC

SECDEF WASHDC//USDP:RSA//

CDRUSACILHI HICKAM AFB HI//TAPC-PED-H//

NSC WASHDC

RUEHC/SECSTATE WASHDC//EAP/VLC//

CIA WASHDC//OEA/SEA/IB/DDO/EA/ICOG//DIA WASHDC

THIS IS A 6 PART MSG COLLATED BY MDU

UNCLAS BANGKOK TH 43258

UNCLASSIFIED 0738 NOV 93

SUBJECT: Detailed Search and Recovery Report of Case 0954.

1. Summary:

REF: 26th JFA Summary Report, BKK, TH DTG200247Z NOV 93.

A. During the period 24 Oct to 8 Nov 93 a Joint United States/Socialist Republic of Vietnam (US/SRV) recovery team traveled to Tuan Giao District, Lai Chau Province, Socialist Republic of Vietnam, to excavate a C-130 E crash site correlated to Case 0954. This case involves the aircraft crash and loss of 11 crew members while conducting a special mission on 29 Dec 67. The site is located at grid coordinate 48QUJ4741096010. The grid coordinate was verified using the Trimble Trimpack Receiver for the Global Positioning System, tracking four satellites. This site is located in a very isolated and mountainous area at elevation of 1457 meters (4780 feet). It is accessible by an arduous 6-hour overland trek, or 2 ½ hour trek from a helicopter landing zone located at grid UJ4386797397. After inserting by helicopter, the team established a base camp approximately an hour's hike from the crash.

End of page 1 of 10

site. Access to the site was along a narrow mountain footpath. The final 30 minutes of the trip required, in many instances, scaling rock faces. This is an aircraft crash site in extremely rugged and dangerous terrain. The immediate area of the site ia a rocky slope 40 to 45 degrees in grade. For some 150 meters (500 feet) below the crash site and perhaps another 60 meters (200 feet) above, the rocky face angles to 60 degrees and more. Working from the lowest elevation of the site to the highest, approximately 17 potential areas of excavation were defined. Each excavation area constituted a separate unit of operation and no attempt was made to establish a site grid, either for mapping or for excavation purposes. Also, given the irregularity of these areas no subgrids were used for excavation; each area was, in effect, its own excavation unit. Excavation procedures consisted of simply removing as much surface rock as was safely practical and scraping up the remaining loose humic debris and soil left behind. All excavated matrix (aircraft debris, human remains and associated soil) was screened through 1/4 inch mesh and carefully scanned for critical aircraft parts, personal effects, and/or human remains. The excavation resulted in the finding of human remains, personal effects and associated pieces of wreckage consistent with those of a C-130 aircraft. 187 pieces of human bone were recovered, which included portions of cranium, vertebra, ribs, humerus, long bone, hand/foot bone fragments, as well as 1 calceneous (heel bone), 1 mandibular fragment (without teeth), and 1 pelvic fragment. 16 teeth were also recovered, of which 6 have dental restorations. Life support equipment recovered from the site include components from a minimum of seven personal parachutes, two oxygen masks, one survival vest, one survival radio and three underarm life preservers. The site was closed by CILHI team leader and anthropologist on 8 Nov 93. Throughout the JFA the U.S. team received very good support and excellent cooperation from their Vietnamese counterparts.

B. United States team members:

-CPT Solseth	Team leader
-1LT Sabin	Assistant team leader
-Dr. Davis	Anthropologist
-SFC Conard	Team Sergeant

End of page 2 of 10

-SFC Maxcy	Explosive ordnance disposal
-MSGT Miller	Life support wreckage analyst
-CT12 Foster	Linguist/analyst
-SGT Hargis	Linguist/analyst
-SFC Thornhill	Medic
-SFC Arnold	Mortuary affairs specialist
-PFC French	Mortuary affair specialist
-SPC Coffin	Photographer

C. Socialist Republic of Vietnam team members:

-Dinh Vu Khuynh	Team leader/VNOSMP
-Nguyen Van Tich	Assistant team leader/VNOSMP
-Nguyen Duc Tuong	Team member/VNOSMP
-Hoang Van Huong	Team member/VNOSMP
-Tran Van Thao	Team member/VNOSM
-Than Du	Team leader/Lai Chau Province
-Nguyen Van Nghi	Team member/Lai Chau Province
-Nguyen Van Thuat	Team member/Lai Chau Province
-Nguyen Thanh Son	Team member/Lai Chau Province
-Vang A Dung	Team member/Lai Chau Province
-Quang Van Pang	District cadre/Tuan Giao District
-Lo Ngoc On	District cadre/Tuan Giao District
-Ngo Van Cu	District cadre/Tuan Giao District
-Giang Van Vu	Village cadre/ Phu Nhung Village
-Vu a Mua	Village cadre/Phu Nhung Village

2. Background:

A. At 0030 hrs on 29 Dec 67 the 11 man crew associated with case 0954 departed Nha Trang, RVN, on a mission over North Vietnam. The mission progressed as planned and a radio report was last received at 0430 hrs. When the aircraft failed to return to base as scheduled, an organized search and rescue was initiated in the mountainous area where the aircraft was believed to be located. Search efforts were terminated on 29 Jan 1968.

B. The site was surveyed on 8 Nov 92 during the 20th JFA. Subsequent to the survey of the site, locals turned over eight bundles of human remains for examination by the U. S. team These remains were repatriated and are currently at the U. S. Army Central Identification Laboratory, Hawaii (USACILHI).

C. The site was surveyed again on 29–30 Mar 93 by

End of page 3 of 10

the JTF-FA Detachment Two Commander.

3. Project location:

A. Near Phu Nhung Village, Tuan Giao District, Lai Chau Province, Socialist Republic of Vietnam.

B. Military grid reference system grid coordinate 48QUJ4741096010. Map edition: 2-AMS; Series L 7014; Sheet: 5752 III; Title: King Khoai; Scale: 1:50,000; Horizontal datum: Indian Datum 1960. The grid coordinate was determined using a Trimble Trimpack Receiver for the Global Positioning System tracking four satellites.

4. Description of project area:

A. The crash site is located at grid coordinates UJ4741096010, in the Tuan Giao District of Lai Chau Province, Socialist Republic of Vietnam. This site is located in an extremely isolated and mountainous area at an elevation of 1457 meters (4780 feet). It is accessible by an arduous 6-hour overland trek, or a 2 1/2 hour trek from a helicopter landing zone located at grid UJ4386797397.

B. This is an aircraft crash site in extremely rugged and dangerous terrain. The immediate area of the site is a rocky slope 40 to 45 degrees in grade. For some 150 meters (500 feet) below the crash site, and perhaps another 60 meters (200 feet) above, the rocky face angles to 60 degrees and more. This is a karst limestone landscape generally covered by a mixed forest or tropical deciduous and evergreen broadleafs with a dense understory of bamboo, bushy shrubs, ferns, vining lianas, and various grasses. The site itself, however, is nearly devoid of vegetation. There is a noticeable, roughly circular break in the trees where the aircraft plunged through the forest canopy. The surface of the site is covered by limestone outcrops and unstable areas of shattered rocks, the latter presumably resulting from the impact of the aircraft against the mountain side. A few pockets of humic soil can be found scattered about

End of page 4 of 10

the crash area. However, for the most part the surface horizon has since eroded downhill. Whatever protective ground cover that may have existed was destroyed by the crash.

A. The site lies on a north to northwesterly facing slope. Overall, the crash area measures 16 meters uphill/downhill and 22 meters across the slope, including lower areas of down-wash, the site extends 55 meters downhill for a total vertical fall of some 35 meters. Although considerable amount of aircraft wreckage litters the main site area and part of steeper slope immediately below, no large pieces of wreckage were seen with the exception of two struts from the main landing gear, the nose gear strut, sections of drive shaft from one of the engines, and four propeller hub assemblies.

The rest of the larger wreckage appears to have been gradually carted away over the years by local villagers "mining" the site for scrap metal. Presumably these were the same people who more recently recovered the remains presented to the survey team during the 20th JFA.

5. Field methods:

A. Because of the extreme ruggedness of the site and the dangerous working conditions inherent on the steep mountainside, field work necessarily proceeded according to the team's ability to remove unstable rock from work areas of the site. This was done first by making a careful reconnaissance of the total potential site area and determining locations of highest potential recovery in relation to the "lay" of the massive amounts of scree (loose rock debris) produced by the crash. Working from the lowest elevation of the site to the highest, approximately 17 potential areas of excavation were needed. These were revised as the excavation proceeded. Each excavation area constituted a separate unit of operation and no attempt was made to establish asset grid, either for mapping or for excavation purposes. Also, given the irregularity of these areas, no subgrids were used for excavation; each area was, in effect its own excavation unit.

B. Excavation began with area 1, defined as the lower boundary of the site area. Work then progressed uphill from one area to the next as each lower area was

End of page 5 of 10

completed. Where possible, adjacent areas were excavated simultaneously, however, for reasons of safety, at no time was any area worked immediately uphill of an area that was still in progress.

A. Excavation procedures consisted of simply removing as much of surface rock as was safely practical and scraping up the remaining loose humic debris and soil left behind. All excavated matrix was screened through 1/4 inch mesh and carefully scanned for critical aircraft parts, personal effects, and/or human remains.

6. Archeological findings:

A. The archeological findings from the Phu Nhung site are summarized as follows:

(1). The overall extent of the site was defined by the distribution of the aircraft debris representing the main airframe, landing gear, and engines. Although scavenged intensively over the years, and despite the natural processes of weather and gravity, it was still possible to identify the main cabin portion of the aircraft from the rear cargo ramp forward to the cockpit.

(2). A total of 17 excavation area were defined and worked in sequence from the lowest elevation of the site to the highest, for a total excavation area of approximately 220 square meters.

(3). The excavation yielded aircraft debris that is consistent with a C-130 type aircraft. An aircraft data plate and several numbered items recovered from the excavation may identify the model; however, further analysis must await return from the field.

(4). Recovery of life-support and other aircrew-related material was restricted to a set of contiguous excavation areas determined to be the main cabin portion of the aircraft. While some life-support and aircrew-related items were found beyond the main areas of concentration, mainly downhill areas of the site as a result of gravity and erosion, there was no evidence for any uphill dispersal of aircrew-related material.

(5). As noted by the life-support specialist,

End of page 6 of 10

the distribution of aircraft debris and aircrew-related material suggests that the aircraft hit the sloping mountain side straight on and then came to rest at and below the impact point without any significant "throw" of debris above the impact point. Furthermore, the recovery of parachute fittings and various other items catalogued by the life-support specialist also suggest that, although only a minimum number of 7 individuals can be accounted for, it is probable that the remaining aircrew members did not leave the aircraft prior to crashing.

(6). Few personal effects were recovered from the excavation: uniform (fatigue) buttons, 2 socks, pieces of boot and boot inserts, the casing of a military-issue wristwatch, a piece of fabric watch band with buckle, and a broken link for an expandable watchband. The distribution of the personal effects mirrored that of the life support and other aircrew-related gear.

(7). Human remains recovered from the excavation include 187 pieces of bone and 16 teeth, 6 of which had dental restorations. As with life-support gear, aircrew related items, and personal effects, the majority of the human remains were excavated from the main cabin of the aircraft.

B. It is significant to note that, despite the amount of damage to the site over the past 26 years, it was still possible to delimit the main cabin area of the crash site where the aircrew would have been at impact. As the excavation proceeded, a consistent pattern of recovery was evident—human remains were forthcoming only from those areas that minimally also yielded life-support and/or other aircrew-related effects. Those areas yielding only airframe, engine, or other non-aircrew related debris did not yield human remains. From this pattern of association between at least two classes of material, it can be concluded that all safely accessible areas of the site have been thoroughly explored and that all safely recoverable human remains are accounted for.

7. Material evidence:

A. Aircraft wreckage:

- Unknown plastic piece with: Lockheed Aircraft Corp. P/n 388612–1a
  End of page 7 of 10
- Data plate: pump, centrifugal, fuel booster p/n rr11640–070725/357
- Data Plate: Vickers Induction Motor A. C. aircraft S/N MX 112594
- Data Plate: Tank Unit Fuel Quantity
- Data Plate: Motor Generator Type No. A5179460600 TI P/N 30732–1
- Data Plate: Airesearch Overhaul Date June 27, 1967
- Aluminum Piece With: 388618
- Aluminum Piece With: 37698
- Unknown Metal Piece With: H-1. Thompson Fiberglass Co.
  Insul-Blkt 12–22206–43 1–24–64 PO Y85605

B. Life Support Equipment:

- Data Plate: Receiver, Transmitter, Radio ACR Rt-10
  FSN 5821–912–4480YY S/N 50142
- Data Plate: Beacon Set, Radio AN/URT-27 S/N 045652
- 3 Ejector Snaps with V-Rings
- 14 Capewell-Type Parachute Canopy Releases
- 29 Parachute Connector Links
- 20 Various Restraint Buckles
- 15 Ejector Snaps
- 9 V-Rings
- 13 Accessory Rings
- Personal Lowering Device Braking Bar
- 3 Pld Line Pieces
- 3 Possible Riser Pieces
- 3 Pieces of Webbing
- 3 Headset Comm Cord Brackets
- 3 Earcup Cushions
- A Headset Earcup
- 2 Oxygen Mask Face forms Type MBU-5/P
- Piece of Oxygen Mask Hose
- 4 Dozen Mask Buckles
- 2 Pieces of Oxygen Mask Hardshell
- 2 Two-Point Oxygen Mask Bayonets

- A Four-Point Oxygen Mask Bayonet
- An Oxygen Mask Receiver
- Survival Vest Lacing Cover
- 2 Pieces of Survival Vest Material
- 10 Life Preserver Buckles

End of page 8 of 10

- 2 Life Preserver Carbon Dioxide Bottles
- Life Preserver Bladder Material
- Multi-Place Life Raft Material
- A Raft Repair Plug
- A Chin Strap
- A Piece of Dark Visor
- 2 Zipper Pull Tabs
- Fire Starter Wrapper
- Piece of Snake Bite Container

C. Aircrew Related Items:

- Wrist Watch Back: DTU-2A/P S/N 105956 Mfg Date DEC 19L6
- 2 Jungle Boot Canvas Tops
- A Blue Sock
- 3 Jungle Boot Insoles
- 3 Pieces of Navigation Map
- 4 .38 Cal Bullets and Shells
- 1 5.56 MM Shell
- Trigger Assembly from a Possible Flare Gun

8. Life support Analyst comments:

Aircraft wreckage observed and recovered are consistent with a C-130 series aircraft. The aircraft impacted the top of a mountainous slope with rugged terrain features. The majority of the wreckage has been scavenged by locals. The remaining items include engine and landing gear components. Life support equipment was recovered in dirt pockets throughout the areas between engine pieces. This indicated the main fuselage area with the cockpit at the top of the slope. Life support equipment recovered from these areas include components from a minimum of seven personal parachutes, two oxygen masks, one survival vest, one survival radio and three underarm life preservers. These items require further analysis. The probability of any successful bailout of any of the crewmembers, prior to aircraft impact, is highly unlikely.

9. Conclusions and Recommendations:

A. The Phu Nhung site is a C-130 crash site; however, the model and vehicle number are as yet unconfirmed.

B. The total maximum extent of the site was delineated by the distribution of aircraft wreckage

End of page 9 of 10

consisting of components associated with the main airframe, landing gear, and engines.

C. Excavation revealed a consistent pattern of association between the recovery of human remains and the occurrence of life-support and other aircrew-related items: i.e. . with the exception of a few pieces of bone washed downhill from the main area of the site, no human remains were recovered from an area that did not also yield life-support or other air crew-related material.

D. Physical evidence in the form of aircraft wreckage, life-support gear, personal effects, and human remains recovered from the site suggest no successful bail out occurred prior to the crash of the aircraft.

E. Based on the foregoing, and having determined that all of the safely accessible areas of the site were thoroughly explored and that all safely recoverable human remains were accounted for, the Phu Nhung site was officially closed on 8 Nov 93 at 1100 hours by the CILHI team leader and anthropologist.

End of page 10 of 10

#4. 17 June 1994 Teletype

Transcribed Teletype message from CJTF-FA Honolulu, HI.

ROUTINE

R 171102z JUN 94 ZYB PSN 858771P36

FM CDR JTF-FA HONOLULU HI//J2//

TO SECDEF WASHINGTON DC//USDP:RSA//

INFO WHITE HOUSE NATIONAL SECURITY COUNCIL WASH DC

RUEHC/SECSTATE WASHINGTON DC//CA/EAP/VLC/CCS/OCS//

JOINT STAFF WASHINGTON DC//J5//

DIA WASHINGTON DC

USCINCPAC HONOLULU HI//J2/J3/J30-M//

USCINCPAC LO WASHINGTON DC

CIA WASHINGTON DC//DEA/SEA/IB/DDO/EA/ICOG//

RUEHBT/USDAO BANGKOK TH//PW-MIA//

CDRUSACILHI HICKAM AFB HI//TAPC-PED-H//

THIS IS A 4 PART MSG COLLATED BY MDU

UNCLAS //N03460//

MSGID/GENADMIN/CDR JTF-FA/252//

SUBJ/Report of Investigation of Leads Pertaining to Possible Remains of U.S. Service Men Reported by a Vietnamese Citizen//

REF/A/RPT/CJTFFA DET TWO/30MAY94//

REF/B/RMG/CJTFFA DET ONE/230220ZNOVJ92//

REF/C/RMG/CJTFFA DET ONE/221030ZNOV93//

NARR/Ref A is the report of information provided by a walk-in source at Det Two on 26 May 94. Ref B is the detailed report of the survey of case 0954 conducted on 8 Nov 92. Ref C is the detailed report of the search and recovery of case 0954 conducted from 24 Oct to 8 Nov 93. Field analysis of the information obtained in Ref A established requirements for the investigation reported below. CJTFFA requested this investigation at the 31 May 94 bimonthly technical meeting in Hanoi.//

RMKS/1. Summary of Investigation: In response to CJTFFA request.

End of page 1 of 10

At the 31 May 1994 Technical Meeting in Hanoi, a Joint U.S./Vietnam investigation team formed in Hanoi on 2 Jun 94, then traveled to Son La Province to investigate recent information alleging that a resident of Son La Province maintained custody of remains and material evidence, including identification media, associated with two unaccounted for individuals from case 0954 (Ref A). Case 0954 involves the 29 Dec 67 loss of eleven U.S. crewmembers aboard a C-130 which crashed in Lai Chau Province. Remains and wreckage associated with this case were turned over by local citizens in 1992. A joint team conducted a survey of the site in November of that year, and the site was excavated in October-November 1993. The 1994 team's primary purpose was to recover from private citizens all remains and personal effects associated with this case. The joint team interviewed two witnesses, obtaining only hearsay information. The team recovered no remains or personal effects. Local authorities believe the limited hearsay information provided by the two witnesses will assist them in locating all individuals who may currently have remains or material evidence associated with this case. Local authorities pledged a strong commitment to continue this investigation unilaterally and recover any remains or personnel effects. No additional joint investigation is planned.

2. Details of Investigation:

A. On 2 Jun 94, the Joint U.S./Vietnam Team formed at JTF-FA, Detachment Two, Hanoi to investigate case 0954.

(1) U.S. Team Members were:

-Mr. K. Gary Flanagan, Team Leader/Casualty Resolution Specialist, JTF-FA Det 2;
-SFC Richard V. McClure, JTF-FA Det 2.

(2) VNOSMP Team Members were:

-Lieutenant Colonel Pham Cong Khoi (Phamj Coong Khooi). Team leader/Ministry of Defense (MOD)
-Mr. Le Thanh Long (Lee Thanh Long), Ministry of Interior (MOI) representative.

(3) Son La Province Team Members were:

- Mr. Nguyen Van Tho (Nguyeenx Vawn Thoj), Province People's Committee, Chairman of the Provgince Foreign Relations Department,
- Mr. Bui Tong'(Buif Tong), Province Task Team;
- Mr. Dao Tien (Daof Tieens), Province Task Team;
- Major Ha Peng (Haf Peeng), Regional Border Defense Force

(4) Moc Chau District Team Members were:

- Mr. Trinh Luong Huu (Trinhj Lwong Hwux), District Committee;
- Mr. Tran Ngoc Dao (Traanf Ngoc Daoj), District Committee;

End of page 2 of 10

- Mr. Luong Van Tho (Lwong Vawn Thoj) District Police Chief.

(5) Song Ma District Team Members were:

- Senior Captain Tran Phuc Thai (Traanf Phucj Thais), District Border Defense
- Mr. Lo Dan (Lop Zaan), District Committee;
- Mr. Le Tan (Lee Taan), District Committee
- Mr. Nguyen Thuan (Nguyeenx Thuaanj), District Committee.

(6) Chien Khuong Village Team Members were:

- Mr. Ha Van Suong (Haf Vawn Swongs) former village party secretary;
- Mr. Deo Van On (Deof Vawn Oon),Village People's Committee;
- Mr. Nguyen Van Quang (Nguyeenx Vawn Quangr), Village People's Committee.

B. The U.S. team leader reviewed all recently obtained information for case 0954 with the Vietnamese team leader. The team members agreed that the objectives for the team were:

(1) Determine what (if any) remains associated with this case may still be in the hands of private citizens;

(2) Obtain all such remains for joint forensic review as quickly as possible;

(3) Determine what (if any) personal effects associated with this case may still be in the hands of private citizens;

(4) Obtain all such personal effects.

The team immediately departed Hanoi. All joint team members agreed that every effort would be made for the team to interview each potential witness for this case.

C. Prior to the team's departure from Hanoi on 2 Jun 94, VNOSMP team members agreed to travel to the locations of Vietnamese citizens associated with the lead information obtained for case 0954 (Ref A), interview each potential witness or alleged participant, and obtain any material evidence related to the case.

D. On 2 June 94, the joint team traveled to Moc Chau District town. The team met with district officials and requested to meet with Mr. Nguyen Chi Dung, who had provided his residential area in Moc Chau Town as a point of contact for an Americana to receive remains for two of the crew members in case 0954. CDRS provided the district team with a description of Mr. Dung to supplement the residence information. After receiving the request, the district team departed for the area listed as Mr. Dung's residence. The team returned less than one hour later with a photograph of Mr. Dung in a border defense force uniform. CRS confirmed that the photograph was the same individual who had visited Det. Two. Dung's neighbors told the district team that he had not returned from visiting relatives near Hanoi. The district team provided the VNOSMP team members with the Hanoi area addresses of two of Dung's brothers.

End of page 3 of 10

The VNOSMP team members returned to the Hanoi area with one vehicle to search for Mr. Dung and bring him back to Moc Chau district town. The U.S. team members remained in Moc Chau in case Mr. Dung returned while the VNOSMP team members were looking for him.

E. On 3 Jun 94, VNOSMP team members returned to Moc Chau District from Hanoi with Mr. Dung. He had been visiting relatives in Ha Tay Province on the outskirts of Hanoi. The joint team re-interviewed Mr. Dung in the presence of district officials and obtained the following additional details (not previously reported in Ref A):

(1) Mr. Luong (Lwongf), an ethnic Thai who lives in Song Ma District, Son La Province, passed the request to Mr. Dung to visit Det Two in Hanoi to see if an American would come to Son La Province to receive the alleged remains of two U.S. crewmembers.

(2) Mr. Luong had alluded to an unspecified number of other individuals who also were aware of the remains but he had not told Mr. Dung their names.

(3) Mr. Dung knows where Mr. Luong lives in Song Ma District and volunteered to lead the joint team to Mr. Luong's home village.

(4) Mr. Dung recalled that Mr. Luong had boasted that one remains was buried very near his home in Song Ma District and could be retrieved very quickly. A second remains was located farther away from his home and would require more than one day to retrieve. Mr.Dung did not have any additional details.

F. On 3 Jun 94, the joint team traveled to Son La Town, Son La Province. The team arrived at the province committee guest house in Son La shortly before sundown. Province officials agreed to meet with the team on the morning of 4 Jun 94.

G. On the morning of 4 Jun 94, the team met with officials from Son La Province and Song Ma District. The final destination of the team, Mr. Luong's home, was determined to be Chien Khuong Village, Song Ma District. The southern village boundary also forms the Lao-Vietnam border and is under the control of the Vietnamese Border Defense Forces. Province officials agreed that the U.S. members of the team could go to Chien Khuong Village, but without central government permission. The border Defense Forces recommended against the trip. The VNOSMP Team Members, acting as Central Government Cadre, in conjunction with the province authorities, cabled Hanoi for authorization for the U.S. team members to go to Chien Khuong. The Joint Team received all necessary permits for the trip to the border area at 0830 hours and departed Son La Town for Song Ma District.

End of page 4 of 10

H. The team traveled by four-wheel drive vehicle for over three hours over extremely difficult terrain, arriving in Chien Khuong Village (48QUJ955127), Song Ma District at approximately 1200 hours. The team walked less than 100 meters from the road to the home of the former village party secretary Mr. Ha Van Suong (Haf Vawn Swongs), an ethnic Thai and lifelong resident of the area. After being introduced to the team and its mission, Mr. Suong indicated that his son, Mr. Ha Van Luong (Haf Vawn Swong), was working in the fields about 800 meters from the team's current location. Village, district, and border defense personnel were dispatched to find Mr. Luong and bring him to Mr. Suong's home for interview. Mr. Suong said that he had never heard of Luong's involvement in any endeavors concerning U.S. remains or personal effects. He said he was unaware of any information concerning U. S. remains or personal effects related to this case, and due to his position of authority within the village community, he should have been aware of any such matters. He would not speculate on why his son sent a messenger to Det Two in Hanoi with remains samples.

I. After about one hour, Mr. Luong arrived at his father's house, escorted by border defense personnel assigned to Song Ma District. Mr. Luong, approx 57 YOA, clean-shaven, crew cut, wearing a freshly-pressed, long-sleeve shirt had been given the opportunity to clean up before meeting with the joint team. Senior Captain Tran Phuc Thai (Traanf Phucj Thais), District Border Defense Force, introduced Mr. Luong to the joint team and asked Mr. Luong to tell the team all he knew about remains and identification media associated with a crash site in Lai Chau Province.

J. Mr. Luong addressed the joint team in a quiet, reserved, and sometimes halting manner. He said he had heard the President of Vietnam during a radio broadcast call for all Vietnam citizens who had remains or information to contribute to the humanitarian effort of resolving the U. S. MIA issue by reporting their information to the authorities. Since he had no personal knowledge of how the MIA program worked, he had simply passed on what little information he had. Mr. Luong said he had some acquaintances who knew of an aircraft that crashed and burned. Some of them had retrieved remains and dog tags from the crash site. Mr. Luong said one of the individuals who told him about the dog tags and remains was Mr. Lo Van Muon (Lof Vawn Mwonf), a resident of Muong Lam (Mwongf Lamj) Village (48QUH636998), Song Ma District. Mr. Luong then changed his mind and said that Mr. Muon lived in Muong Sai (Mwongf Sai) Village (UJ 959187), Song Ma District.

End of page 5 of 10

K. Mr. Luong said he had not seen the dog tags or the remains except for the few bone samples he asked Mr. Dung to give to the U.S. MIA Office in Hanoi. Mr. Luong said he had no personal knowledge of the source of the dog tag rubbings, said he had never seen any pieces of survival map, and did not remember who had given him the information. Mr. Luong said that he had no further information to provide the joint team. Mr. Luong disavowed any knowledge of any other remains and then remained silent.

L. Mr. Dung, the witness who had passed the information leading to this investigation, sat behind Mr. Luong and remained silent until this point.

When Mr. Luong appeared to have finished his statement, Mr. Dung said that Mr. Luong had changed his story. Mr. Dung said Mr. Luong had told him that the remains of one U. S. pilot was nearby and another was a considerable distance from the village, reburied in the jungle. The two men argued over who was telling the truth for about one minute. Then LTC Khoi asked to introduce the joint team.

M. LTC Khoi introduced the joint team and its mission. He explained the U.S. and SRV Government policies, respectively, of providing no rewards or favors in exchange for U.S. remains or information. LTC Khoi explained when remains prove to be those of U.S. servicemen, the SRV Government can reimburse Vietnamese citizens a reasonable sum of money for labor, transportation, and storage costs. LTC Khoi emphasized that this is a humanitarian mission, there are no hidden or unofficial programs for rewards, and that the Vietnamese members of the joint teams operate under the strict directives of the government of Vietnam that this is solely a humanitarian issue. He advised Mr. Luong that he should provide the joint team with all information concerning this case. He advised Mr. Luong to turn over all remains and personal effects in his possession. He also advised Mr. Luong to inform the joint team of all persons who have knowledge of remains or personal effects pertinent to this case.

N. LTC Khoi invited CRS to ask questions or provide any details. CRS reiterated the team's humanitarian mission, reviewed the joint efforts that had culminated in the excavation of the 0954 site in Lai Chau Province in Nov 93. CRS then invited Mr. Luong to provide any additional details which might assist the joint team in resolving the mystery of the latest information concerning the remains and identification media associated with this case.

O. Mr. Luong was hesitant to respond, but finally began speaking, this time in a monotone without looking at the joint team members.

End of page 6 of 10

He said that he had heard that people (an unspecified number) in Lai Chau had located seven remains at a crash site where an aircraft had burned. The people had taken one of the remains for their own purpose. He did not know the disposition of the other six remains. After a short pause, Mr. Luong said that it was his people's experience that in dealing with outsiders they always held some information back. He said it was their insurance against the unscrupulous dealings of outsiders. Also, he said it was not uncommon for his people to pass information by word of mouth from one person to another without identifying all of the individuals involved. He remembered another man named Lao (Laof), who was also involved with these remains and dog tags, but he did not know the man well enough to say his full name or where he lived.

P. Apparently shaken, Mr. Luong said he had nothing more to offer and became silent. After a brief pause, central, province and district authorities conferred and agreed that the interview was over. The team thanked the former party secretary Mr. Suong for the use of his home to conduct the interview and departed Chien Khuong Village for Muong Sai Village, the reported residence of the potential witness, Mr. Lo Van Muon. On the way into Muong Sai Village, Senior Captain Thai inquired from other residents of the village about the location of a Mr. Muon. No one provided distinct answers. Once the team reached Muong Sai Village residents said they were certain that no one by the name of Muon lived in Muong Sai Village.

Q. While the team was stopped in Muong Sai Village, Major Ha Peng, representative of the Regional Border Defense Forces, said that he was well acquainted with Mr. Luong, since they were first cousins. Major Peng opined that Mr. Luong was not a man of good character and was not a respected member of his community. He said he was aware of the events which transpired in both Son La and Lai Chau Provinces which eventually led to the joint excavation of site 0954. With the information he gained by listening to Mr. Luong, Major Peng said he believed that he and the border defense forces in the district and the region could follow the trail of information and recover all remains and personal effects which might pertain to case 0954. He assured CRS that Mr. Luong's reluctance to discuss the circumstances of the remains and personal effects in the hands of private citizens was not inconsistent with the manner of the local people when dealing with outsiders. Major Peng said that not only were the U.S. team members considered outsiders but so were the VNOSMP team members. Major Peng assured CRS that he had a plan to obtain all of the remaining details of this case and to recover all remains and personal effects that might still be in the hands of private citizens.

End of page 7 of 10

R. Major Peng then asked Mr. Nguyen Chi Dung, the individual who passed information to Det Two concerning this case on 26 May, if he would be willing to assist the joint team. Mr. Dung had previously served with the border defense forces in the Chien Khuong Village area. He is well known in the village and surrounding area and is not considered an outsider. Mr. Dung volunteered to do whatever he could to resolve this problem. Major Peng asked Mr. Dung to return to Chien Khuong Village and consult with Senior Captain Thai of the border defense forces. Mr. Dung would remain in Song Ma District until he determined the disposition of the remains and personal effects for this case. Once Mr. Dung obtains the necessary information he will report this to the border defense forces. Province and district representatives on the team agreed that this plan should proceed and recommended against the joint team returning to Chien Khuong Village. The team departed for Son La Town, and Mr. Dung went back to Chien Khuong Village.

S. On 5 June 94, the joint team met at the Son La Province guest house to discuss the investigation of the information associated with case 0954. LTC Khoi reported the following:

(1) Authorities of the central government, Son La Province, Song Ma District, and the Regional Border Defense Forces approved of Major Peng's unilateral plan to follow up with residents in the area.

(2) Major Peng will supervise the activities of the border defense forces for this case and will conduct all necessary coordination between the authorities of Son La and Lai Chau Provinces to determine all individuals in this chain of information and recover all possible remains, personal effects, or material evidence.

(3) Mr. Tho, representing Son La Province, made a strong commitment that Son La Province Task Team would cooperate on all actions for this case.

4. Material Evidence: No remains or material evidence were collected during the investigation of this case.

5. Recommended Future Actions:

A. Recommend no additional joint investigation activity on this case.

B. Recommend the VNOSMP continue to work with appropriate regional authorities to locate witnesses, recover material evidence and make available for joint forensic review all remains and personal

End of page 8 of 10

effects associated with this case which may be in the possession of Vietnamese citizens.

C. Recommend that Major Peng report the results of the Border Defense Force Unilateral effort to the U.S. side via the VNOSMP.

D. Recommend that VNOSMP assess the unilateral progress made by local authorities on this case and receive all remains and personal effects which may have been obtained for joint forensic review.

6. Comments:

A. U.S. and VNOSMP team members rate the reliability of the witness Mr. Luong as suspect. Local officials commented that Mr. Luong is not a well-respected or trusted member of the community.

B. VNOSMP team members and local officials are working to locate all participants in the chain of information concerning this case which extends from the site in Tuan Giao District, Lai Chau Province to Song Ma District, Son La Province. Regional Border Defense Force Representative Major Peng provided his assurances that the Border Defense Forces would assist in locating all possible material evidence associated with this case. Major Peng was aware of the individuals involved in the events leading up to the discovery of the 0954 site, the unilateral turnover of remains, the joint survey, and the subsequent joint excavation. He said his personal knowledge of the unilateral and joint activities for this case, including the Vietnamese citizens who have previously provided information and remains, would help him to follow the new leads effectively.

C. CRS received outstanding support during all aspects of this investigation. Officials in Moc Chau District, Son La Town, and Song Ma District had one day's notice (or less) that the joint team would be arriving in their respective locales. Despite little or no notice, authorities in each locale complied with every request made by the team and allowed the team access to every location requested.

D. CRS received official assurance from all Vietnamese officials who participated in this investigation that the information chain of alleged remains and identification media would soon be resolved.

E. Major Peng said he believes there may be some remains and personal effects in the hands of private citizens. Based on his previous knowledge and experience with this case, he is certain that he has a sound plan to recover any such remains or personal effects.

F. Major Peng explained that the names provided by the witness Mr. Luong to describe the other two individuals who claim to have remains could loosely be translated as "this guy" and "that guy" in the village vernacular.

G. The number of remains (7) referenced by Mr. Luong, although

End of page 9 of 10

clearly hearsay information indicates the information passed to Det Two is related to remains unilaterally previously turned over to a joint team in Nov 92. Witnesses available for joint interview at that time were unwilling to reveal names of other participants in the unilateral recovery of remains at the site.

H. There was no advance party for this investigation. Local officials had no ability to screen the information in advance. This unscheduled investigation was undertaken by a small joint team to follow leads and obtain any remains or personal effects which could possibly pertain to Case 0954. LTC Khoi and Mr. Long were assigned as the VNOSMP cadre for this team with one day's notice.

End of page 10 of 10

Appendix C

Combat Talon Aircraft Losses

Stray Goose and Combat Talon C-130s proved to be appropriate aircraft for conducting special air operations in all the nation's conflicts since the Vietnam War. It is very likely that they will continue in this vital role as long as Lockheed keeps producing C-130s. They have managed to remain on the cutting edge of evolving technology by taking advantage of innovations that made them formidable assets to the country's military capability.

There were eight losses of Combat Talon aircraft from their first deployment to Vietnam in 1966 through 2013. Six of these resulted in air crew losses. There was also one loss of Combat Talon crew members who flew in an EC-130E in support of the Iranian hostage rescue attempt.

The first aircraft loss occurred at Nha Trang Air Base in Vietnam on 25 November 1967, during a Vietcong mortar attack on the air field. It was one of the original C-130E(I) Stray Goose Combat Talons number 64–0563 that belonged to Detachment 1 of the 314th Troop Carrier Wing. A direct mortar hit destroyed the aircraft completely and damaged the other three Talons that were parked in the area under attack. There were no personnel injuries.

The second no-loss-of-life aircraft loss occurred on 29 December 2004 in Iraq during a nighttime landing on a runway that was undergoing maintenance. It was a Combat Talon II, MC-130H, #90–0161 that belonged to the 15th Special Operations Squadron from Hurlburt Field in Florida.

The first air crew loss occurred on 29 December 1967, when a C-130E(I), tail number 64–0547, crashed into a mountain east of Dien Bien Phu during a nighttime leaflet drop and resupply mission. Lost were the following S-01 crew members:

Capt. Edwin N. Osborne Jr.—Aircraft Commander

Capt. Gerald G. Van Buren—Pilot

Maj. Charles P. Claxton—Pilot

Lt. Col. Donald E. Fisher—Navigator

Capt. Gordon J. Wenaas—Navigator

Capt. Frank C. Parker III—Electronic Warfare Officer

TSgt. Jack McCrary—Flight Engineer

SSgt. Wayne A. Eckley—Flight Engineer

SSgt. Edward J. Darcy—Loadmaster

Sgt. James Williams—Loadmaster

SSgt. Gean P. Clapper—Radio Operator

The second air crew loss occurred on 5 December 1972 in a mid-air collision between Pope AFB–based C-130E(I), tail number 64–0558, that belonged to the 318th Special Operations Squadron, and an F-102A from McEntire Air National Guard Base during an airborne interceptor defense training mission. Fatalities were all twelve Combat Talon crew members and the interceptor pilot.

Lt. Col. Donald E. Martin—Aircraft Commander

Capt. Douglas S. Peterson—Pilot

2nd Lt. Douglas L. Thierer—Cadet Pilot

Maj. Keith L. VanNote—Navigator

Capt. John R. Cole—Navigator

Cap. Marshall J. Dickerson—Electronic Warfare Officer

Capt. Louis R. Sert—Electronic Warfare Officer

TSgt. Claude L. Abbott—Flight Engineer

TSgt. Robert E. Doyle—Flight Engineer

SSgt. Billy M. Warr Sr.—Flight Engineer

SrA. Gerald K. Faust—Loadmaster

SSgt. G. A. Mickley Jr.—Radio Operator

The third air crew loss occurred on 25 April 1980 during Operation Eagle Claw at Desert One in Iran when a Sea Stallion RH-53D helicopter collided with an EC-130E that had refueled it on the ground. EC-130E was flown by Combat Talon crew from the 8th Special Operations Squadron at Hurlburt Field in Florida.

Capt. Harold L. Lewis—Aircraft Commander

Capt. Lyn D. McMillan—Pilot

Capt. Richard L. Bakke—Navigator

Capt. Charles T. McMillan II—Navigator

TSgt. Joe C. Mayo—Flight Engineer

The fourth air crew loss occurred on 26 February 1981 in the sea off Tabones Island, Philippines, when an MC-130, tail number 64–0564, crashed during a low-level turn during a return to Clark Air Base. It belonged to the 1st Special Operations Squadron. The aircraft's eight-man crew and fifteen passengers perished.

Maj. James M. Kirk—Aircraft Commander

Capt. Norman L. Martel—Pilot

Capt. Thomas D. Patterson—Navigator

Capt. Gregory S. Peppers—Navigator

SSgt. John T. Felton—Flight Engineer

MSgt. Barry R. Chumbley—Loadmaster

TSgt. Gary W. Logan—Loadmaster

TSgt. Stephen A. Blyler—Radio Operator

15 Passengers

The fifth loss of life occurred on 12 June 2002 near Sarthe Band Airport in Afghanistan when a Combat Talon II, MC130H, tail number 84–0475, crashed shortly after takeoff. Aircraft was from the 15th Special Operations Squadron at Hurlburt Field. Two crew members and one passengers were lost.

TSgt. Sean M. Corlew, loadmaster from the 16th SOW at Hurlburt Field

SSgt. Anissa A. Shero, loadmaster from the 16th SOW at Hurlburt Field

USA Sgt. 1st. Class Peter P. Tycz II from the 3rs SFG at Fort Bragg

The sixth air crew loss occurred on 7 August 2002 when a Combat Talon II, MC-130H, tail number 90–0161, crashed after takeoff from the Roosevelt Roads Naval Station in Puerto Rico. It belonged to the 15th Special Operations Squadron at Hurlburt Field. The entire six-man crew and four passengers were lost.

Maj. Michael J. Akos—Pilot

Capt. Christel A. Chavez—Co-pilot

Maj. Gregory W. Fritz—Navigator

1st Lt. Nathanial Buckley—Electronic Warfare Officer

TSgt. Robert S. Johnson—Flight Engineer

SSgt. Robert J. McGuire Jr.—Loadmaster

SSgt. Shane H. Kimmett—DSO

Capt. Panuk P. Soomsawasdi—STT Liaison Officer

Kentucky ANG SSgt. Martin Tracy—STT

Kentucky ANG TSgt. Christopher Matero—STT

The seventh air crew loss occurred on 31 March 2005 when Combat Talon II, MC-130H, tail number 87–0127, that belonged to the 7th Special Operations Squadron at RAF Mildenhall, crashed on a night training mission in Albania. All nine crew members were lost.

Capt. Todd R. Bracy—Aircraft Commander

Cap. Surender Kothakota—Pilot

Capt. James S. Cronin—Navigator

Capt. Gil C. Williamson—Electronic Warfare Officer

1st Lt. Ray C. Owens Jr.—Electronic Warfare Officer

CMSgt. Lawrence B. Gray—Flight Engineer

TSgt. James R. Henry—Loadmaster

SSgt. Patrick R. Pentico—Loadmaster

TSgt. Glenn P. Lastes—Linguist Det. 2

List of Abbreviations

AAA	Anti-Aircraft Artillery
ACS	Air Commando Squadron
ADI	Attitude Direction Indicator
AFMPC	Air Force Military Personnel Center
AFROTC	Air Force Reserve Officer Training Corps
AFSOC	Air Force Special Operations Command
AFSOF	Air Force Special Operations Forces
BOQ	Bachelor Officers' Quarters
CCK	Ching Chuan Kang Air Base in Taiwan
CCT	Combat Crew Training
CCTS	Combat Crew Training Squadron
CIA	Central Intelligence Agency
CILHI	Central Identification Laboratory, Hawaii
CINCPAC	Commander in Chief in the Pacific
CJTFFA	Commander Joint Task Force Final Accounting
DCSO	Deputy Commander for Special Operations
DIA	Defense Intelligence Agency
DNIF	Duty Not Involving Flying
DOD	Department of Defense
ECM	Electronic Countermeasures
E&E	Escape and Evasion
ELINT	Electronic Intelligence
EWO	Electronic Warfare Officer
FE	Flight Engineer
FLIR	Forward Looking Infrared
FOIA	Freedom of Information Act

GCI	Ground Control Intercept
GS	Ground Speed
HIS	Horizontal Situation Indicator
IAS	Indicated Air Speed
IE	Investigation Element
ILS	Instrument Landing Systems
IRAN	Inspection and Repair as Necessary
JACK	Joint Advisory Commission, Korea
JCS	Joint Chiefs of Staff
JTF-FA	Joint Task Force—Final Accounting
JUWTF	Joint Unconventional Warfare Task Force
KIA	Killed in Action
KTAS	Knots True Air Speed
LM	Loadmaster
MAC	Military Airlift Command
MACV-SOG	Military Assistance Command, Vietnam—Studies and Observations Group
MACV	Military Assistance Command, Vietnam
MIA	Missing in Action
MOU	Memorandum of Understanding
MPC	Military Payment Certificate
MRE	Meals Ready to Eat
MTT	Mobile Training Team
MWR	Morale, Welfare, and Recreation
NATO	North Atlantic Treaty Organization
NOK	Next of Kin
NPRC	National Personnel Recovery Center
NSC	National Security Council
nm	nautical mile
NVA	North Vietnamese Army
OPCON	Operational Control
OPLAN 34A	Operations Plan 34A
OSS	Office of Strategic Services
R&R	Rest and Recuperation
RE	Recovery Element
REFNO	Reference number for recovery of Americans lost in Vietnam

RO	Radio Operator
RTAFB	Royal Thai Air Force Base
RTU	Rotational Training Unit
SACSA	Special Assistant for Counterinsurgency and Special Activities
SAM	Surface to Air Missile
SAR	Search and Rescue
SAWC	Special Air Warfare Center
SCO	Summary Court Officer
SEA	Southeast Asia
SECDEF	Secretary of Defense
SECSTATE	Secretary of State
SOG	Studies and Observations Group
SOS	Special Operations Squadron
SOW	Special Operations Wing
SRV	Socialist Republic of Vietnam
SRVG	Socialist Republic of Vietnam Government
TAC	Tactical Air Command
TACAN	Tactical Aid to Navigation
TAS	True Air Speed
TAW	Tactical Airlift Wing
TCW	Troop Carrier Wing
TDY	Temporary Duty
TFR	Terrain Following Radar
TOT	Times on Targets
USCINCPAC	US Commander in Chief, Pacific
USCINCPAC IO	US Commander in Chief, Pacific, Information Officer
USO	United Service Organizations
USSDP	Uniformed Services Savings Deposit Program
Vietcong	Communist political and military organization in South Vietnam
VN	Vietnam
VNOSMP	Vietnamese Office for Seeking Missing Personnel

Notes

Chapter 1

1. Dean, *Air Force Role in Low-Intensity Conflict*, 88–89.
2. Ibid., 90–91.
3. Thigpen, *Praetorian STARShip*, 13–14.
4. Grimes, *History of Big Safari*, 247–50.
5. Ibid., 16–17.
6. Trest, *Air Commando One*, 169.
7. Ibid., various book pages.
8. Thigpen, *Praetorian STARShip*, 105.
9. Momyer, *Air Power in Three Wars*.

Chapter 2

1. Thigpen, *Praetorian STARShip*, 82.

Chapter 3

1. Lt. Col. Doug Forsythe, USAF-Ret., phone interview with author, 14 Jul 2013.
2. Briscoe, "Jack Air Operations, Korea, 1951–1953," 122.
3. Plaster, *SOG: The Secret Wars of America's Commandos in Vietnam*, 23.
4. Thigpen, *Praetorian STARShip*, 78.
5. Moore, *Vietnam's Most Secret Squadron*, 36–37.
6. Col. John F. Lewis, USAF-Ret., e-mail message to author, 17 May 2013.

Chapter 4

1. Thigpen, *Praetorian STARShip*, 103.
2. MSgt. Melvin Gibson, USAF-Ret., phone interview, 21 Jun 2013.
3. Lt. Col. Jean Lesieutre, USAF-Ret., e-mail message to author, 21 May 2013.
4. Thigpen, *Praetorian STARShip*, 111.
5. Ibid., 89.
6. www.nhatrang-reunion.org/nhatrang_history.html.
7. Col. John M. Patton, USAF-Ret., telephone interview with author, 14 Jun 2013.
8. Collins. "Doctrine Development for the Employment of Tactical Air Forces."
9. Lt. Col. Howard Reeve, USAF-Ret., phone interview with author, 13 May 2013.

10. Lesieutre, e-mail message to author, 21 May 2013.
11. Col. Arthur Heaphy, USAF-Ret., phone interview, 10 Jul 2013.
12. Lesieutre, e-mail message to author, 21 May 2013.

Chapter 5

1. Plaster, *SOG: The Secret Wars of America's Commandos in Vietnam*, 229.
2. Lt. Col. John Drohan, USAF-Ret., "COMBAT TALON I: The First Deployment."
3. Capt. Patrick Watson, USAF, phone interview with author, 28 Sep 2013.
4. Thigpen, *Praetorian STARShip*, 102–3.
5. CMSgt. Mel Hendrickson, USAF, "Monkey and I," unpublished memoir, 2.
6. Ibid., 3.
7. Plaster, *SOG: The Secret Wars of America's Commandos in Vietnam*, 309.
8. Ibid., 229.
9. Ibid., 227.
10. Briscoe, "JACK Air Operation, Korea 1951–1953," 131.
11. Col. John Lewis, USAF-Ret., phone interview with author, 15 Jun 2013.

Chapter 6

1. Col. John Gargus, USAF-Ret., "Air Force Special Operations Command," *US Special Operations Forces*, 201.
2. Columbus Dispatch, 29 Oct 1993.
3. HQ. AFMPC/DPMCB, letter to MSgt. Charles R. Timms, 12 Oct 1993.
4. Steven McCrary, e-mail to the author, 25 Sep 2000.
5. Suzanne Parker, letter to the author, 21 Sep 2000.
6. Teletype message. CJTFFA Det. One Bangkok, TH 230220Z Nov 92, 1.
7. Wendy Darcy, e-mail to author, 25 Aug 2000.

Chapter 7

1. www.jpac.pacom.mil, Mission Overview—What we do at JPAC 1.
2. www.jpac.pacom.mil, Mission Overview 1.
3. www.jpac.pacom.mil, Mission Overview—Investigation and Analysis 1.
4. www.jpac.pacom.mil, Release # 11–9, 5 Apr 2011.
5. www.jpac.pacom.mil, Mission Overview—Recovery 1–2.
6. www.jpac.pacom.mil, Mission Overview—Identification 1–2.
7. www.jpac.pacom.mil, Mission Overview—Closure 1.
8. Teletype message. CJTFFA Det. One Bangkok, TH 230220Z Nov 92, 1–2.
9. Ibid., 2.
10. Ibid., 3.
11. Memorandum for Commander US Army CILHI, 9 Mar 2000, 1–2.
12. Teletype message. CJTFFA Det. One Bangkok, TH 230220Z Nov 92, 4–5.
13. Ibid., 4.
14. Ibid., 4–5.
15. Ibid., 3.

16. Ibid., 5–6.
17. Ibid., 6.
18. Teletype message. CTF-FA Honolulu, HI 160002Z Dec 93, 1.
19. Ibid., 6–7.
20. Fax message. CDR Det. 2 to CJTF-FA, 31 Mar 1993.
21. Teletype message. CJTFFA Det. One Bangkok, TH 221030Z Nov 93, 5.
22. Ibid., 1–6.
23. Memorandum for Commander US Army CILHI, 7 Jan 2000, Encl. 1, 2.
24. Memorandum for Commander US Army CILHI, 9 Mar 2000, 8.
25. Ibid.
26. Memorandum for Commander US Army CILHI, 9 Mar 2000, 2.
27. Teletype message. CJTFFA Honolulu, HI 171102Z Jun 94, 7.
28. Ibid., 9–10.
29. Memorandum for Commander US Army CILHI, 9 Mar 2000, 3.
30. Teletype message. CJTFFA Honolulu, HI 171102Z Jun 94, 6.
31. Ibid., 1–2.
32. Ibid., 2–4.
33. Memorandum for Commander US Army CILHI, 9 Mar 2000, 4.
34. Teletype message. CJTFFA Honolulu, HI 211757Z Aug 98, 4.

Chapter 8

1. JTF-FA letter to HQ AFMPC, 3 Dec 1992.
2. Air Force Personnel Center Internet home page as of Apr 2013.
3. HQ AFSVA/CCQ letter to author 26 Sep 2005.
4. HQ AFPC/DPDXI letter to author 31 Aug 2005.
5. AFPC/DPDXI letter to Col John Gargus, 22 Sep 2005. AFPC/DPDXI letter to Col John Gargus, 22 Sep 2005.
6. Columbus Dispatch, 29 Oct 1993.
7. Allen, *Until the Last Man Comes Home*, 143–45.
8. USAF (AFPMSC) letter to AFPMC, 3 Dec 1968.
9. DPMPC letter to HQ USAF/DPM, 30 Mar 1978.
10. AFMPC/DPMC Staff Summary Sheet, 3 Apr 1978.
11. HQ USAF DPM letter to HQ AFMPC/DPMC, 27 Apr 1978.
12. Allen, *Until the Last Man Comes Home*, 144.
13. Ann R. Fisher, phone interview with author, 28 Jun 2013.
14. Patricia C. Claxton, e-mail message to author, 26 Jun 2013.
15. HQ AFMPC/DCPMB letter to Mrs. Claxton, 3 Feb 1993.

Appendix A: The Last Mission of Combat Talon's S-01 Crew

1. This story was first published for the families at the dedication of the memorial pedestal at Hurlburt Field's Memorial Air Park in 1998. Then it was published in the Air Commando Association newsletter. After that it was picked up by Col. Jerry Thigpen who included it in his book *The Praetorian STARship*. It is available in several inputs by military buffs on the Internet.

Bibliography

Books, Articles, and Monographs

Allen, Michael J. *Until the Last Man Comes Home: POWs, MIAs, and the Unending Vietnam War*. Chapel Hill: University of North Carolina Press, 2009.

Briscoe, Charles H. "JACK Air Operation, Korea 1951–1953." *Veritas* 9, no. 1 (2013).

Chinnery, Philip D. *Any Time, Any Place*. Annapolis, MD: Naval Institute Press, 1994.

Collins, David C., Lt. Col. "Doctrine Development for the Employment of Tactical Air Forces." *Air University Review* (November–December 1967).

Collins, John M. *Military Strategy*. Washington, DC: Brassey's, 2002.

Dean, David J. *The Air Force Role in Low-Intensity Conflict*. Maxwell Air Force Base, AL: Air University Press, 1986.

Drohan, John, Lt. Col., USAF-Ret. "COMBAT TALON I: The First Deployment." Unpublished memoir.

Gargus, John, Colonel USAF-Ret. *The Son Tay Raid: American POWs in Vietnam Were Not Forgotten*. College Station: Texas A&M University Press, 2010.

Grimes, Bill. *The History of Big Safari*. Wright Patterson Air Force Base, OH: 645th Aeronautical Systems Group, 2013.

Haas, Michael E. *Apollo's Warriors: United States Air Force Special Operations during the Cold War*. Maxwell Air Force Base, AL: Air University Press, 1997.

Hendrickson, Mel, CMSgt. USAF. "Monkey and I." Unpublished memoir.

Jolly, Randy. *Air Commandos*. Garland, TX: Aero Graphics, 1994.

McRaven, William H. *Special Ops*. Novato, CA: Presidio Press, 1996.

Momyer, William W., Gen. USAF-Ret. *Airpower in Three Wars*. Washington, DC: Department of Defense, Department of the Air Force, 1978.

Moore, Bernard II, Col. USAF-Ret. "Vietnam's Most Secret Squadron." *Tip of the Spear* (January 2010).

Plaster, John L. *SOG: The Secret Wars of America's Commandos in Vietnam*. New York: Simon and Schuster, 1997.

Pushies, Fred J. *US Air Force Special Ops*. Osceola, WI: MBI Publishing, 2000.

Sasser, Charles W. *Raider*. New York: St. Martin's Press, 2002.

Schemmer, Benjamin F. *The Raid*. New York: Harper and Row, 1976; Ballantine, 2000.

Schemmer, Benjamin F.; John T. Carney, Col. USAF-Ret.; Peter J. Schoomaker, Gen. US Army-Ret.; John M. Collins, Col. US Army-Ret.; John Gargus, Col. USAF-Ret.; George R. Worthington, RADM US Navy-Ret.; and Roxanne Merritt. *US Special Operations Forces.* Westport, CT: Hugh Lauter Levin Associates, 2003.

Thigpen, Jerry L., Col. USAF-Ret. *The Praetorian STARShip: The Untold Story of the Combat Talon.* Maxwell Air Force Base, AL: Air University Press, 2001.

Trest, Warren A. *Air Commando One: Heinie Aderholt and America's Secret Wars.* Washington, DC: Smithsonian Institution Press, 2000.

Memoranda

Memorandum for CDR US Army CILHI (internal) 9 March 2000. Subject: Identification of six sets of remains 193–284-I-01 through 05 and 193–284-G-01.

Memorandum for CDR US Army CILHI through S-3. 7 Jan 2000. Subject: Search and Recovery Report 1994/CIL/002, A C-130E (#64–547) Aircraft Associated with REFNO 0954 near Phu Nung Village, Tuan Giao District, Lai Chau Province, Socialist Republic of Vietnam, 24 Oct through 8 Nov 1993.

Teletype Messages

From CDR JCRC Barber's Point, HI to AFMPC Randolph AFB, TX 051902Z Mar 87, Subject: Congressional Inquiry, SSgt. Gean Clapper, USAF.

From CJTF-FA Det One Bangkok to CDR JTF-FA Honolulu, HI 230220Z Nov 92, Subject: Detailed report of survey of case 0954.

From CJTF-FA Det One Bangkok to CDR JTF-FA Honolulu, HI 221030z Nov 93, Subject: Detailed search and recovery report of case 0954.

From CDR JTF-FA Honolulu HI to USCINCPAC, Honolulu HI 141913Z Dec 93, Subject: Repatriation of remains from Socialist Republic of Vietnam.

From CDR JTF-FA Honolulu HI to HQ AFMPC Randolph AFB TX 160002Z Dec 93, Subject: Analysis of Material Evidence Associated with REFNO 0954

From CDR JTF-FA Honolulu HI to SECDEF Washington DC//USDP: RSA 171102Z Jun 94, Subject: Report of investigation of leads pertaining to possible remains of US service men reported by a Vietnamese citizen.

From CDR JTF-FA Honolulu HI for information to White House National Security Council et al., 211757Z Aug 98, Subject: Interview of two Vietnamese citizens about remains of REFNO 0954.

Fax Messages

From CDR Det. 2, JTF-FA, Hanoi, SVR to JTF-FA, Camp Smith, HI, 31 Mar 93, Subject: FAX 102–93, Case 0954.

Reports

Forensic Anthropology Report. CILHI 1993–284-G-01, 20 Oct 1999.

Forensic Anthropology Report. CILHI 1993–284-G-01, 2 Nov 1999.

Personal contacts:

Bannon, Holland B. Master Sergeant USAF-Ret., Loadmaster (S-04).

Cartwright, Bert Jr. Master Sergeant USAF-Ret., Flight Engineer (S-04).
Claxton, Patricia.
Connaughton, John M. Colonel USAF-Ret., Pilot (S-06).
Dalton, Julie.
Dambach, Robert. Senior Master Sergeant, Loadmaster (SG-3).
Darcy, Wendy.
Fitzwater, David A., Crew Chief of MC-130 #64–0563.
Fisher, Ann R.
Forsythe, William D. Lieutenant Colonel USAF-Ret., Pilot (SG-2).
Gibson, Melvin B. D. Chief Master Sergeant USAF-Ret., Loadmaster (SG-5).
Guenon, William A. Major USAF-Ret., Pilot (SG-1).
Heaphy, Arthur J. Colonel USAF-Ret., Navigator (SG-1).
Hess, Lee. Colonel USAF-Ret., Aircraft Commander (S-38) and Squadron Commander 1983–85.
Hines, Thomas F. Colonel USAF-Ret., Commander 1968.
Hobson, James L. Jr. Major General USAF-Ret., Pilot (S-07) and AFSOC Commander.
Holbein, Jack R., Jr. Major General USAF-Ret., Talon Navigator and SOCPAC Commander.
Hovan, Richard. Staff Sergeant USAF, Crew Chief of MC130 #64–0567.
Kelley, Larry J. Lieutenant Colonel USAF-Ret., Navigator (S-03).
Lesieutre, Jean M. Lieutenant Colonel USAF-Ret., Electronic Warfare Officer (SG-4).
Lewis, John F. Colonel USAF-Ret., Electronic Warfare Officer (S-05).
Mason, Herbert A., Jr. GS-13 AFSOC Historian.
Mattingly, David. Pilot (SG-2).
McClam. Lieutenant Colonel USA-Ret.
McCormick. Lieutenant Colonel USAF-Ret., Navigator (S-05).
McCrary, Steve.
Miller, Thomas E. Lieutenant Colonel USAF.
Osborne, Catherine J.
Parker, Suzanne M.
Reeve, Howard. Lieutenant Colonel USAF-Ret., Aircraft Commander (SG-5).
Rhodes, Donald L. Master Sergeant USAF Ret., Loadmaster (S-06).
Rogers, Dow A., Jr. Lieutenant Colonel USAF-Ret., Commander 1966–67.
Rowe, Ron.
Schramm, Fred. 353rd Special Operations Group Historian.
Sell, Richard H. Pilot (SG-5).
Smith, James L. C. "Les." Navigator (SG-5).
Thompson, Roy L. Colonel USAF-Ret., Mission Planner 1967.

Index